In God's Image

In God's Image

Recognizing the
Profoundly Impaired as Persons

—

Peter A. Comensoli

EDITED BY Nigel Zimmermann

CASCADE Books • Eugene, Oregon

IN GOD'S NAME
Recognizing the Profoundly Impaired as Persons

Copyright © 2018 Peter A. Comensoli. All rights reserved. Except for brief quotations in critical publications or reviews, no part of this book may be reproduced in any manner without prior written permission from the publisher. Write: Permissions, Wipf and Stock Publishers, 199 W. 8th Ave., Suite 3, Eugene, OR 97401.

Cascade Books
An Imprint of Wipf and Stock Publishers
199 W. 8th Ave., Suite 3
Eugene, OR 97401

www.wipfandstock.com

PAPERBACK ISBN: 978-1-62564-632-3
HARDCOVER ISBN: 978-1-4982-8537-7
EBOOK ISBN: 978-1-5326-5284-4

Cataloguing-in-Publication data:

Names: Comensoli, Peter A., author. | Zimmermann, Nigel, editor.

Title: In God's name : recognizing the profoundly impaired as persons / Peter A. Comensoli ; edited by Nigel Zimmermann.

Description: Eugene, OR : Cascade Books, 2018 | Includes bibliographical references and index.

Identifiers: ISBN 978-1-62564-632-3 (paperback) | ISBN 978-1-4982-8537-7 (hardcover) | ISBN 978-1-5326-5284-4 (ebook)

Subjects: LCSH: People with disabilities—Religious aspects—Christianity.

Classification: BT135 .C65 2018 (print) | BT135 .C65 (ebook)

Manufactured in the U.S.A.   APRIL 9, 2018

For Peter and Marco, and for all who live their lives at the extremes
of the human condition.
Friends of God, one and all.

Et ait Deus:
'Faciamus hominem ad imaginem et similitudinem nostrum …'
Et creavit Deus hominem ad imaginem suam;
ad imaginem Dei creavit illum;
masculum et feminam creavit eos.
—GENESIS 1:26, 27

Remember we are but travellers here.
—ST. MARY OF THE CROSS MACKILLOP

CONTENTS

Acknowledgments ix

Introduction Persons among Persons? Picturing the Profoundly Impaired in a Non-impaired World 1

chapter 1 Life Lived at the Extremes: A Catholic Voice amid the Human Peripheries 15

chapter 2 "People Just Like Other People": Reinders' Reimagined Anthropology of the Profoundly Impaired 32

chapter 3 A Thoroughly Human Enterprise: The Place of Friendship in a Christian Anthropology 63

chapter 4 Friendship-Made: Friendship, Humanity, and the Profoundly Impaired 88

chapter 5 Being a Creature: Recovering the Human Project 111

chapter 6 The Pilgrim Creature: Hope and Human Life 133

chapter 7 *Imago Dei*: "The Nature That We Have" 156

chapter 8 Drawing Near to Christ: Measuring the Human Condition 184

Conclusion "Beyond Inclusion!": Humanity Lived under the Condition of Impairment 213

Bibliography 225

Index 235

ACKNOWLEDGMENTS

With sincere and grateful thanks to:

Oliver O'Donovan and Fergus Kerr, OP, who were my patient, wise, and insightful doctoral supervisors, the thesis of which this book originates.

The many friends and colleagues at New College, Edinburgh University, who surrounded me with scholarly collaboration and ecumenical friendship over the years of research and writing.

Hans Reinders, that tower of theological accompaniment with the profoundly disabled, who encouraged me to publish this work, knowing that I am a critical friend of his own work.

Nigel Zimmermann, who has been my good friend, theological companion, and attentive editor.

INTRODUCTION

PERSONS AMONG PERSONS?

Picturing the Profoundly Impaired in a Non-impaired World

THERE ARE PEOPLE WHO live their lives at the extremes of the human condition because of some gross intellectual, cognitive, neurological, or developmental impairment to their human nature. Included among such individuals with profound cognitive impairments (or more simply, the profoundly impaired) are: human beings with extremely retarding congenital conditions and complex intellectual disabilities, the severely brain injured, those living in a post-coma unresponsive state, those suffering from acute mental illness, and those at an advanced stage of progressive neurological degeneration.[1] What makes the profoundly impaired an identifiable group of human beings is that their cognitive faculties of reason, will, and self awareness—those characteristics of human beings commonly associated with the moral status of being a person—are, or have come to be, grossly undermined or entirely absent.

While the nature of such conditions of impairment is often perplexing in the extreme, and while the lives of those so conditioned are often considered a tragic mystery to the unimpaired, under normal societal circumstances (and granted post-natal survival) their dignity is generally fostered and their wellbeing attended to. Evidence of such practices towards the profoundly impaired is widespread, at both domestic and

---

1. The language around "impairment" and "disability" has always been hotly contested and terminology has changed regularly (and will likely again) in line with current sensitivities. For the sake of clarity, however, a consistent terminology must be chosen and settled on, without seeking to curtail the linguistic debate. Consequently, from now on the shorthand term "profoundly impaired" will be used to refer to those people living with a profound cognitive impairment, as outlined in the text.

public levels, lending merit to the intuition that the profoundly impaired are generally acknowledged and respected as moral peers within the human community. The profoundly impaired are recognizably persons among persons in all the unremarkable and unremarked ways in which their personal status is acknowledged and respected in practice. Given that the personhood of the profoundly impaired is commonly acknowledged in social practices—given that they are recognizably persons among their peers—there is good reason for granting moral weight to the intuition which underlies the practice.

Yet what might the argument for such a presupposition look like? In other words, how is it that the profoundly impaired are recognizably persons amongst fellow persons, given that they are ordinarily treated as persons in practice? Furthermore, why is this an important question to ask? Two suggestions present themselves in response to these questions. First, the very asking of the question of personhood about the profoundly impaired suggests that there is something at stake in the recognition of persons. Being recognizably a person makes a difference. Whatever else might be said about the question of personhood, it is at least a question of normative significance for human beings, including the profoundly impaired. Secondly, human beings are recognizably persons by virtue of their being human, that is: in virtue of their living of a human life. This suggests that it is the lives that human beings live, precisely in the condition under which they live it, that is significant for recognizing persons. The question of how it is that the profoundly impaired are recognizably persons, therefore, can be seen as a question that acknowledges that there is indeed something at stake in their being the particularly conditioned human beings that they are. It is in responding to this question that this book will be concerned.

Pictures of Human Life Lived at the Extremes

If the significance of the question about how the profoundly impaired are recognizably persons is to hinge on the twin claims that something is at stake in this recognition and that it has to do with their being human, then an initial word is called for on what these claims are about. To this end, consider the following word-picture:

> The duke scowls. He paces; he rattles a little; at last he bursts out, "Damn it all, Cromwell, why are you such a . . . person? It isn't as

if you could afford to be." He waits, smiling. He knows what the duke means. He is a person, he is a presence.[2]

In grudgingly acknowledging that Thomas Cromwell is a person, the Duke of Norfolk recognizes something about the man before him that had previously gone unacknowledged by him. In recognizing that Cromwell is a person, Norfolk is forced to acknowledge that a claim had been made on him as a fellow person. Cromwell is, unavoidably, a subject to contend with, and not a mere object of more or less tangential significance. Something happens in the recognition of Cromwell as a person: Norfolk scowls and Cromwell smiles. It makes a difference to both of them, thereby speaking of a certain normative dimension to being a person. A person occupies an acknowledged position—an unavoidable presence—within the world of other persons; a person can be ignored, but not denied. It says that personhood, among the many other things that might be said about it, constitutes a moral claim for human beings on human beings. Something is at stake in the recognition of persons; it makes a real difference.

What is it about this moment of personal recognition such that it would unsettle Norfolk and entertain Cromwell? The use of the personal pronoun gives away the answer. Its use is not to do with the fact that Cromwell is a man—that he is a human being; it may be assumed that Norfolk is not suddenly rattled by the fact of Cromwell's human nature. Rather, it has to do with Cromwell, the man—him being the human being that he is. When it comes to recognizing persons, there is a real difference between "being human" (being the human being that one is) and "human being" (the factuality of one's humanity). It is in how this distinction plays out that something is revealed about how someone is recognizably a person. All that Cromwell has, and that by which Norfolk's mind is turned, is the particular life he is living. The condition of his humanity is significant, but not for the content of that condition; wealth did not win the argument. Personhood is not some determinative condition, some qualitative measure, to be achieved by a human being. Rather, someone is recognizably the person that he is by means of nothing more than the living of his own conditioned human existence.

The picture of personhood thus conveyed in the encounter between Norfolk and Cromwell not only reminds us that the question of personhood is properly an anthropological one, but it also suggests something

2. Mandel, *Wolf Hall*, 163.

notable about how the profoundly impaired are recognizably persons. If what is at stake about one's personhood has to do with being human, and if being human is about living the life that one has in the condition under which one finds it, then a quite remarkable claim is being made about the profoundly impaired. They are recognizably persons precisely because of the lives they are living in virtue of the impaired condition of their lives. The condition of their lives is not the reason why they are recognizably persons, yet it is only in the condition of their lives that they can be recognizably the persons that they are. It is the case both that their impairment has nothing to do with them being persons, and that they are the persons that they are in the living of their impairment.

Herein lies the importance of the question that is our concern: any position that does not allow for the personhood of the profoundly impaired precisely because of the nature of their impairment, or that does uphold the personhood of the profoundly impaired precisely by sidelining their impairment, gets the anthropological question of the profoundly impaired wrong. This is because the condition of impairment has, at one and the same time, both nothing and everything to do with how the profoundly impaired are recognizably persons. In the picture at hand—a picture still in need of an argument—"person" is not a designating term for that particular kind of human being who has come to exert a personal presence among the community of persons. Rather, "person" is the answer to the question of how a human being is who he is; it is the *nomen dignitatis* for being human. "Being human"—being someone of human kind, living a human life—is simply "being a person." It is in the discovery of this dignifying name that the personal presence of a human being is declared and recognized. Only by being attentive to the question of how it is that the profoundly impaired are recognizably persons will the significance of such an anthropological picture emerge.

To state again: the point of departure for asking the question of how the profoundly impaired are recognizably persons is the presupposition that the commonplace practices of the human community towards them provides good reason for granting moral weight to recognizing their personhood. However, this is not an anthopological move that is universally supported. There are those who would make a categorical distinction between the biological reality of human beings and the moral status of persons.[3] Furthermore, some human beings, because of the extremity at

---

3. The philsopher Peter Singer is at the vanguard of this position. His so-called anti-anthropological notion of speciesism is most fully developed in his well-known

which they live their lives, are not, or may never be recognized as occupying a personal presence amongst the community of persons. Or so the argument goes.

This is not to say that the profoundly impaired may not be afforded some greater or lesser place within the community of persons. It is to hold, however, that the extension of a personal moral standing to them is precisely an act of inclusion by those from within the community of persons to those without.[4] As such, there is nothing about the profoundly impaired, in and of themsleves, by which they may lay claim, for themsleves, to a share in the dignity and moral status of persons. Instead, they are allowed to do so only on the grounds that a paradigm of inclusion is adopted by persons towards non-persons.

Such philosophical pictures of persons tend to neglect the fact that personhood is always a lived reality, and not some abstract category then to be applied to things in the world.[5] The moral claim that the profoundly impaired make upon the human world is made via the condition of their lived humanity. It is not about finding ways in which they might first be categorised, before extending to them a moral status. They also neglect to account for the indesputable evidence that human life is inherently marked by dependency, vulnerability and disability.[6] This reality is an

---

book of moral philosophy, *Practical Ethics*. As he states in the same work, "There are many beings who are sentient and capable of experiencing pleasure and pain, but are not rational and self-conscious and so not persons . . . [N]ewborn infants and some intellectually disabled humans [fall into this category] . . . [T]hose beings who do lack self-consciousness cannot be said to have a right to life, in the full sense of 'right'" (101). Another highly influential argument in the same vein is to be found in Derek Parfit's more nuanced, though equally reductionist, position on personal identity, *Reasons and Persons*.

4. This is the position, for example, taken by the Christian philosopher Tristram Engelhardt in his widely read textbook on bioethics. Human non-persons are to be afforded the moral status of persons only as a matter of religious imperative. Engelhardt, *Foundations of Bioethics*, 135–39.

5. As Elizabeth Anscombe states as the second of her commonly held philosophical errors, "A human being comes to be a person through development of the characterisitics which make something into a person. A human being in decay may also cease to be a person without ceasing to be a human being. In short: being a person is something added to a human being who develops properly, and that may disappear in old age or imbacility. The concept of a person becomes an instrument in propaganda for muder. Persons must be respected; not so human beings, who are not yet or no longer persons." Anscombe, *Twenty Opinions Common among Anglo-American Philosophers*, 2 (https://symblogia.files.wordpress.com/2012/01/anscombe-20-opinions.pdf.).

6. This is a point made by the philosopher John Haldane: "The dominant image

abiding feature of every person, impaired and unimpaired alike. In this particular picture of personhood the underlying presupposition is an entirely negative one: no human being, in virtue of being human, is recognizably a person, and the bridging of the recognitional gap of personal presence for the profoundly impaired is determined by a factor of "unless and until."

Christian Anthropology Theologically Re-imagined

But if not this anthropological picture for the profoundly impaired, then which one? It is worth noting at this point that speech about the recognition of persons has its origins in theological declarations, and specifically Christian ones. This has to do with the way in which the word "person" took on its distinctive anthropological shape during the christological debates of the early Church, culminating in the Council of Chalcedon in the fifth century. It was there that the Church settled on a language and concept—"person"—to use for talking about the man, Jesus Christ, and in so doing for talking about humanity in general. As has been noted of this historal fact,

> Without Christian theology we would have had no name for what we now call "persons," and, since persons do not simply occur in nature, that means we would have been without them altogether. That is not to say that we can only speak intelligently of persons on explicitly theological suppositions, though it is conceivable that the disappearance of the theological dimension of the idea could in the long run bring about the disappearance of the idea itself.[7]

If this theological, specifically Christian, foundation of personhood is to be affirmed, then there ought to be ways of approaching the recognition of the personal presence of the profoundly impaired from a theological perspective. The widespread and constant practice of the Christian

---

[in moral philosophy] has been of intelligent, educated, healthy and mobile adults, fashioning rewarding lives consisting of largely unimpeded activities. The mentally retarded, the physically disabled, the deformed, the senile, and others of similar conditions hardly feature in mainstream philosophical thinking about how to live." Haldane, *Practical Philosophy*, 80. He is developing here an insight of Alasdair MacIntyre in *Dependent Rational Animals: Why Human Beings Need the Virtues*. Martha Nussbaum takes up a similar theme in *Hiding from Humanity: Disgust, Shame, and the Law*.

7. Robert Spaemann, *Persons*, 17–18.

churches towards the profoundly impaired (and all those at the margins of society for whatever other reason) already speaks of a pastoral affirmation for pursuing such a theological response. With this background what might a Christian theology look like, such that it addresses the presupposition that the profoundly impaired are indeed recognizably persons, by providing cogent argumentation as to how they are the persons that they are?

The beginnings of a contemporary concern for the profoundly disabled from a theological perspective might best be located in the eugenics debates of the early part of the twentieth century and the abortion debates of the mid- to late twentieth century, both of which took up questions pertaining to the moral status of the disabled, the handicapped, the retarded, and so on.[8] The turn towards a more focused theological reimagining of the disabled, however, is often associated with groundbreaking thinking done in the 1980s and 1990s by the American theologians Stanley Hauerwas and Nancy Eieslands, who (separately) sought to break through a perceived ethical objectifying of the disabled and to treat them properly as subjects (Hauerwas) and participants (Eiesland) in society.[9] The themes and insights of these two authors have since become the theological point of departure for a growing number of theologians working in the area of disability theology, including Deborah Beth Creamer, Hans Reinders, Thomas Reynolds, John Swinton, and Amos Yong, to name the more prominent theologians who have written books in the area (not to mention those who have published articles).[10] Separately and together,

---

8. For a treatment of the questions of eugenics, foetal testing and abortion, see the articles by Amy Laura Hall ("To Form a More Perfect Union," 75–95.) and Mary B. Mahowald ("Aren't We All Eugenicists Anyway?" 96–113.) in *Theology, Disability and the New Genetics*. As far as I am aware, none of the other so-called theologians of disability have drawn on earlier thinking in terms of the disabled that emerged from the eugenics and abortion debates.

9. Hauerwas, *Suffering Presence*, and Eiesland, *The Disabled God*. As far as I am aware, none of the other so-called theologians of disability have drawn on earlier thinking in terms of the disabled that emerged from the eugenics and abortion debates.

10. Medi Ann Volpe has noted this phenomenon of privileging Hauerwas and Eiesland in an article where she surveys and reflects on three contemporary works in disability theology, offering a useful précis of Hauerwas' and Eiesland's theological proposals in the process: Volpe, "Irresponsible Love: Rethinking Intellectual Disability, Humanity and the Church," 490–501. This is also reflected in the publication, some two decades later, of a positive examination of Hauerwas' contribution. John Swinton, ed, *Critical Reflections on Stanley Hauerwas' Theology of Disability*. For the key work of Creamer, see *Disability and Christian Theology*. For Reinders, see *The Future of the*

these Christian theologians are seeking to shine a light onto those living with profound and complex cognitive disabilities or conditions.[11]

A distinctive feature of this emerging body of work is a call for theologians to address the challenges thrown up for such people by anthropologies that deny their personhood, and to consider the lives of the disabled in terms of a re-imagined personhood that does not define them by the condition of their disablement.[12] The key question for these so-called disability theologians is this: How can people who seem to live at the very outer extremes of human life nonetheless be included in the fellowship of the human (and faith) community?

Behind this call for a theological re-imagining of Christian anthropology lies a suggestion that the Christian theological tradition of the past has somehow failed in securing the humanity of the severely disabled, and their moral status within the human community. As their marginalization from participation in the community of persons has grown, the

---

Disabled in Liberal Society and *Receiving the Gift of Friendship*. For Reynolds, see *Vulnerable Communion*. For Swinton, see *Resurrecting the Person* and *Dementia: Living in the Memories of God*. For Yong, see *Theology and Down Syndrome*, More recent books by John Gillibrand, *Disabled Church—Disabled Society*, and Molly C Haslam, *A Constructive Theology of Interllectual Disability*, have been published since the major writing of this work, and therefore do not feature in it.

11. The anthropological reality of the disabled as a specific theological theme is still fledgling, and presently confined almost exclusively to the above-mentioned theologians, almost exclusively from various Protestant traditions, working together in the English language. On the British scene, there is John Swinton and Brian Brock, among others, at the Centre for Spirituality, Health and Disability, Aberdeen University (http://www.abdn.ac.uk/cshad/). In the United States, William Gaventa, and various editorial consultants, are producing the only peer journal of disability theology, the *Journal of Religion, Disability and Health* (http://www.tandf.co.uk/journals/WRDH). There are those, most notably Hans Reinders, who are associated with the European Society for the Study of Theology and Disability (http://www.abdn.ac.uk/cshad/EAS-DT.htm). Apart from what is generated from these sources, theological work specifically directed towards the disabled is slim and scattered (although not unsubstantial, as will be seen), or treated as a sub-theme in bioethics. A collection of symposium papers was published in the French language, from the interdisciplinary study center Pôle Handicaps, Dépendance et citoyenneté, l'Université catholique de Lille (http://www.univ-catholille.fr/etablissements/handicaps-dependance.asp). However, there are no French language sources referenced, and the one theological contribution to the anthropological question of disability is a survey of the literature in English from the sources just mentioned. Foyer, Greiner, and Jacquemin, eds., *Oser parler du handicap: Approches éthiques et théologiques*. See especially the articles by Dominique Greiner, Dominique Foyer, and Vincent Leclercq.

12. For example, see Swinton, "Introduction," 8–12. See also Swinton and McIntosh, "Persons in Relation," 175–84.

INTRODUCTION: PERSONS AMONG PERSONS? 9

Christian tradition has not been able to stem the tide. Therefore, a new way of imagining humanity is needed, one that will secure the inclusion of the profoundly disabled amongst the community of persons without making the condition of their humanity an obstacle to their moral status. Key to this anthropological re-imagining is the adoption of a paradigm of inclusion, around which the condition of human disablement is separated out from the question of human nature. The profoundly disabled, so the argument goes, can be seen to be included in the community of persons when the condition of their disablement is not made to be determinative of their claim to being human.

The turn towards a matrix of inclusion in which to raise theological questions concerning the disabled may be accounted for, at least in part, by a biographical attentiveness towards the lives of those who are disabled. This is a striking point worth noting: unlike the conceptual picture of persons previously described, the re-imagined anthropological picture of these theologians is often motivated by the personal lives of those living with disability. They have sought to bring into the open those whose lives are hidden and marginalized and who are rarely considered as having a voice in theological inquiry. The biographical motivation manifests itself in the search for concepts and language that will provide the profoundly disabled with a way of belonging within the community of persons. Consequently, a paradigm of inclusion towards the disabled, born from a personal involvement in the lives of the disabled, has deeply influenced the subsequent theological inquiry of these theologians.[13]

As a strategy, however, the adoption of a paradigm of inclusion is not to be undertaken without some anthropological risk attached. The German theologian Bernd Wannenwetsch has identified this risk in a brief but insightful commentary on the project of re-imagining Christian anthropology in favor of the profoundly disabled. As he notes,

> Since being referred to as persons, as well as referring to others by this notion, is something we usually take for granted, we are tempted to understand the predication of a disabled human being as "person" as a kind of benevolent stretching of the concept from the usual case toward the unusual. In other words, we are led to think of this "including" of the disabled within

13. Even a cursory survey of the article titles in the peer reviewed *Journal of Religion, Disability and Health* reveals that the relationship between inclusion and the disabled has been consistently and frequently raised as an issue to be attended to, both theologically and pastorally.

the protected zone which we inhabit—"even the disabled!"—as a required *moral act*. Christian contributions to the discussion have often attempted to provide reasons for the adequacy or even necessity of this moral act of inclusion.[14]

The extent to which a paradigm of inclusion is central to the strategies of those concerned for securing the humanity of the profoundly impaired, is the extent to which this warning will need to be heeded in the ensuing arguments.

The Anthropological Project of Hans Reinders

With this brief outline of the general strategy of those working within the area of disability theology, we have a (very rough) sketch of what a re-imagined Christian anthropology in favor of the profoundly impaired might look like: motivated by a paradigm of inclusion, it seeks to secure the humanity of the profoundly impaired without the condition of their humanity becoming an obstacle to their moral status within the community of persons. Of the various authors involved in this theological project, it is the Dutch theologian Hans Reinders who has made the answering of the anthropological question of the profoundly disabled most central to his own work. His major book, *Receiving the Gift of Friendship: Profound Disability, Theological Anthropology, and Ethics*, has attracted considerable scholarly attention and has already reshaped the theological debate.[15] Reinders alone has intentionally produced a sustained work focused on Christian anthropology and profound disability. He is not concerned with articulating pastoral implications, but with proposing theological foundations for the inclusion of the profoundly disabled amongst the community of humanity. It will be his project, therefore, that will be of particular interest to us.

Reinders is concerned with two related claims in *Receiving the Gift of Friendship*: that the profoundly intellectually disabled are "people just like other people" and that, therefore, whatever it is that makes human beings distinctive "it cannot be the human faculties," those features of

---

14. Wannenwesch, "Angels with Clipped Wings," 183. See especially 183–85 for Wannenwetsch's argument.

15. Reinders has written extensively on the question of the profoundly intellectually disabled and specifically from the perspective of Christian anthropology. Both the cover blurbs to *Receiving the Gift of Friendship*, and subsequent peer reviews of it comment on the significance of this book in reshaping the theological debate.

personhood that the profoundly disabled do not have.[16] His basic thesis in relation to these dual claims may be summed up as follows: the humanity of the profoundly disabled cannot be secured by appealing to the traditionally held Christian doctrine of the *imago Dei* because it holds that personhood is something intrinsic to human beings, not normative for them. As the profoundly disabled lack in their natures the requisite characteristics of personhood, especially rationality, volition and self awareness, then the theological anthropology inherent in the *imago Dei*, understood as the measure of humanity's closeness to God by nature, cannot secure for them any claim on humanity. As a counter to this intrinsically moribund notion of the *imago Dei*, Reinders proposes that the extrinsic gift of the friendship offered by God as the good of being human, unencumbered by the reality of the immanent human condition, is the only way of securing the moral status of their lives outside of their impaired natures. It is only in being chosen as a friend by God that the lives of the profoundly disabled are seen to transcend the intrinsically impaired condition of their lives.

According to this picture "person" is not the *nomen dignitatis* of human beings, and the traditional anthropological doctrine of the *imago Dei* is entirely essentialist in meaning. Therefore, "being human"—being someone of human kind living a human life and thereby recognizably a person in God's image—simply cannot secure the humanity of the profoundly disabled. The upshot of this position is that the humanity of the profoundly impaired can be assured only by adopting an anthropology that will sideline their impairment. If this is an accurate summary of Reinders' project—and it will be a major task of the book to show that it is—then it is clearly opposed to the intuition about the humanity of the profoundly impaired that is the principle premise of this book. Therefore, it will be incumbent upon the ensuing theological arguments concerning how the profoundly impaired are recognizably the persons that they are, in virtue of the lives they are living, to show that Reinders' project of re-imaging Christian anthropology for the sake of the profoundly disabled cannot do what it claims to do.

Why is it important for Reinders to secure the humanity of the profoundly disabled in a way that eschews the tradition of the *imago Dei* and the theological provenance of personhood? The simple answer is that any anthropology that makes the condition of their nature central to their

16. Reinders, *Receiving the Gift of Friendship*, 2.

inclusion amongst the community of persons will pose an insurmountable problem for the securing of their humanity. Consequently, he needs to find a way of including them such that the problem that their human nature has for their humanity, because of the condition under which they are living their nature, may be overcome. In other words, Reinders is committed to framing the anthropological question of the profoundly impaired within a paradigm of inclusion, and this commitment leads him to reject a place for their impaired condition in determining the moral status of their humanity.

In engaging with Reinders' position, the challenge ahead will be twofold. Negatively, the task will be to criticise this theological re-imagining of Christian anthropology centered on a paradigm of inclusion and a commitment to separating out the question of one's condition from the question of one's humanity. The significance of such a rejection should not be missed: to argue for a position contrary to the current trend is to cut against the dominant theological grain adopted amongst those concerned for the lives of the profoundly impaired. The more positive task ahead will be to see if the Christian anthropological tradition centered on the doctrine of the *imago Dei* can be retrieved in a way such that the condition of the lives of the profoundly impaired is not the determinative reason why they are recognizably persons, yet it is only in their so-conditioned lives that they can be recognizably the persons that they are.

The Christian Anthropological Tradition from a Catholic Perspective

The relationship between conditioned nature, personhood, and the *imago Dei* has been central to the tradition of Christian anthropology. On the face of it, this relationship proposes a remarkably affirming picture of the personhood of the profoundly impaired. Consider, for example, the following remark by Pope John Paul II, which is a distillation of this tradition from a Catholic perspective:

> The starting point for every reflection on disability is rooted in the fundamental convictions of Christian anthropology: even when disabled persons are mentally impaired or when their sensory or intellectual capacity is damaged, they are fully human beings and possess the sacred and inalienable rights that belong to every human creature. Indeed, human beings, independently of the conditions in which they live or of what they are able to

> express, have a unique dignity and a special value from the very beginning of their life until the moment of natural death.... The wounded humanity of the disabled challenges us to recognize, accept and promote in each one of these brothers and sisters of ours the incomparable value of the human being created by God to be a son in the Son.[17]

The notion that there is something profound at stake simply in being the human beings that we are, impaired or unimpaired, is certainly present in John Paul's statement; but of course, this affirmation of the profoundly impaired is not a theological argument in response to the anthropological question of how the profoundly impaired are recognizably persons. That theological task is what lies ahead. However, it does propose a place in which the argument might be fruitfully grounded, namely: that human beings are recognizably persons—that they possess a unique dignity and incomparable value—because they are the created children of God. Being created in the image of God, therefore, is being presented not as a definition of personhood, but as the reason why all human beings are recognizably persons; and being such a creature is all that counts for being a person.

This is a proposition which says that the personal presence of the profoundly impaired among other persons is not to be denied to them, nor only extended to them as a means of belonging, nor simply eschewed of them so that they may thereby be included by other means. Instead, we have a picture which gives expression to the anthropological amplitude of the second creation narrative from the book of Genesis: "In the image of God he created him; male and female he created them" (Gen 1:27).[18] The Catechism of the Catholic Church draws out this insight in the following way: "Being in the image of God the human individual possesses the dignity of a person, who is not just something, but someone."[19]

The implication is that human beings who are—or who have become—profoundly impaired are recognizably persons because they are made in the image of God. It may be proposed, therefore, that this picture places the doctrine of the *imago Dei* at the heart of Christian anthropology as its proper normative structural underpinning. Consequently, it

---

17. John Paul II, *Message on the Occasion of the International Symposium on the Dignity and Rights of the Mentally Disabled Person*, §2.

18. Unless otherwise noted, all scriptural quotations will be taken from the New Revised Standard Version of the Bible.

19. *Catechism of the Catholic Church* §357.

may also be claimed that the doctrine of the *imago Dei* is thereby to be placed at the structural center of any theological account of the personhood of the profoundly impaired. It will be the intention of this book to address the question of how the profoundly impaired are recognizably the persons that they are by theologically working within a Catholic anthropological imagination. So, it is first to the task of clarifying the theological nature of this Catholic imagination that we must turn.

1

LIFE LIVED AT THE EXTREMES
A Catholic Voice amid the Human Peripheries

A Catholic Voice

THE STORY OF PERSONHOOD, as was noted in the Introduction, cannot be told in isolation from Christian language and history. Consequently, to take up the question of how it is that the profoundly impaired are recognizably persons—how it is that they are acknowledged and respected as moral peers within the human community even though they live at the extremes of the human condition—will mean finding a specific theological voice at which to pitch the question.[1] That voice will be a Catholic one. As a Catholic voice, it is manifestly concerned with reaching out to persons at the "peripheries," as Pope Francis puts it.[2]

In terms of a more general Catholic perspective on personhood, there is no lack of recent scholarly work to draw on.[3] Yet, there is a no-

---

1. This does not mean, however, that the philosophical voice must go unheard; the philosophical and the theological are interwoven, as Hans Urs von Balthasar has noted: "Now in the Christian era, the general (or philosophical) concept [of 'person'] must already exist if it is to receive its special theological content. Yet the unique Trinitarian or Christological content that the concept acquires in theology casts its light back upon the general (or philosophical) understanding without the latter having, therefore, to leave the realm of what is generally human." Balthasar, "On the concept of person," translated by Peter Verhale, in *Communio: International Catholic Review*, 19.

2. Pope Francis, *Evangelii Gaudium*, 20.

3. Both Spaemann's *Persons* and von Balthasar's "On the concept of person" are good examples of Catholic scholarship on the more general question of personhood.

ticeable lack of specific anthropological reflection focused on the lives of the profoundly impaired from a Catholic theological perspective.[4] There is, of course, a very extensive body of literature in Catholic bioethics dealing with moral and pastoral questions in situations of extreme impairment, but this body of work does not generally concern itself with a theological anthropology of those who are so impaired.[5]

The reason for the theological lacuna may have something to do with a tendency amongst Catholic scholars to receive doctrinal pronouncements of an anthropological nature—like John Paul II's statement concerning the disabled—as raising questions best dealt with by philosophical ethics, leaving issues of engagement with the impaired to play out in bioethics and pastoral theology. Be that as it may (and the reason why this is the case will not be pursued any further in this book), the lack of specifically theological voices from within the Catholic tradition

---

Another noteworthy example is Ratzinger, "Retrieving the Tradition: Concerning the notion of person in theology," in *Communio: International Catholic Review*, 439–54. For a philosophical work that seeks to take account of historical themes that have come to dominate questions about personhood, see Kavanaugh, *Who Counts as Persons? Human Identity and the Ethics of Killing*. Working from a similar engagement with historical authors, but taking a phenomenological line, is Robert Sokolowski, *Phenomenology of the Human Person*. For a theological account of the historical development of a specifically Catholic anthropology, see Servais Pinckaers, *The Sources of Christian Ethics*, translated from the third edition of *Les sources de la morale chrétienne*, by Noble.

4. Apart from the French language contribution already mentioned, *Oser parler du handicap*, as far as I am aware, only three Catholic theologians—Emmanuel Agius, a Maltese bioethicist; Mary Jo Iozzio, an American moral theologian; and Pia Matthews, a British ethecist—have written explicitly on questions of theological anthropology and the lives of the profoundly impaired. Agius gave a paper on some theological aspects of disablement at a conference in Europe in 2007, entitled "Disability, Bioethics and Human Rights" (I received an electronic copy of the paper directly from the author himself). Iozzio has written two articles touching on issues of impairment and disablement: Mary Iozzio, "Genetic Anomaly or Genetic Diversity: Thinking in the Key of Disability," 862–81; and "The Writing on the Wall . . . Alzheimer's Disease: A Daughter's Look at Mom's Faithful Care of Dad," 49–74. Matthews' work explores the status of people with profound intellectual disabilities who some regard simply as "non-acting": *Pope John Paul II and the Apparently "Non-acting" Person*.

5. Perhaps the most well-known—and certainly highly regarded—English language textbook in Catholic bioethics currently in circulation is Ashley, deBlois, and O'Rourke, *Healthcare Ethics*. Yet, while it addresses issues pertaining to disability, mental illness, and degenerative impairment, it does not raise as a theological question their status as persons. See especially chapters 5 and 6.

contributing to the anthropological questions thrown up by the lives of the profoundly impaired is, at the very least, something worth redressing.

The other reason for raising a specifically Catholic theological voice has to do with the fact that it has mostly been the Catholic anthropological imagination that has been challenged for contributing to the problem of securing the humanity of the profoundly impaired such that the condition of their humanity is not a central determining factor. Two reasons may be posited for this questioning of the Catholic provenance. Firstly, there is a perception that the Catholic anthropological imagination overly emphasizes ontological and substantialist accounts of personhood (which are then read in essentialist terms). The shape of this perception will become abundantly clear as we make our way through each stage of this book. It is sufficient to note here that this is manifestly the case with Reinders' project of theologically re-imagining the humanity of the profoundly disabled in terms of friendship, over and against the traditional doctrine of the *imago Dei*. It is also the case, more generally, that any theologian who would favor some form of epistemological or relational re-imagining of personhood will have to contend with the Catholic anthropological imagination. Secondly and perhaps more prosaically, the very breadth and depth of the Catholic doctrinal, philosophical, and theological tradition provides a readily available resource with which present-day theologians may engage.

By adopting a specifically Catholic voice in the task ahead, the question that arises is this: How might a Catholic anthropological imagination respond in the face of the challenges posed by the lives of the profoundly impaired, and what theological resources might be drawn from it to aid in that response? To that end, an appropriate initial task will be to give some shape to this Catholic anthropological imagination, for the Church certainly lays claim to offering a privileged perspective on the anthropological question, as the following statement makes abundantly clear:

> As an expert in humanity, [the Church] is able to understand man in his vocation and aspirations, in his limits and misgivings, in his rights and duties, and to speak a word of life that reverberates in the historical and social circumstances of human existence.[6]

---

6. Pontifical Council for Justice and Peace, *Compendium of the Social Doctrine of the Church*, 2004: Pt. 1, Ch. 2.I.a, §61. The provenance of the phrase "expert in humanity" is Pope Paul VI's encyclical letter of 1967, *Populorum progressio* (§.13). The phrase itself has become commonplace in the magisterial teachings of the Church.

Are They Human? Puzzlement and Expertise

The first word to be said about this shape, however, would seem to be one of puzzlement and not expertise. Unlike the certainty of the psalmist writing in Psalm 139 about the constitution of his own humanity, some people appear not to have been properly "knit together in their mother's womb" or apparently their humanity has subsequently become unraveled (Ps 139:13). How is it that they are recognizably the answer to the question: Human being? We are presented with a factual puzzle when faced with the deeply mysterious nature of the humanity of the profoundly impaired. The further removed in appearance someone is from the biological norm the more pronounced the puzzlement becomes about his or her hold on a human nature.

This is an acknowledgment of how very limited is the extent to which the mystery of human life lived at the extremes is penetrable. So when the Catholic Church lays claim to being "an expert in humanity" we may fairly ask how this is the case, because "being puzzled" would seem to be a more apt way of characterizing how the Christian tradition—along both Catholic and Protestant lines—has approached those people whose lives are lived at the extremes of the human condition.

In acknowledging this factual puzzlement, we may also acknowledge that the Catholic Church's present-day claim to anthropological expertise is not meant to be read as some kind of claim to special knowledge utterly independent of science and philosophy. Presumably, the Church is offering instead some qualified notion of expert knowledge. What this might be is hinted at in the list of paired aspects about human life associated with the the claim to expertise: vocation/limitation; aspiration/misgiving; right/duty.[7] None of these pairings tells us anything about the constitutional makeup of human beings; they do not answer the qualitative question: What is a human being? They do, however, point out where to look if the question is about the recognition of the unique individual human being living his or her life. Two distinctive ways of accounting for human beings are identifiable, therefore: one that is factual and the other

---

Pope Benedict XVI declared: "The Church has no technical solutions to propose but, as an expert in humanity, offers to all the teaching of Sacred Scripture on the truth about mankind, and proclaims the Gospel of Love and justice." *Midday Angelus*, 12 July 2009.

7. Reminiscent, no doubt, of the opening line of the Second Vatican Council's "Pastoral Constitution on the Church in the Modern World," §.1.

that is normative. This distinction is another way of expressing the distinction previously noted between "human being" and "being human."

What is significant about this distinction, such that it should make a difference to the claim of expertise? A quip attributed to G. K. Chesterton helps bring it out: "We speak of a manly man, but not of a whaley whale."[8] While the Church may puzzle over the nature of the "man," the factuality of a human life, concurrently she may express knowledge (born of a reasoned faith) about the nature of the "manly," the living of a human life. The former is a qualitative question; the latter is a recognitional one. To be a man—to acknowledge the person that one is—always involves both a third-person perspective and a first-person one, yet the factuality of someone's human nature is only resolved in the recognition of him or her being human, and not the other way around. A human being is always someone, and never only something; being the human being that one is—being a person—is the *modus existendi* of human beings.

The expertise that the Church claims for herself is a knowledge and understanding of what is genuinely human about being a human being, that is, about living a human kind of life, and not the significance of any factual differences that may distinguish one human being from another. Thus,

> The dignity of the person is not touched by such observations [of factual human differences], for the dignity of human beings as persons is not an object of observation but of recognition.... If we say that someone is a person, we are saying that he or she is someone, a unique Individual; and this cannot be understood as the chance implication of one predicate, or even of an ensemble of predicates. *What* he or she may be besides does not settle *who* he or she is. The *what* we can observe and comprehend; the *who* is accessible to us only as we recognize something ultimately inaccessible.[9]

The lives of those who live at the extremes of human life do raise factual doubts about their humanity. However, once the fact of the matter is established—or charity demands a favorable reading—then the claim to being human, even if it is lived in terms of a grossly deformed nature, overrides all other considerations. Resolving the factual question of a human being is of significance only to the extent that it involves laying claim

---

8. Quoted in Schmude, *G. K. Chesterton*, 20.
9. Spaemann, *Persons*, 39.

to the *modus existendi* of being human, and this, in turn, is to lay claim to a unique place in the order of creation.

Being human always involves a normative claim, regardless of the deformity of one's nature or departure from the biological norm. Despite the puzzlement that may arise in asking the factual question, therefore, the broad Christian tradition has consistently held that deformity of nature or departure from the norm is not in itself a morally significant factor once a human life is taken to be present. From a Catholic perspective, once the factual reality is affirmed then no other criterion is required to establish the moral status of that individual. The question: "Human being?" is always a question that requires more than a factual answer because a human being always exists as someone, the unique individual of normative import that he or she is. There is always something at stake when it comes to a living human being. It is in affirming this reality that the Catholic Church lays claim to her expertise.

An Existential Anthropology: The *imago Dei* in *Gaudium et Spes*

This claim finds conciliar confirmation in the anthropology adopted by the Catholic Church at the Second Vatican Council, in the Pastoral Constitution *Gaudium et Spes* (GS).[10] The document itself is acknowledged to be the first time the Church had articulated a specific anthropology in its own right.[11] It did this by doctrinally affirming the scriptural notion of the *imago Dei*: that human beings are made according to (or after) the image of God. This adoption of the notion of the *imago Dei* as the hermeneutical key to the Church's anthropology is made explicit at the beginning and end of the chapter on the human person. In so doing, GS notes both the creational and christological dimensions to the *imago Dei*, as it is found in Sacred Scripture (Gen 1:26 and Col 1:15, respectively). Thus, the Council Fathers taught:

> For Sacred Scripture teaches that man was created "to the image of God," is capable of knowing and loving his Creator, and

---

10. Vatican II, *Gaudium et Spes*. See especially "Part I: The Church and Man's Calling; Chapter I: The Dignity of the Human Person."

11. As the German theologian Cardinal Walter Kasper has noted, "*Gaudium et Spes* signals the first time that a council has consciously endeavored to set forth a systematic account of Christian anthropology in an independent thematic context.... Prior to Vatican II no council had produced a 'general outline' of Christian anthropology." Kasper, "Theological Anthropology of *Gaudium et Spes*," 129.

was appointed by Him as master of all earthly creatures that he might subdue them and use them to God's glory. (GS 12)

He Who is "the image of the invisible God," is Himself the perfect man. To the sons of Adam He restores the divine likeness which had been disfigured from the first sin onward. Since human nature as He assumed it was not annulled, by that very fact it has been raised up to a divine dignity in our respect too. (GS 22)

In turning to the notion of the *imago Dei* as the anthropological key, the Council Fathers saw in it a way of bringing the order of creation into line with the redemptive and eschatological order, such that the origin and destiny of humanity would be seen in its integrated whole. The *imago Dei* is the linchpin, as it were, between the two poles of creation and redemption, placing anthropology into its proper and fulfilling christological setting.

Without denying or undermining the significance of the christological configuration of the anthropological question, however, our interest in the hermeneutical role of the *imago Dei* lies mainly in the creational dimension. This is because our focus on the humanity of the profoundly impaired is not about raising as a question the extent to which each individual human being, in being human, comes to live according to the true image of God found in Jesus Christ. Rather our focus is on how someone who is profoundly impaired exists according to the image of God in which all human beings exist, and by which they are destined in Christ.[12] It is the human being who is firstly created in the image of God, he who has his origins in that image, who is then to be redeemed as the image of God. This is, as the Council Fathers noted, the vocation—the God-given destiny—proper to each and every human being in his being human, and the source of his dignity (GS 21).

It is this existential configuration of the *imago Dei* that is especially noteworthy about GS. The Council Fathers were not concerned with responding to the factual questions of human beings, but with that one

---

12. Of the relationship between these two dimensions of the anthropology espoused in GS, David L. Schindler has noted, "The tension that arises [between Art. 12 and Art. 22] is thus between a potentially 'theistically-colored and to a large extent non-historical view' of man, which can result from Article 12's omission of Christology from its theology of creation, and the more concrete view of man which results form Article 22's Christological integration of the orders of creation and redemption-eschatology." Schindler, "Christology and the *Imago Dei*," 158.

living human being who, representatively, stands before the world making a claim of acknowledgment on it.

> Man is not wrong when he regards himself as superior to bodily concerns, and as more than a speck of nature or a nameless constituent of the city of man. For by his interior qualities he outstrips the whole sum of mere things. (GS 14)

To be a man, to be a living human being, is to be someone who, by virtue of being human, reaches out beyond a merely descriptive presence amidst the world of things into presenting a personal presence to the world. He is superior not in qualitative terms (in what he is), but in terms of his personal existence (in who he is). It is precisely in his personal existence that he locates the dignity of the human vocation: to live his life according to the image of God that he is. Doctrinally speaking, therefore, the manner in which the interpretive key of the *imago Dei* is adopted in GS points to the framing of the Church's anthropological position in existential terms, and not essentially. Being a human creature—existing as a human being—is what matters for grounding the dignity and vocation proper to every human being, because by virtue of the creaturely existence proper to being human, they are in the image of God.

Being Treated as a Person: *Donum vitae* and the Profoundly Impaired

How does this general anthropological imagination of the Catholic Church play out in the lives of the profoundly impaired? To this end, we may turn to a doctrinal position repeated on a number of occasions in recent years, but first adopted in the magisterial Instruction *Donum vitae* of 1987 (DV). While DV is concerned with addressing issues pertaining to the beginnings of human life, its anthropological insights are equally pertinent to the lives of the profoundly impaired. It begins by noting what the Church can and cannot say anthropologically:

> Certainly no experimental datum can be in itself sufficient to bring us to the recognition of a spiritual soul; nevertheless, the conclusions of science regarding the human embryo provide a valuable indication for discerning by the use of reason a personal presence at the moment of this first appearance of a human life: how could a human individual not be a human person? The Magisterium has not expressly committed itself to an

affirmation of a philosophical nature, but it constantly reaffirms the moral condemnation of any kind of procured abortion. This teaching has not been changed and is unchangeable.[13]

Evidently here the Church remains unwilling to make a definitive declaration on the qualitative question of what constitutes a human being. That question is properly approached from scientific and philosophical criteria, and the Church makes no claim to revealed knowledge in this regard. Factual puzzlement—expressed in a more humble submission to the mysteries of what constitutes a human life biologically and philosophically—is an abiding acknowledgment of the Church concerning what constitutes a human being. Yet, the statement also notes the basic stance adopted by the Church in favor of defending and protecting human life in its absolute condemnation of willed abortion, thereby overriding any constitutional mystery. The statement is affirming the constant (and radical) Christian practice adopted from earliest times to oppose abortion and infanticide.[14]

Significantly in this context, the notion of personhood is not introduced in qualitative terms. The Church is not concerned with first establishing what is required to constitute a human being as a person, as if personhood is some quality pertaining to a particular nature. Instead, by employing the phrase "personal presence" DV proposes that the appropriate way to approach the question of personhood is adjectivally, which has the effect of positioning personhood in terms of being human. As a consequence, the word "person" is the name for the mode in which a human being exists, and not as the fact of human existence or as something that human beings may (or may not) have. The claim of the Church, therefore, is that she relies on the expertise of science and philosophy to help with the qualitative question about what constitutes a human being, but then brings her own expertise to the table with knowledge about the manner of human existence, namely: human beings exist personally.

---

13. Congregation of the Doctrine of the Faith, "Instruction on Respect for Human Life in its Origin and on the Dignity of Procreation" *Donum vitae* (22 February 1987): I.§1. This statement was confirmed by Pope John Paul II in his encyclical letter "The Gospel of Life," §60, and reaffirmed by the CDF in its "Instruction on Certain Bioethical Questions," *Dignitas personae*: I.§4.

14. For example, the ancient Christian text of the *Didache* states, "You shall not kill a child by abortion nor shall you kill it once it is born" (V.2). This is a very early expression of the Church's radical opposition to the culture of the time where the exposure of fetuses and infants was practiced.

The implication of this approach for the profoundly impaired is revealed in the way in which DV goes on to speak about how being human determines the way all human beings are to be regarded.

> Thus the fruit of human generation, from the first moment of its existence, that is to say from the moment the zygote has formed, demands the unconditional respect that is morally due to the human being in his bodily and spiritual totality. The human being is to be respected and treated as a person from the moment of conception; and therefore from that same moment his rights as a person must be recognized, among which in the first place is the inviolable right of every innocent human being to life. This doctrinal reminder provides the fundamental criterion for the solution of the various problems posed by the development of the biomedical sciences in this field: since the embryo must be treated as a person, it must also be defended in its integrity, tended and cared for, to the extent possible, in the same way as any other human being as far as medical assistance is concerned.[15]

Particularly noteworthy in this part of the statement is the fundamental criterion upon which a judgment about human life is to be made, namely: absolute equal regard for human beings from the moment that the factual question is resolved. As with the tradition it is following, DV is making clear that there is to be no distinction between human beings relative to the constitutive condition of their nature, no matter what level of deformity or stage of underdevelopment. Of course, the Church is laying out a doctrinal position here, and not arguing for it. Nonetheless, a significant theological nuance is made in regard to this criterion with the use of the word "as," in the sentence: *The human being is to be respected and treated as a person.*

One possible way of interpreting the word is to understand it to be making a claim that the Church has, for doctrinal reasons, adopted a practical policy of treating human beings as persons, even while conceding the theoretical possibility that some may not be. It is an assertion, based in faith, to see personhood as integral to being human, but not necessarily co-extensive of human beings. In this reading of "as" personhood is a predicate applicable to human beings synthetically, not analytically: "person" is ascribable to human beings, not a word for "human being." As such, it implies a distinction of a moral kind between human nature

15. *Donum vitae*, I.§1

and personhood. This is not, however, how the notion of personhood is presented more generally according to the anthropology of GS, nor is it how it is set up in the first half of the quotation from DV. So there is good reason to assume that the "as" in the second half is not indicating a practical stance taken in relation to a synthetic proposition about personhood.

For the two parts of the quotation to be consistent with each other, and to understand GS and DV as presenting one coherent teaching of the Church, consider the following way of reading the "as" sentence: *Human beings always exist as persons, that is, personally, because "person" is the mode in which human beings are who they are.* The implication is no longer one of making a distinction between nature and personhood, but one of recognizing a nature as being personal in kind. To acknowledge the presence of a human being is to acknowledge a personal presence.

Accordingly, human beings are to be respected and treated as persons because that is precisely what it means for them to be human: a person is a living human being. Even if we are left puzzled on scientific and philosophical grounds about how the humanity of someone who is profoundly impaired is constituted, we are to acknowledge them to be the persons that they are in the acknowledgment of the humanity that they have. This is what is especially significant about the word "as" as it is being proposed anthropologically in DV. It allows for the factual puzzlement thrown up by the lives of some human beings living at the extremes of human life, which the Church continues to acknowledge, while insisting on the personal status of being human, which the Church has always practiced.

Recalling that DV presents a doctrinal position and not a theological argument, we may now at least recognize in it a specifically Catholic point of reference to bring to the theological task ahead of accounting for how we recognize the personhood of the profoundly impaired. While DV does not explicitly use the language adopted in GS to give expression to a Catholic anthropology, the doctrine of the *imago Dei* is very much in mind when it teaches that there is a personal presence at the first appearance of a human life. Therefore, DV is both a faithful articulation of the Christian anthropological tradition, as that has come down to the present day in teaching and practice, and a specific articulation of that tradition in terms of those who are living at the extremes of the human condition. It is also enough to have picked up along the way something of how this doctrinal stance articulates the distinction between "human being" and "being human."

An Anthropology of Childlikeness

Admittedly, Sacred Scripture, the primary resource for a theological argument that would give flesh to the doctrinal bones of GS and DV, does not make the task easy. The profoundly impaired, at least as they are being characterised here, are conspicuously absent from the canons of both the Hebrew and Christian Testaments. They do not appear as characters integral to the unfolding drama of God's self-revelation nor as specific subjects of concern in Jesus' manifestations of the Kingdom. No healing of Jesus ever involved someone profoundly impaired; he spoke no direct word to or of them.[16] They do not receive mention in the list of the blessed (Matt 5; Luke 6) nor in the list of the least (Matt 25). This lack of direct textual reference does not mean the Bible is devoid of valuable theological and ethical insight into the lives of the profoundly impaired. As it is, Scripture is permeated with images of our littleness and weakness with respect to God, and of his care for us in our insignificance.

The theme of childlikeness is a curious undercurrent that flows through both the Hebrew and Christian scriptures, yet it seems to have been unconsidered in Christian anthropology. One such example is to be found in Psalm 131 where a fully-grown adult, with all his faculties intact and functioning, nonetheless finds himself in the image of a newly weaned infant. Another example, one that is worth a closer look, is the story common to all three Synoptic Gospels (Matt 19; Mark 10; Luke 18) where Jesus was blessing little children presented to him.[17] Here is Luke's version:

> People were bringing even infants to him that he might touch them; and when the disciples saw it, they sternly ordered them not to do it. But Jesus called for them and said, "Let the little children come to me, and do not stop them; for it is to such as these that the kingdom of God belongs. Truly I tell you, whoever does not receive the kingdom of God as a little child will never enter it." (Luke 18:15–17)

---

16. But what of the various healings of the so-called possessed (e.g., Mark 5; Matt 8; Luke 4 and 8)? Do they not point to a deep attentiveness of Jesus towards the severely mentally ill? The difficulty with this class of healings is that they are presented as manifestations of an externalized, spiritual force imposed on an otherwise unimpaired subject. There is no clear indication that Jesus ever treated them in terms of exhibiting manifestly permanent conditions of human impairment.

17. Matthew splits the story into two separate pericopes: Matt 18:1–5 and Matt 19:13–15.

There is an obvious meaning to this story concerning trust and simplicity of heart with which the children reach out to Jesus; what he has observed in children he looks for in turn in his disciples. Jesus makes it clear that adult disciples are to look to how young children live out their humanity to learn how they are to live their own. There is no deferment to an elevated anthropology present here. Jesus presents little children, and not mature adults fully capable of exercising their reason and will, as the model of living a fully human life. The implication is that while human capacity is a feature of human beings, it is not the gospel measure of being human. It is not what human beings are capable of that reveals whether or not they have their humanity well or fully. Jesus does not negate these God-given gifts, but looks for their humble submission into a different vision of human living. One can reason and will to one's heart's content, so long as it is in the manner of the young child who does not rely on these faculties to live his or her life to the full.

This childlike undercurrent in the Bible is worth noting, even if briefly, because it is suggestive of a way in which to approach the anthropological question of the profoundly impaired. The gospel intuition moves our thinking away from what has been called "our society's obsession with the images of mastery and autonomy," without denying a proper place for a human nature grounded in reason and will.[18] The theological question arising from this scriptural note is sounded well by the Swiss-born spiritual master, Br. Roger of Taizé: "What does it mean for someone who is fully an adult to combine the spirit of childhood and the maturity that comes with long years of experience?"[19] To which we may add: How does the experience of living a profoundly impaired life likewise combine with being the human being that he or she is? What lies behind this question, and the biblical theme of childlikeness that prompts it, is the issue just identified: How can we account for the meaning of human life such that the condition of any one individual living that life is not disregarded? In its turn, this question highlights the need to avoid any theological argument that treats the lives of the impaired and unimpaired as anthropologically different.

18. Wannenwetsch, "Angels with Clipped Wings," 192.
19. Roger of Taizé, *Path of Hope*, 21–22.

One Anthropology for All

With this note of warning in mind, we may turn with approval to one of the very few statements made by the Catholic Church specifically directed towards the lives of the profoundly impaired as support for adopting this position. It is a *Message* given by Pope John Paul II on the occasion of a symposium on mental retardation.[20] The key doctrinal sentence from the *Message* is this:

> Indeed, human beings, independently of the conditions in which they live or of what they are able to express, have a unique dignity and a special value from the very beginning of their life until the moment of natural death.

John Paul then draws out the implication of this claim:

> The disabled person, with all the limitations and suffering that scar him or her, forces us to question ourselves, with respect and wisdom, on the mystery of man. In fact, the more we move about in the dark and unknown areas of human reality, the better we understand that it is in the more difficult and disturbing

---

20. Vanier, that great advocate for the humanity of the profoundly impaired, had this to say about the *Message*: "I consider this document by John Paul II to be one of the most important writings about the affirmation of the transformative power of people with disabilities." Jean Vanier, *Our Life Together*, 549, note '*'. What adds to the significance of this comment is Vanier's sense that the Pope had grown into this understanding of the profoundly disabled: "John Paul II was another person who came to truly understand L'Arche, but perhaps only when he became ill with Parkinson's disease. I remember the first time I had breakfast with him (in 1987, when he was still well) and I explained to him how a disabled person . . . was a healing presence in L'Arche. ... John Paul said to someone afterwards that he hadn't understood what I meant. It's after he become sick that . . . he understood how someone 'made little' by severe handicap could transform others" (548–49). The mention of the year 1987 is important because Reinders also sees John Paul as a source for understanding the profoundly disabled, and refers not to the 2004 *Message*, but to something written in 1981, long before Vanier had perceived a genuine understanding coming from the Pope. Cf. *RGF*: 19, 88 & 120–22. Furthermore, the document Reinders refers to does not seem to be from the pen of John Paul at all. Certainly it does not appear in either the *AAS* or in the list of documents attributed to the Pope on the official website of the Holy See. What it does seem to refer to is an anonymously written article in the *L'Osservatore Romano*, the quasi official newspaper of the Holy See, on the occasion of the International Year of the Disabled in 1981. Therefore, the understanding of the Church's position Reinders draws from it must be called into question, and the 2004 document may be considered a more authoritative articulation of the Church's doctrinal position.

situations that the dignity and grandeur of the human being emerges.[21]

What John Paul seems to be indicating is that any reflection on the lives of the profoundly impaired needs to reflect back onto the lives of all human beings if it is to be an authentic expression of a Catholic anthropology. There can be only one anthropological account of being human, not different accounts for different classes of people; the lives of the profoundly impaired inform that account in a way that is applicable to the lives of all. Significantly, John Paul links this anthropological intuition directly to the puzzlement that we have noted in the Christian tradition concerning those living their lives at the extremes of the human condition. It is by being attentive to the dark and unknown areas of human reality that the full meaning of the lives of all human beings will emerge. As Jean Vanier, the French-Canadian founder of the L'Arche communities, has pointed out on many occasions and in various ways:

> People with disabilities can be a paradox. Sometimes we are not quite sure who they are nor how to react to them. Their presence obliges us to look more deeply into our own lives and to reflect on what is really important.[22]

In seeking to look into our own lives through the prism of the lives of the profoundly impaired, there is one feature of Catholic anthropology (and Christian anthropology more generally) that has consistently and characteristically been distinctive about it, but which, on the face of it, would appear to raise a specific and seemingly devastating problem for the profoundly impaired. It is this: however else human life might be conceived, the faculties of reason and will—that is, subjective human agency—have always been a defining feature of that conception. We may simply note the far-reaching influence of Boethius' definition of a human person—*naturae rationalis individua substantia*—to appreciate the extent to which it is the rational and volitional human being who has come to dominate Christian anthropological thinking.[23] Human nature is a rational and volitional nature.

While debate will continue over how reason and will combine to play their part in human living, their presence in the anthropological context

---

21. John Paul II, *Message on the Occasion of the International Symposium on the Dignity and Rights of the Mentally Disabled Person*, §2.

22. Vanier, *Befriending the Stranger*, 38.

23. Boethius, *De persona et duabus naturis*, c.ii.

is entirely uncontroversial. Yet evidently, some human beings—including those we are attending to—do not fit into this anthropological picture. In the most extreme cases, they do not show even a minimal indication that personal agency plays any role whatsoever in their lives. So herein lies the issue: Are their lives truly human lives, given that they have never had, or no longer have, the capacity for subjective human agency?

Even a cursory survey of contemporary Christian moral theology will quickly reveal the lack of attention given to the specifically human dimensions of the profoundly impaired. Consider the following example from the Belgium Thomist Servais Pinckaers, OP, one of the most eminent Catholic moral theologians of the late twentieth century and early twenty-first, who was deeply indebted to the anthropological insights of Thomas Aquinas, who in turn took his cue from Boethius (ST I.29.2).

> No concept of humanity, no anthropology can adequately grasp the best and noblest qualities of the human person. The source lies in actions and thoughts; it is these that make the person.[24]

What is evident in this example (and many more like it from other eminent Catholic theologians) is what might be called an elevated view of anthropology, whereby subjective agency is presented as the decisive moral factor in human living. There is little room here to allow for the manner in which the profoundly impaired live their lives. On the face of it, it is difficult to see how the profoundly impaired are meant to find a genuinely human place at all within a picture that privileges the reasoning and willing human being. Yet undoubtedly, the rational and volitional nature of human beings continues to play a central role in traditional accounts of the Christian—and specifically Catholic—anthropological imagination.

It is at this seemingly contradictory juncture that Hans Reinders takes up his own anthropological re-imagining in favor of the profoundly disabled such that a transcending concept of humanity centered on receiving the gift of friendship replaces an immanent conception reliant on a capacity-based explanation. His point is that any anthropological view based on the things that the human faculties allow people to do or to have, as being the things that make people human, is manifestly inadequate when it comes to accounting for the lives of the profoundly disabled. Without at least the capacity for human agency and the future prospect of exercising it, how can a claim be made on living a fully human life? This,

---

24. Pinckaers, *Sources of Christian Ethics*, 88.

at least, seems to be the tenor of Reinders' difficulties with traditional Christian anthropology, specifying the Catholic-supported doctrine of the *imago Dei* as being especially tarred by this brush. Reinders' project, therefore, comes down to this: To what extent can we talk about human life without reference to reason and will? To take this question seriously is to dispense with the notion that something is at stake for humanity generally in retaining a central place for reason and will in the living of a human life, all for the sake of including the profoundly impaired.

This is a radical move indeed. If the dividing of some human beings from others, because of their deviation from the conceptual norm, is wrongheaded, then so too is the dividing of some from others, because of their possessing rationality and free will. Reinders is certainly correct to say that the answer to the question of one's humanity "depends very much on how we understand our own being as humans."[25] Radically re-imagining the Christian anthropological tradition, for the sake of including certain human beings, raises fundamental theoretical issues for theology, both about whether or not the anthropological alternative (in this case friendship) is up to the task, and about any abiding strength in the traditional approach.

Thus, a question may now be posed to Reinders' reaction against the supposedly elevated anthropology of the Christian tradition: Is reason and will central to the living of all human lives such that the condition under which any one individual living that life is not disregarded? Reinders says "no"; the Catholic anthropological tradition seems to say "yes." The task ahead will be to show how it is that the former gets the answer wrong (if not the question), and to show how the latter has the resources for getting it right. We begin with Reinders' re-imagined anthropology of friendship.

---

25. Reinders, *Receiving the Gift of Friendship*, 11.

2

"PEOPLE JUST LIKE OTHER PEOPLE"

Reinders' Reimagined Anthropology of the Profoundly Impaired

Reinders' Assumptions

AT THE HEART OF Hans Reinders' project in *Receiving the Gift of Friendship* is the claim that the only sure path to full inclusion amongst the community of persons for the profoundly disabled lies in their being chosen as a friend. He acknowledges that the increased political awareness of disability in many societies over recent decades has brought about a change for the better for people with profound disabilities, especially in terms of their participation as citizens of society. Reinders' contention, however, is that it is not in the domain of citizenship (to use his phraseology) that the one kind of good that matters most to the profoundly disabled will be located, but in the domain of intimacy, in being befriended.[1] Thus:

> Despite the success they have found in strengthening their status in the public sphere, people with disabilities—particularly intellectual disabilities—experience loneliness and isolation in the sphere of their personal lives. . . . This is the reason why we need to think beyond rights and justice. In many cases, the lives of persons with disabilities lack the blessing of intimacy: that is, they lack friends, which is the one kind of good that rights and justice claims cannot achieve.[2]

1. Reinders, *Receiving the Gift of Friendship*, 6.
2. Ibid.

The crucial task Reinders sets himself, therefore, is to move the argument pertaining to the humanity of the profoundly disabled beyond the political realm of citizenship and participation, centered on justice and the rights of the disabled, and into the more personal realm of the goods that people pursue in their lives, and especially friendship. In making such a move, the notion of friendship is presented as not just a question that may be asked about the humanity of the profoundly disabled, but the specific anthropological solution to the question of the profoundly disabled. It is this notion of the good of friendship to which Reinders turns to make this argument.

Reinders has in mind a specific aspect of the good of friendship to do the anthropological work for the profoundly disabled: "contemporary moral culture disseminates conceptions of a good life that hardly help us to imagine someone with an intellectual disability as a friend."[3] It is this particular notion of the disabled being chosen as a friend—of the unimpaired imaging themselves as befriending the impaired—that Reinders wants to pair up with a more general notion of the good of friendship. Therefore, to get at the heart of the structure underpinning Reinders' understanding of friendship, which in turn underpins his entire project, it is necessary to examine critically the way in which he brings together "friendship," "goodness," and "being chosen." This, then, is the task at hand.[4] It will provide the basis upon which subsequently to judge (in the next chapter) whether or not his anthropological grounding of friendship holds up to scrutiny, and whether or not his project in favor of being chosen as a friend can ensure the personal presence of the profoundly impaired amongst the community of persons.

A Transcending Concept of Humanity

It will be helpful to begin this task by noting at the outset where Reinders seeks to go with his anthropological notion of the good of friendship. He begins with a fixed position: being chosen as a friend is the only sure way of grounding the humanity of the profoundly disabled, because their inherent incapacities—specifically, their lack of purposive agency—will always fail to secure for them a claim to being fully human. With this

---

3. Ibid., 7.

4. Reinders addresses the question of the relationship between friendship and goodness in ibid., chapter 4.

end in mind, Reinders goes looking for "a transcending concept of what it means to live a truly human life," one which will provide "a universally valid answer" suitable for the profoundly disabled.[5] Locating this universalizing transcending concept of what it is to be a human being is a question of articulating "what it is to be a *flourishing* human being," whereby "the question of the meaning and purpose of being human coincides with the question of the human good."[6] The task that flows out of that question is this:

> to conceive of the ultimate human good [i.e., the good of human being] in such a way that the result does not regard the lives of human beings with profound disabilities either as "defective" or as only marginally participating in the good.[7]

The task Reinders has set for himself, therefore, is one of searching for the various facets of this one transcending idea pertaining to the good of human being that will support and secure the choice in favor of friendship over and against inherent capacity (which he believes the Christian tradition treats as being synonymous with personhood).[8]

In Reinders' thinking, the goal of being chosen as a friend contains within it a certain programmatic means to the end. At each juncture of his argument he will employ the same conceptual commitment—that is, the transcending-concept-of-the-human-good—to secure the goal. When it comes to securing the humanity of the profoundly disabled, the choice between what pertains to "friendship" and what pertains to "capacity-person" involves a single, repeatable parting of the ways determined by the transcendence criterion. Thus, Reinders identifies a series of binary opposites—philosophical/theological; ontological/teleological; origin/end (purpose); intrinsic/extrinsic; active/passive—based on the imminent/transcendent divide, each of which neatly belongs in either the "capacity-person" or the "friendship" camp. In other words, it would seem that human life is conceived of in two fundamentally opposed ways, one of which is consistently and systematically chosen over the other because

---

5. Ibid., 154.
6. Ibid., 124 (original italics).
7. Ibid., 125.
8. Thus, for example, Reinders claims that the identity of capacity and personhood is at the heart of Catholic anthropology: "Clearly, this statement [referring to §48 of the 1993 encyclical *Veritatis Splendor*] entails the conception of the human person as defined by the embodied capacity for reason and will." Ibid., 96.

of what it apparently offers in terms of the humanity of the profoundly disabled. With this in mind, the chief work to be done in the critical task ahead will be to show that Reinders has indeed made this the decisive, recurring (and, as will become evident, peculiar) move in his argument as it unfolds, and to uncover why he does it.

As the answer has already been hinted at in the preceding paragraph, the question as to why Reinders goes looking for the transcending good of friendship to secure the humanity of the profoundly disabled can be dealt with quickly. The presupposition that human life is presentable from two different conceptual perspectives is the key. For Reinders, only a transcending conception can be inclusive of the humanity of the profoundly disabled as the other presumes that the fullness of humanity is closed to them because of their lack of purposeful capacity, of personhood.[9] If the profoundly disabled are to be "one of us" (as he puts it), if they are to have a share in our humanity, then the conception of the "us" must be one such that it can accommodate the "one" in a non-capacity-based way.[10] It must be a conception that is different from, and entirely unencumbered by, the traditional conception grounded in personhood. Of course, this is nothing more than a restatement of his reason for the entire project.[11] It has the advantage, however, of highlighting the importance that Reinders places on the issue of inclusion of the profoundly disabled in the human community. Inclusion is the underlying motivation-giving purpose to the project; it is why he finds it necessary to go looking for a different conception of human life, one based on the transcendent good of receiving the gift of friendship.

If inclusion gives us reason to think that Reinders might want to be adopting a comprehensive approach to the anthropological question of the profoundly disabled, then the question as to whether or not he does indeed make this move may be approached as a question of how he does it. To do this, it will be helpful to gain some sense of how the immanent and transcendent concepts of human life operate, as well as a sense of why it is precisely a conceptual difference that is being asserted. Consider the following remark:

9. "If human beings with profound intellectual disabilities are to be dignified, then the ground of their dignity cannot be found in human capacity." Ibid., 11.

10. Chapter 1 is entitled "One of Us." Ibid.

11. "I do believe that human beings with profound intellectual disabilities are people like other people, and I do believe that the best way to understand human beings is not found in the human faculties." Ibid., 2.

> The important distinction here [in terms of human subjectivity] is the distinction between the *gift* of life and the *givenness* of life. When "choice" dominates one's moral view, life appears as *datum*, but not necessarily as *donum*. *Datum* refers to "gift" as contingency: there is givenness, but there is no giver. In contrast, *donum* refers to givenness that implies purpose. The gift of life implies a giver who may have had a purpose in mind by "sending" whatever it is that happens to you.[12]

Reinders' stated purpose in drawing such a distinction between *datum* and *donum* is to re-conceive human subjectivity away from "choosing," centered on a paradigm of human acting, and onto "receiving," a paradigm of responding.[13] The point of making this shift is to discount the possibility of viewing the goodness and purpose of human life as conferrable on people's lives "by virtue of their own authorisation" (hence, the "choosing" paradigm), because this would automatically exclude the profoundly disabled from participation in such human goodness and purpose.[14] Herein lies the reason why Reinders is looking for a transcending concept of human life: in one conception the profoundly disabled are excluded from a personal presence among the community of persons because of what they intrinsically lack; while in the other personal presence is not even a question needing to be asked of them because the purpose of their lives is established in what has been given to them extrinsically.

These two perspectives on human life do not operate simply as different modes of expressing human life, which are ultimately reconcilable in the individual life of each human being. Instead, these two ways of conceiving of human beings are incommensurable leitmotifs about human life and its goodness. To commit to the *datum*/act/choosing motif is to pursue a classification of human being as determined by a taxonomy of personally enabling capacities supposedly inherent in human nature. It is to conceive of a human life as intrinsically constructed. To commit to the *donum*/response/receiving motif is to pursue a universally common purpose to human life unencumbered by the limitations imposed on participation by a profoundly disabling condition. This is to conceive of human life as extrinsically constituted. The former falls into the realm of an immanent conception of human life, while the latter envisages human life as a transcendent concept. They start from different places, so

---

12. Ibid., 137.
13. Ibid., 136.
14. Ibid., 137.

they pursue different outcomes. These two perspectives on human life are properly leitmotifs, therefore, of which one excludes the profoundly disabled from the human community and the other includes them in it. There can be neither a commixture of them in their various elements, nor can they be reconciled at some deeper level of unity.

At least, this seems to be the anthropological stance advocated by Reinders, to be fleshed out in terms of the binary opposites noted earlier. We must ask whether this is a fair reading of his position. This can be answered by considering the way in which he compares his approach to the humanity of the profoundly impaired to that of four other theologians who have likewise grappled with the anthropological question of their lives.[15] Reinders takes these four theologies and examines the extent to which they are either free of or undermined by boundary blurring between the two motifs, based on the immanence/transcendence divide. To make the point, it will suffice to consider David Pailin's so-called "theology of human being," which is the one Reinders most favors.[16]

What Reinders finds appealing in Pailin's thinking is a determination to eliminate the ranking of inherent differences between human beings as a reason for excluding some individuals, and to embrace diversity of human life such that it includes all individuals. All human beings are limited, restricted, finite, says Pailin; there is simply a diverse expression of this reality. That view of human life which promotes difference in human beings is good, but that approach to human life which differentiates between human beings is not. The profoundly disabled are not different from the abled in such a way that they are excluded from the "embrace" of being human. Rather, they are (along with everyone else) an expression of the immense diversity of human being. Thus, says Reinders: "it is clear where Pailin is heading: the worth of human beings is not grounded intrinsically; it is not inherent in their being but comes from elsewhere."[17] This "elsewhere" where all human beings are included in a universal embrace of worth is, for Pailin, in their creaturely-ness before the unconditional love of God, the Creator of all value. Therefore, the value of being human is entirely something to be received, and Reinders takes this to mean: "a theocentric basis for the fundamental worth of being human

---

15. Ibid., 159–226. The four contributions are: Eiesland, *The Disabled God*; Block, *Copious Hostin*; Hauerwas, *Suffering Presence*, among other of his works; and Pailin, *A Gentle Touch*.

16. Reinders, *Receiving the Gift of Friendship*, 206ff.

17. Ibid., 210.

requires that we humans speak in the passive voice."[18] Here, then, is an anthropological position in which two differing perspectives on human life are presented and weighed in terms of a transcending criterion.

Reinders, however, is concerned that Pailin does not then take the final step of discounting altogether as irrelevant the participatory involvement of the profoundly disabled in human living as persons. His assertion is that Pailin continues to advocate an ongoing subjective role for the disabled, in virtue of which there exists an I-Thou relationship with other persons, something of which the profoundly disabled are incapable. Subjectivity implies an inherent capacity, thereby making a personal contribution relevant to human value, which Reinders is not willing to countenance in terms of the profoundly disabled, who are inherently incapable of contributing to human living. According to Reinders, this would mean falling back into an anthropocentric dependency that renders the theocentric perspective conditional. It is precisely a blurring of the boundaries between leitmotifs that Reinders will not countenance:

> Thus the worth of any human being is neither instrumentally nor intrinsically but always extrinsically grounded, not in the value they have for others, not in the quality they have in themselves, but in the love of God . . . [Therefore, Christians must] resist the idea that, when a profoundly disabled child is born, something must have gone wrong. Not because this claim is necessarily mistaken but because it is at best *irrelevant* and at worst *obstructive* in terms of how we represent God's love for this child.[19]

The error of boundary blurring, which Reinders finds in Pailin (and even more markedly in the other three theologians), he finds continually repeated in various other ways as his argument develops. The slippage from a purely transcendent grounding of the value of human life into intrinsic justifications is the one recurring error he finds repeated from ancient times through to the present. He offers three examples: while looking favorably on the relational theology of John Zizioulas, whereby "human being is freed from ontological necessity," he argues that Zizioulas "remains captive to a focus on subjectivity" in establishing human freedom.[20] When he considers Paul Wadell's reading of St.

18. Ibid., 218.

19. Ibid., 220 and 226.

20. Ibid., 254–73. Thus: "[T]he problem with Zizioulas's account of relational personhood . . . is that it fails to acknowledge the primordial aspect of our receptivity: it

Thomas Aquinas' account of friendship with God, one that is focused on the supernatural end of human being as graced friendship with God, he criticises it for relying on ontological categories of virtue and natural fulfilment to make the argument.[21] Even though he approves of Henri Nouwen's story about his friendship with a profoundly disabled child named Adam, wherein Adam "teaches" Nouwen a new vision of human being whereby the presence of Adam "transforms" his perspective from an anthropocentric comparison ("from below") to a theocentric recognition ("from above"), he laments his slide into the language of reciprocity, with all that that entails in terms of capacity.[22]

These various examples are enough to show that Reinders does indeed adopt an anthropological approach that presents two ways of conceptualizing human beings that are incommensurable leitmotifs about human life and its goodness. The point Reinders wants to keep driving home is that any position that slips from a transcendent conceptualization into an immanent one will, by means of that slippage alone, fail the test of inclusion for the profoundly disabled in the human community. We may take it to be the case, therefore, that Reinders has committed himself to something of an ideological approach to human life, in that he has identified one single parting of the ways that leads him to take the same turn at each successive crossroad in the quest for securing the humanity of the profoundly disabled. With this established, it is now possible to examine in detail the nature and content of this transcending

---

is a gift that can only be received. . . . [H]e has lost track of the fact that human freedom cannot be conceived in analogy to divine freedom, because it does not originate from an analogous act of self-affirmation [as is the case within the Trinity]." Zizioulas, *Being as Communion*, 270–71.

21. Reinders, *Receiving the Gift of Friendship*, 288–302. Thus: "[W]e must insist on the primacy of God's love from beginning to end. Only the primacy of his self-giving love will answer whether or not we will attain the fullness of life independently from the 'quality' of our response. Whatever there is to the fullness of life, it must be God's gift from beginning to end, unless one is willing to accept that there are human beings who are excluded from it." Ibid., 301; Wadell, *The Primacy of Love*. Reinders relies entirely on Wadell's account of Aquinas on friendship to make his argument.

22. Ibid., 340–45; 369–74. Thus: "Now that [Nouwen] has been transformed, he has left the 'need for comparison' behind. Now he is capable of seeing Adam 'from above,' which enables him to see his friend's 'real self' . . . Now he sees Adam's humanity for what it is, 'full humanity,' not humanity diminished by his disabilities, which then allows him to say that there is a brotherly love between them, and that it is reciprocal. . . . Being transformed by God's love [however] entails embracing Adam's human being for what it is; it does not necessarily entail the discovery of a 'real self.'" Nouwen, *Adam*, 371–72.

concept of human goodness and how it is supposed to pertain to being chosen as a friend.

"The Good That Human Beings Have" and "the Good of Being Human"

To state the essential assertion that Reinders seeks to defend: a thoroughly transcendent conception of the good of human life—one that will carry the argument for human goodness from the beginning to the end of "human being"—is the only sure way of securing the humanity of the profoundly disabled and ensuring a path for them to inclusion. Given there are any number of goods that may be associated with living a human life, what kind of human good will fit such a conception? To respond to this question, Reinders begins his defense of a transcending concept of the human good by identifying the kind of good it needs to be, and the kind it ought not to be:

> If the human good is "really" good, it must be good with respect to each of our lives. Therefore, we cannot be content with a concept that some of our lives are not fully human lives because of the goods that cannot be realized within them. . . . There is no other way of defeating the claim that living with a profound disability is a life not worth living than arguing for a conception of the good that shows this judgement to rest on a mistake.[23]

Two kinds of good are being envisaged here by Reinders. First, there is the good that pertains to the kind of life that human life is. This is a singular, and unqualifiable good of being a human being. It is the conception "good" as it applies to "human being." Then there is the understanding of good, present in the form of a plurality of goods, which qualifies the life as it is being lived. This kind of good may be called the good(s) that human beings have. It is "good" in a relative and concrete sense. Reinders has this to say about how these two goods are related in human beings:

> [T]he notion of the good life can have at least two different meanings. One refers to the enjoyment of the collection of various goods that is acquired during one's lifetime; the other refers to a conception of the ultimate good as the end of living a human life, which transcends the meaning of these various

---

23. Reinders, *Receiving the Gift of Friendship*, 130.

goods, and from which the importance of these goods can be evaluated.²⁴

Each kind of good is identified with a specific conception of human life, but only the former, we are told, fulfils the criterion of being the "really good" good that is inclusive of every human life. The latter kind of good cannot secure the full humanity of the profoundly disabled because, as the earlier quotation implies, some of the goods of this kind—and we may note here purposive agency—cannot be realized within them. Because such goods cannot be ascribed to the profoundly disabled, therefore their humanity is correspondingly devalued in comparison with those who are so endowed. It is a conception of the human good that implies that the lives of the profoundly disabled are "an anthropological subdivision with regard to the good life."²⁵

It is Reinders' use of the word "within" in relation to this conception of the good that human beings have that carries the weight of the argument. With it he attributes an entirely intrinsic locale and understanding to goods of this kind, meaning: they are wholly realized from within the nature of the individual human being, and draw their value from that realization. These goods are, to recall Reinders' language, self-authorizing goods, and consequently they cannot speak to the good of being human as such. Accordingly, human goodness of this kind is a function of immanent human potency; the human good is conceived of as that which human beings participate in inherently, by way of self possession.

We may fairly associate this kind of human goodness with Reinders' *datum* conception of human life, noted earlier; the goods of this kind are contingent givens of a human life, but they do not tell us anything about the purpose of being human as such. While they are goods that human beings may have because they are human beings, they are not able to secure the human good with respect to human life itself. It is precisely because this kind of good is intrinsically grounded—realized within—that Reinders believes that it generates a mistaken conception of the human good, one that necessarily undermines the humanity of the profoundly disabled. They are barred from participation in it because they do not have the intrinsic capacities that generate such a human goodness.

If the good that human beings have is of a kind that belongs to a *datum* conception of human life, that is to say: if the goods intrinsic

24. Ibid., 127.
25. Ibid., 130.

to human life speak to the immanent participation of someone in that goodness, then its conceptual opposite, the good of being human, must be taken to be a function of an intervening transcendent purpose given to human life. To suit Reinders' purposes, such a good could not be intrinsically self authorizing; it would have to be a good extrinsically conferred: a gift, *donum*. Whatever goods of the first kind that someone may or may not have, it does not exhaust the meaning of human goodness. Instead,

> [it] presuppose[s] another kind of good, conceptually at least, that lies beyond the variety of goods that [people] are accumulating, which is the kind of good that is "ultimately necessary."[26]

This second kind of good, which Reinders identifies as "the ultimate good of being human," is precisely the transcending concept of the human good he is looking for.[27] It is the good that "lies beyond," by which human life is given its definitive purpose and value. It is a good unencumbered by the need for a conception of human goodness—an accumulating good—that is only realizable from within. As such, it is a concept of goodness that is inclusive of the profoundly disabled for it does not require of them to bring anything of their own to the table of human life; the good that most matters to them is the kind that has been conferred on them extrinsically. What, then, is Reinders' transcending concept of the human good? Not what is *datum*, but *donum*; not what is chosen, but received; not what is self authorised, but conferred; not what is intrinsic, but extrinsic; not what is within, but beyond.

While the two kinds of goods proffered by Reinders may sit side-by-side in every human being, they are clearly treated as offering conceptually different understandings of human beings. They give expression to two fundamentally distinct leitmotifs on human life that stand independently of each other and are of no influence upon one another. They are incommensurate conceptions of human goodness. Yet, Reinders insists that a choice can be made between the two, and that the judgment is to be made in favor of the transcendent good of being human over the immanent good that human beings have. What determines this choice is the outcome each appears to offer the profoundly disabled in terms of their claim on humanity. By means of the former they come to belong to the human community; by means of the latter they do not. It is worth

---

26. Ibid.
27. Ibid., 132.

noting how peculiar and philosophically confused this move is: a relative measure is being taken between two supposedly incommensurate goods.

As it turns out, it is this evaluative and relative choice being made by Reinders that reveals much about the content of his transcending concept of the human good as it relates to friendship. Achieving the outcome of belonging—of being included—dominates his structural landscape, as he makes abundantly clear: "I will pursue this question [of what is ultimately necessary for a fully human life] in terms of belonging. . . . [T]he ultimate good is about belonging."[28] What is appealing about making the outcome of belonging critical to his argument is its apparent other-dependency: "wherever you belong, you only belong there because significant others in your life will confirm that you do."[29] In other words, belonging is treated as an outcome extrinsic to the one who is recognized as belonging; its achievement for the individual lies beyond the capacity of the individual.[30] Therefore, it may be placed on the transcending side of the leitmotif divide, which is precisely where Reinders locates it.

Furthermore, because the outcome of belonging is achieved by placing it on the transcending side of the divide, creating a sense of belonging depends on establishing a relationship that is itself not established by way of a natural necessity, which would bring it back into the realm of the immanent leitmotif. Such a relationship cannot be self authorised; it must be conferred, received. Thus:

> A full sense of belonging does not depend on choice but on being chosen. Therefore, it is more properly found in relationships with friends than within the family.[31]

So, "being chosen as a friend" is thereby placed at the heart of Reinders' project for securing the humanity of the profoundly disabled,

---

28. Ibid., 131.

29. Ibid.

30. A beautiful and richly theological account of the complexities of selfhood is presented in the important work *Dementia: Living in the Memories of God* by John Swinton. For patients living through Dementia, the grasp that one has over oneself is non-static, difficult to describe, and perhaps cannot be understood outside the categories derivative to Christian theology, in which our creation and redemption sit within the power of the divine, and paradoxically is the only means of discovering what is truly significant in the human being, including their memories and the memories others might have of them.

31. Ibid.

emerging as the central anthropological notion driving the choice for the outcome of inclusion. Yet, as Reinders warns, "This argument can only work if it does not make friendship dependent on human agency."[32]

Augustine on Goodness and Reinders' Leitmotifs

To ensure that the good of friendship is not conceived of in this way, to argue that the good of friendship for the profoundly disabled can only be secured if it is extrinsically grounded, Reinders turns to Book XIX of St. Augustine's *De civitate dei* for support. His argument is that Augustine's account of goodness provides a theocentric warrant for his own transcending concept of the human good, and in so doing he proposes that this points to a conceptual divide between ontological and teleological accounts to human life. Reinders' basic claim is this: it is God—the utterly Other and the source of all value—who can be the only true giver of inclusion, meaning that humanity is not dependent in any way on an intrinsic self authorisation, but entirely on an extrinsic conferral. For Reinders, the teleological question about being human—the purpose or end of human life—is answerable only from a theocentric perspective such that friendship becomes the utterly passive, thoroughly extrinsic, singular good of being embraced by God's unconditional love.

It is this position, Reinders maintains, that is present in Augustine's theology of goodness:

> "Nature" . . . does not define "goodness," at least not in the Christian (i.e., Augustinian) understanding of being human that I will defend in my analysis. Within the Augustinian perspective, the final end (*telos*) of being human is properly understood in terms of a relationship with God.[33]

Reinders further claims that Augustine argues for such a position by discriminating between those kinds of goods desired and pursued by people in their lives, and an ultimate good, the good of being human, which is conferred by God. Thus:

> there are many possible goods in our earthly existence; but they can only be properly appreciated from the point of view of our destiny, which for Augustine is to be residents of the "city of

---

32. Ibid., 132.
33. Ibid., 155.

God," in which we will enjoy God's friendship ... So the lives of persons with profound disabilities can be evaluated from two perspectives on the good life: in one view, their lives are good when they enjoy a list of particular goods; in another, their lives are good, just as all other human lives are good, when they answer to a higher purpose, an ultimate goal, or a final end.[34]

As is implied in these two quotations, Reinders is proposing that an expression of his own demarcation of the two leitmotifs is found in Augustine's "two cities" metaphor, as he applies it to human goodness.[35] He insists that Augustine advocated a real and incommensurate distinction between an ontological conception of human life and a teleological conception. In Reinders' thinking, each of these binary opposites asks a different question of human beings. The ontological question is concerned with the origins of human life, of "who counts as a human being," while the teleological question asks about the end or purpose of human life, of "what it means to be human."[36] For Reinders, the humanity of the profoundly disabled can only be secured when the latter question is asked, for it is only with that question that an extrinsic aspect is present. It is the ontological/teleological divide that drives Reinders towards the need for a transcending concept of the human good in the first place, and to finding its association with Augustine.

Reinders takes from Augustine the notion that the various goods that originate in human beings and to which people give value (the ontological goods bound to the earthly city) are fundamentally different from the good that comes from God and which gives value to human beings (the teleological good originating in the heavenly city). This ultimate good of being human—the good that gives human beings their

---

34. Ibid., 151–52. Later on, Reinders makes substantial use of a relational notion of personhood, drawn from the Trinitarian theology of Orthodox theologian John Zizioulas, as his principal theological support "for the ecstatic nature of human being as extrinsically grounded," 252 (see 252–75 for his discussion of Zizioulas). While this provides Reinders with a way of linking the passive "being chosen as a friend" with the dynamic personhood of the triune God, it is what he first draws from Augustine on goodness that provides the more basic architectural structure. Therefore, it is Reinders' reading of Augustine, and not his subsequent adoption of Zizioulas, which underpins his argument.

35. Ibid., 129n5. Reinders points specifically to Book XIX.4 as support for his own argument. Significantly, however, he does not actually quote Augustine, or paraphrase him, at any stage.

36. Ibid., 51.

ultimate purpose—is different in kind from other goods, is sourced differently from other goods, and trumps all other goods.[37] And, according to Reinders' reading of Augustine, this kind of goodness is dependent upon—and only dependent upon—the relationship of human beings with the God of unconditional love, who chooses to be in a relationship with us. The ultimate good of being chosen as a friend, therefore, is nothing more than the teleological meaning to being human that God unconditionally gives to human beings.

The question that arises from Reinders' association of his own incommensurate leitmotifs with Augustine's teleological underpinning of human goodness is whether or not Augustine's theology in fact does what Reinders draws on it to do. This is both a question of whether or not Augustine actually holds to what Reinders says he does, and a question of whether or not Augustine's theology provides the requisite structure to the leitmotifs. In other words, can his thesis sit comfortably on an Augustinian foundation? As it is only to Chapter 4 of Book XIX of *De civitate dei* that Reinders directs his attention, it is thereto which we turn in order to answer these questions.[38]

The broader task Augustine sets himself in Book XIX is to discuss the two respective ends of the earthly and heavenly cities. These ends are compared and contrasted in terms of human happiness; and happiness, in its turn, is compared and contrasted in terms of its pursuit in the midst of human affairs. The ends in view, then, can be seen as "horizons of action that generate . . . contrasting moral characters."[39] Behind this task, however, lies Augustine's earlier configuration of these cities in terms of love. Thus:

---

37. As Reinders puts it, "[Augustine] argues why the wide variety of good things that people value cannot be equivalent to the ultimate good. . . . [T]he nature of these goods is such that they can be lost, can be changed into their opposites, and, therefore, cannot be relied on. Augustine's argument aims at a conception that locates the ultimate good in the heavenly city, that is, in the life hereafter, but this does not alter the logical point: that the ultimate good is different in kind from the variety of goods people usually seek in their lives." Ibid., 129n5.

38. Augustine, *De civitate dei*. I will curtail my own reading of XIX.4 to the specific issue of goodness, bracketing out Augustine's broader focus on political theology, which is widely regarded to be the central concern of Book XIX. See O'Donovan, "Augustine's *City of God* XIX and Western Political Thought," first published in 1987, reprinted in D. Donnelly, ed., *City of God*, 135–38.

39. O'Donovan, "Political Thought of City of God," in O'Donovan and O'Donovan, *Bonds of Imperfection*, 49.

> We see then that the two cities were created by two kinds of love: the earthly city was created by self-love . . . , the Heavenly City by the love of God . . . The former looks for glory from men, the latter finds its highest glory in God. . . . Consequently, in the earthly city its wise men who live by men's standards have pursued the goods of the body or of the mind, or of both. . . . In the heavenly city, on the other hand, man's only wisdom is the devotion which rightly worships the true God . . . (XIV.28)[40]

Augustine sets about his task of examining the two ends, by first expounding the ancient philosophical position about the nature of human happiness, as represented in the thought of Marcus Terentius Varro (XIX.1–3), and then by proposing the Christian counter-view (XIX.4). The lesson to be learned from a reliance on philosophy is that the earthly city's tendency to locate the end of goodness in the pursuit of the goods of this world that are intrinsic to our nature—namely, pleasure or virtue or both—is bound to fail because they are determined by contingency, prone to evil, and burdened by the vagaries of life. Whereas to locate the supreme good in the eternal life founded in God, and not in this world and its corrupted goods, is to rely on the gracious help of God to receive what is given to us as our ultimate good. Therefore, Augustine locates the supreme good in the surety of eternal life rather than in anything dependent upon the vagaries of this life. Only eternal life, "the true end of human action," can guarantee happiness.[41] The goods of human life, according to this understanding, are inadequate in themselves as good ends to pursue; human beings cannot come to their good end without the aid of God. Thus, and as Gerard O'Daly has commented,

> From the outset Augustine is critical of philosophical teleology, but not of the teleology principle as such, which he accepts. The ultimate good for the Christian is eternal life . . . and living rightly entails living by faith, by divine grace. Thus two principles of philosophical enquiry are rejected: the principle that the good sought, and thus happiness, is to be found in our temporal, earthly existence, and the belief that happiness, and so virtue, can be found by unaided human effort.[42]

---

40. O'Donovan sees this configuration as one whereby the two cities "were distinguished by polar opposite moral principles [of good and evil] . . . and by final separation on the day of judgement." O'Donovan, *Desire of Nations*, 202.

41. O'Donovan and O'Donovan, *Bonds of Imperfection*, 50.

42. O'Donovan, *Augustine's City of God*, 199.

Augustine's two cities correspond to two fundamentally different ends—the *summum malum* and the *summum bonum*—and these are determined by either anthropocentric or theocentric outlooks, respectively. Interestingly, however, the supreme end of goodness is configured by that good towards which all human beings strive for its own sake, and for the sake of all other goods. Something is not good for someone unless it is configured to the final good. This is how something comes under the definition of "good" in the first place. Consequently for Augustine, all sorts of goods for human beings—goods that are immanent to human beings—are oriented to the good of being human when they are oriented towards the supreme end of goodness in God. In other words, while, for Augustine, there can be a plurality of goods to pursue in one's life, they can only be good to pursue for one's life because they are united under the one supreme good. That which does not conform to this configuration is evil—*malum*—and is to be avoided.

Certainly for Augustine, there are two polar ends towards which one may orient one's life, but structurally each end will determine differently that which is pursued as being either good or evil. The thing pursued, however, is the same: there is not one list of things that are "good" and then pursued, and another list of "evil" things that are then pursued. Rather it is in the orientation of their pursuit that they are seen to be either good or evil. There is, therefore, a teleological principle inherent to human life, and all human goodness—both "good for" and "good of"—is structurally determined by this principle. To be sure, those intermediate goods that are good for human beings—the goods for human beings precisely because of the subjects that they are—require the grace of God for them to be oriented towards the supreme good of eternal life (an eschatological transformation, let us say). Nonetheless they are teleologically configured.

Now compare this structure of goodness to that of Reinders. For him, there are two ends (like Augustine), but they correspond to two different kinds of good: the good of being human, which is ultimate, universal and extrinsic; and the human goods that are instrumental, contingent and intrinsic. In other words, Reinders' configuration of goodness seems to be a complete reversal of Augustine's.

How has Reinders come to believe that Augustine's structure of goodness supports his own architecture, when they appear to be completely opposite? It would seem to be located in the issue of whether or not our human nature is ordered for the pursuit of human fulfilment.

Reinders, of course, does not deny that human beings have a human nature. He does, however, discount the relevance of that nature for securing human fulfilment; it is not necessary for securing human fulfilment other than by being a kind of receptacle for humanity. Therefore, it can never be considered ordered towards the pursuit of human fulfilment. Augustine, on the other hand, argues that the corruption of human nature is not insurmountable, because God provides what is lacking for the sake of pursuing fulfilment. In this sense, nature is relevant because it has to do with human beings having natures that are ordered towards fulfilment. Human nature is the (graced) means by which human beings—because they are ordered for fulfillment—pursue fulfillment.

If this claim is true, then we can expect to find evidence for it in Augustine's thinking. Instructive in this regard is Augustine's discussion in Book XIX of the content of the supreme good—namely, peace (eternal life). First, he establishes that the true end of human goodness, which lies in the heavenly city, is the supreme good of eternal peace (XIX.11), and then he goes on at some length to discuss how peace is nonetheless an integral and instinctive feature of our "miserable" mortal life. His conclusion is that the supreme good for human beings finds a real echo in the goods pursued by human beings in earthly life—"there cannot exist a nature in which there is no good" (XIX.13)—and that this relationship is ordered to human life. Thus:

> Every mortal who uses aright such goods, goods designed to serve the peace of mortal men, shall receive goods greater in degree and superior in kind, namely, the peace of immortality, and enjoyment of God and of one's neighbour in God. (XIX.13)[43]

Note that Augustine is talking of a common object of goodness, the supreme good of peace, that is shared in by both cities. Although differently configured, it is not different in kind, as Reinders would have it, but simply more completely fulfilling in eternity. Secondly, he assumes that this good is to be pursued, not simply received. Finally, it is a good—at one and the same time designed for earthly living and better qualified

---

43. O'Donovan notes how Augustine makes a threefold summary of this argument in XIX.20: (i) the eschatological claim that the supreme good is eternal peace; (ii) the negative conclusion that this mortal life is inherently unhappy; and (iii) the positive qualification of a qualified happiness here and now so long as this life is lived with a view to the eternal life. What links the third point to the first two is the "common objects of love" that are the focus in both cities. See O'Donovan and O'Donovan, *Bonds of Imperfection*, 54.

and more abundantly had eternally—proper to the nature of human beings. In other words, Augustine is concerned, in this life, about overcoming an inadequate possession by human beings of the ultimate good, and not with an already adequate ordering of human beings to that good.

By implication (and to bring us back to the broader issue in hand), the profoundly disabled must be, by nature, already ordered to the supreme good of human fulfilment. Indeed, the condition of their humanity is not relevant to their achieving of this fulfilment. What makes it irrelevant is different between Reinders and Augustine. For Reinders, either agency is an issue, leading to the exclusion of the disabled, or agency is irrelevant altogether. Either way, the place of agency is the determining factor as to which leitmotif is being pursued. For Augustine, on the other hand, there are no competing leitmotifs because the ultimate good is the common object of goodness in both mortal life and eternal life, and therefore agency is irrelevant because it is not determining anything. Consequently, the profoundly disabled are freed from the leitmotif stance and are no longer made the point of demarcation between ontological questions and teleological ones, opening up both sets of questions to play a role in securing the full humanity of the profoundly disabled.

The upshot of this discussion is that Reinders' claim that he gets his separation of leitmotifs from Augustine does not hold. Whatever else might be said of Reinders' use of Augustine on human goodness, the text itself does not support the notion of a separation of the intrinsic from the extrinsic, which is so crucial to Reinders' thinking. The human good and the goods for humans are not incommensurate conceptions, nor do they undermine each other. Not only does the text itself fail to confirm Reinders' claim, there exists another source, unreferenced by Reinders, which can be seen as confirmation that Augustine cannot be the source of his leitmotif stance. In 415 AD, around a decade before he wrote Book XIX, St. Augustine penned a letter to St. Jerome (*Letter CLXVI*) seeking his views on the question of the origin of the human soul.[44] It is of

---

44. Augustine of Hippo, *Letter to Jerome*, 165–203. The dating of this letter is of some assistance in fleshing out the structural argument revealed in Book XIX of *De civitate dei*. O'Donovan points out that the argument of Book XIX completes a promise made in Book II. Cf. O'Donovan & O'Donovan, *Bonds of Imperfection*, 52. As it is, Book XIX is dated as late as 425 AD, as much as ten years after Letter 166, which might suggest that Augustine's thinking could have changed markedly in the ensuing decade. Book II, however, was finished by 413 AD, which would indicate that his structural thinking did not change significantly over the ensuing years, given that the argument in Book XIX follows on from that set out in Book II. Consequently, it is reasonable

particular interest to us that he had the status of children and the intellectually impaired in mind when he broached this question with Jerome.

The question of the origin of the human soul had greatly perplexed Augustine throughout his Christian life, and he had returned to it at some considerable length many times in his writings, always failing to solve the issue of which theory was orthodox.[45] He was now seeking Jerome's opinion as to which was the best to follow.[46] The theories themselves are not important for our purposes, but the context in which Augustine approaches them is. How is it that some children—who have rational souls proper to human beings because they are human beings, but who have yet to reach that stage in their development when they can exercise this rational faculty for their own good or ill (i.e., virtuously or sinfully)—pay the penalty of a form of suffering not of their own cause or fault, given that God can only create a good soul (CLXVI.16–17)?

While Augustine offers no solutions to this line of questioning, the way he raises it is instructive. In this one instance where the lives of the profoundly impaired are considered, it is an ontological question that is raised: What is it about the nature of the human soul in terms of its origins that children suffer so? Yet it is thought through in terms of teleology: What kind of soul is it they have, such that they are nonetheless included amongst the just?[47] In other words, he looks for an answer about the nature of the human soul, which is an ontological concern, by considering the various aspects of its manifestation and purpose, which are teleological issues.[48] We may reasonably conclude, therefore, that Au-

---

to posit that what Augustine has to say in his letter to Jerome is in keeping with, and substantially the same as his thinking in Book XIX, allowing us to read the issues he raises in the former as shedding light on his conclusions in the latter, and vice versa.

45. See, for example, the commentary on the Book of Genesis, *De genesi ad litteram* (393/394 AD); the treatise *De anima et eius origine* (420–21 AD); and a letter to Optatus, numbered 202A (420 AD).

46. As things transpired, Jerome made no attempt to take up the challenge! Letter CLXXII, from Jerome to Augustine (416 AD).

47. Augustine makes one other reference to the mentally impaired in *De anima et eius origine* (Book IV.6[7]). In a section considering the question of how human beings come to know what they know, Augustine makes the following comment: "I pass over mention why many, who try to learn these things [about the body], are unable. By reason of a slowness of wit [*impediuntur ingenio*] they are prevented from learning from others things they themselves do within themselves. How strange this is!" This remark is so obscure and oblique, however, that we can, like Augustine, pass over it without it concerning us. See Augustine, *The Nature and Origin of the Soul*.

48. As far as Augustine is concerned this is a different question from the one of theodicy. See CLXVI.18.

gustine was consistent in arguing for a real and necessary relationship between the ontological and teleological perspectives of our humanity, even if in this instance he was unable to resolve the perplexing question posed by the phenomenon of profoundly disabled children. For our purposes, however, the evident structural consistency in the arguments employed by Augustine in both *De civitate dei* and *Letter CXLVI* precludes any attempt to read into his anthropology a leitmotif stance.

Reinders and Nygren

A new question now arises: If not Augustine, then is there another theological position, reminiscent of the leitmotif stance, that Reinders might be drawing on in developing a Christian anthropology favorable to the inclusion of the profoundly disabled, or is he proposing an entirely new architecture? By way of a response to this question, a significant hint is given by Reinders himself in the only place where Augustine is actually quoted in *Receiving the Gift of Friendship*. In a discussion where he rejects any substantial understanding of human being connected with the doctrine of the *imago Dei*, Reinders draws attention to the supposedly Augustinian doctrine of the *reliquiae*, "the 'remnants' of the divine image in humankind that remained intact despite the condition of total degradation [of fallen human nature]."[49] While he applauds the anti-substance bearings of a remnantist anthropology—"it habitually starts with the rejection of any analogy of being between God and man"—he rejects the immanentist trap it supposedly falls into: "this tradition nonetheless returns at some point to thinking about Christian anthropology in terms of the human faculties independent of an actual relationship with God."[50]

Whatever else might be said about the doctrine of the *reliquiae*, what is instructive for us about Reinders' rejection of it is the anti-relational aspect he sees embedded in it. For it is precisely the relationality of being human, and not the substantial human nature, that conforms to the transcendent criterion. This is a further indication of the radical extent

---

49. Reinders, *Receiving the Gift of Friendship*, 235. He quotes Augustine in footnote 20 on the same page, designating him as the source of the doctrine. In the discussion in which this quotation occurs, Reinders seeks to reject the so-called "double portrait of humanity" he finds in St. Irenaeus' reading of the *imago Dei* (distinguishing "image" and "likeness"), and subsequently absorbed into Catholic and Protestant traditions. See ibid., 231ff.

50. Ibid., 235.

to which Reinders drives home his own anthropological sensitivity: the utter degradation of fallen human nature must be presumed, so that the work of God's grace in humanity may be absolutely determinative of human nature. This is the leitmotif stance being played out on the grandest scale of all: the transcendent sovereignty of (the relationship of) grace over and against the immanent servitude of (the substance of) nature. This was never Augustine, but it is Reinders: a relational anthropology, over and against a substantial one; friendship conferred, over and against innate personhood; a transcendent criterion, over and against an immanent one; God's extrinsic grace, over and against humanity's intrinsic nature. Where, then, does this place Reinders in relation to the Christian anthropological tradition?

As it happens, there is an influential theological position that may be associated with such a radical anthropological stance. In the 1930s the Swedish Lutheran theologian Anders Nygren applied a so-called motif-research methodology to the Christian concept of love, comparing and contrasting the motifs of *eros* and *agape*.[51] Nygren's work quickly become the point of departure, either positively or negatively, for a renewed theological interest in Christian love, including friendship, among theologians of various traditions.[52] Nygren proposed an antithetical distinction between his two fundamental motifs: *eros* as a need and desire-based, egocentric, acquisitive love, and *agape* as an unmotivated, spontaneous, unconditional, theocentric, self-giving love. As Nygren argued, "Between Vulgar Eros and Christian Agape there is no relation at all," and this is because "Eros recognises [sic] value in its object—and loves it. Agape loves—and creates value in its object."[53] Nygren was quite strident in his arguments for separating out these two kinds of love, and he made it clear that friendship-love, *amor amicitiae* or *philia*, belonged under the self-centered love of *eros*.[54] Only God's unmotivated love for humanity

---

51. Anders Nygren developed his theory of love over two volumes, published in 1930 and 1936 respectively, under the title *Den kristna kärlekstanken gonem tiderna. Eros och Agape*. I will refer to the unabridged, combined English translation: Anders Nygren, *Agape and Eros: Part I—A study of the Christian Idea of Love & Part II—The History of the Christian Idea of Love*.

52. Alan Vincelette provides a substantial list of theologians in recent decades who have been influenced by Nygren's thesis. P. Rousselot, *The Problem of Love in the Middle Ages*, translated with an introduction by A. Vincelette, 11n1.

53. Nygren, *Agape and Eros*, 51, 211. See 210 for Nygren's tabulation of the differences between the two motifs.

54. Ibid., 186; 641ff.

could be the true source of Christian love of neighbor. Thus, says Nygren (in words that would sit comfortably with Reinders),

> Agape-love is directed to the neighbour himself, with no further thought in mind and no side-long glances at anything else. . . . [N]o reason for my loving him can be found in his own character or conduct. . . . There is no motive for the love in the loved object itself, and no motive must be found outside the object, in some ulterior purpose, or else the love will not be true and unfeigned, will not be Agape.[55]

The level of correspondence between Nygren's fundamental motifs and Reinders' leitmotifs is remarkable. Structurally, they are nearly identical. The only difference seems to be that Reinders uses the word "friendship" to designate his theocentric love, whereas Nygren would reject such a naming. Yet, Reinders associates it with a meaning that matches Nygren's unmotivated, utterly altruistic agape-love; Reinders' "friendship" and Nygren's "agape" mean the same thing, and both conform to the same transcendent criterion. This may be confirmed in the fact that for both of them, there is nothing in the object towards which such love is to be directed, nothing about the recipient, that is in any way relevant to the giving of agape/friendship-love. The friendship that matters for Reinders—the love of God for the profoundly disabled—does not ask for anything; it is simply given by God and simply received by the person. There is no internal dynamic of giving and receiving to this kind of relationship because there is nothing on the part of human beings, and proper to human nature, that can be given and that could make a difference; there is no place for mutuality because there is no need of it. This is precisely the structure of Nygren's agape. As Nygren put it, "The presence of Agape is marked by a receptive attitude"; and as Reinders echoes, "The call to share one's life with a profoundly disabled person will not be properly heard unless one is prepared to receive the presence of that person as a gift from God."[56]

The Failure of Reinders' Transcending Concept

It is now time to draw together the various threads of Reinders' project and to ask if his transcending conception of the good of friendship—the

---

55. Ibid., 215-16.
56. Ibid., 221; and Reinders, *Receiving the Gift of Friendship*, 350.

good of which is neither sourced from Augustine nor like Augustine, but which is structured according to a Nygrenian approach—which is extrinsic, theocentric, teleological (in Reinders' understanding of that word), universalist, transcendent, and utterly incommensurate with any conception which might bleed into an immanentist conception of nature—actually does what he wants it to do, namely, secure the humanity of the profoundly disabled. As it turns out, Reinders himself provides a means of doing so. A truly telling lacuna—perhaps unexpectedly—of *Receiving the Gift of Friendship* is that the human relationships of Jesus of Nazareth barely feature in it.[57] The stories from the Gospels of the encounters of the incarnate God with others are not put forward as exemplars of the kind of love Reinders calls friendship and Nygren calls *agape*. In fact, there is only one occasion where Reinders presents a passage from Sacred Scripture for reflection, that being the story of the man born blind from the ninth chapter of John's Gospel.[58] Significantly, however, it is not put forward as a study of Christ-like friendship as such, but as a model for "coming to see" the world from the perspective of the leitmotif of theocentric love. Both the general lack of reference to Sacred Scripture and the particular meaning given to Jesus' healing of the man born blind are pertinent.

Noting Jesus' claim that the man was born blind "so that God's work may be revealed in him" (John 9:3), Reinders correctly points to the dialectic between sightedness and blindness being played out on different levels in John 9; it is not simply a story being told about a miracle. This is especially evident in the spiritual blindness exhibited by the Pharisees compared to the new sight—physical and in faith—the healed man has of Jesus. Reinders stresses how the healed man comes to bear witness to the way God's love works. By testifying to the restoration of his sight by Jesus he reveals to others willing to see how God sees him (and has always seen him):

> It is not primarily about the man's blindness, nor about his healing, but about his relationship with God. . . . He should not be seen as a sinner, nor should his disability be seen as a sign of

---

57. Perhaps the lacuna should not be so unexpected. Given that Reinders gets his separation of leitmotifs from Nygren, a theological representative of a post-Kantian tradition, it ought not to be surprising that he can make nothing subsequently of the gospel tradition.

58. Ibid., 322–35.

sinfulness . . . Instead, he should be seen as chosen by God to shame those who reject the Son sent by the Father.[59]

Key to this reading of John 9 is Reinders' concern to expose the "ways of seeing" the profoundly disabled, which have come to dominate their lives: he names the medical model of dealing with a pathology, the social model of interpreting a behavioral malfunction, and the political model of advocating for representation.[60] Each focuses in on a particular light shone on the disabled by others, but not by God. The consequence of each of these ways of seeing, we are told, is that they are forms of blindness whereby the lives of the disabled are determined in terms of their disabilities. In contrast to these, John 9 presents a Christian model of seeing whereby the disabled shine a light on us, and our need for healing.

> This need concerns the self-images that get in the way of our friendship with God because, in relying on our own judgement about other people and about ourselves, we misunderstand God's friendship. . . . What I wish to suggest is that the "mission in life" of people with disabilities, even profound disabilities . . . is to help us to do that.[61]

The upshot is that sightedness and blindness have come to exist within one and the same situation: two sides of the same coin, so to speak, yet each face is permanently turned away from the other. So a choice must be made: the way of sightedness or the way of blindness.

Reinders' reading of John 9 suggests that it is only by seeing according to the way of Jesus—not seeing the man's blindness but seeing the love of God—that we can learn to receive the profoundly disabled as friends and, therefore, as fully human. Only by shifting from a focus on (our) agency and activity to a focus on (their) non-agency and passivity will we come to see God's way of befriending. There are two difficulties with this way of reading John 9, however. First, it does not actually deal with the friendship of God for the man but with the question of how we are to know the man. The issue being presented in this reading is an epistemological one, not an anthropological one. It is about learning to see the profoundly disabled from a different perspective: it is about coming to know them in the light of Christian faith. However, none of this has to do with the notion of friendship as such, of the way God loved the blind

59. Ibid., 326.
60. Ibid., 328–29.
61. Ibid., 328.

man as revealed in Jesus. It presents theocentric love as an attitudinal matter: to see in the way God loves is a matter of being rightly disposed.

The other related difficulty is that it removes from the story the significance of the healing act itself. Recall Reinders' structure: friendship orders humanity. There can be no internal dynamic of giving and receiving in Reinders' structure because nothing in human beings can make a difference to God's love. To heal is to bring motivation into the equation: there is something about the one who is unwell that motivates the healer to act. Reinders, reminiscent of Nygren, rejects such a move. The healing becomes irrelevant in the reading of John 9, yet the healing is crucial to the story's unfolding; there is no Johannine sign without it. The problem with Reinders' reading of John 9 can be put in question form: If it is not the man's blindness that is at issue, but our blindness to seeing him as irrelevantly blind, then why does Jesus heal the blindness of the man?

Perhaps a response to this question, and the one Reinders' reading seems to imply, is that Jesus healed him so as to make a point to others (the Pharisees, the disciples). An obvious problem with such an interpretation, however, is that this would instrumentalize the man himself; his healing becomes the all-important means to making a point, and the man himself becomes irrelevant. Let us take it that Reinders is not suggesting this because that would mean the man was not being loved for his own sake, without motivation. Yet, Jesus healed him; and this is the only evidence we have to ground the claim that Jesus loved him. The healing is the only answer we have to the question of God's friendship for the man.

So the question arises: What is important about healing him with regards to loving him? What connection does the healing have to the loving? The very notion of any such connection is antithetical to Reinders' claim that the (immanent) condition of the man is irrelevant to the (transcendent) loving of him. Yet, to ask who it is that Jesus sees before him, the story reveals not just the object of God's glory, as Reinders would need it to be, but a man, a subject, who is blind and glorious. It is the personal presence of this particular man, blind and glorious, whom Jesus receives as a gift from God and, as an integral part of that dynamic of love, heals him. What, in turn, does it mean for this man to receive the gift of God's love in Christ? It means his healing from disability. The healing cannot be separated from the loving; the man's blindness makes all the difference in the world, for him and for Jesus. Yet, the blindness is irrelevant in Reinders' thesis.

The rather stark conclusion lying at the heart of Reinders' structure, therefore, is that it is unable to accommodate an incarnate God, whose theocentric love is directed to the conditioned beloved. It is as if there is to be no place for healing of the disabled in Reinders' thinking, no purposeful need for bringing about a change in their human condition, because it makes no difference to securing their humanity and, therefore, their inclusion: that is all that matters. Yet, it makes a difference to Jesus that a man born blind is healed, and this difference has to do with the man himself whom Jesus befriends. The healing action of Jesus suggests that the man's condition was relevant to the way Jesus loved him, and teleologically so. Jesus did not heal him meaninglessly; he healed for a purpose and that purpose was for the good of the man himself. This conclusion is further testified to by the lack of any other engagement with the Scriptures in Reinders' book. None of the healing actions of Jesus are mentioned as exemplars of theocentric friendship. Perhaps none of them can be mentioned because they do not fit into Reinders' structure of friendship.

Broaching the Question of Friendship Itself

All that remains to do in this chapter is to draw together the various implications about Reinders' notion of friendship to see what they amount to. To recall: Reinders seeks a notion of friendship that will secure the humanity of the profoundly disabled, and he proposes a structure that is dependent upon a transcending concept of the human good: one that is extrinsically grounded, passively received, and universally applicable. Such a friendship is theocentric because it locates its meaning in God's unconditional love for all humanity, including the profoundly disabled. The kind of friendship Reinders envisages is one that addresses the overarching concern for inclusion by rendering the human condition (viewed through the prism of non-agency) irrelevant.

We have now seen, however, how this leads to the positing of a non-predicated, categorical subject as the perceived object of friendship. Furthermore, and contrary to his claim to be in the provenance of St. Augustine, Reinders' theocentric friendship is structurally identical with Anders Nygren's agape: theocentric friendship is, from a human perspective, what agape's spontaneous, unmotivated bestowal that excludes any need for mutuality is, from God's perspective. Reinders' leitmotif stance matches Nygren's opposing fundamental motifs. Consequently, Reinders sets up the work that friendship must do for the sake of inclusion as a choice—a judgment—between fundamentally opposing visions of the world. Thus, the question of "seeing" replaces the question of "being," a move borne out by Reinders' reading of John 9 in such a way that any significance in Jesus' healing of the man born blind is trumped by learning to see him as "friend of God."

Perhaps the most striking point to emerge from the preceding analysis of Reinders' structure of friendship is that he never actually addresses the question of friendship itself. He spends a great deal of time describing how friendship would need to operate within the context of inclusion: as belonging; as gift/bestowal; as conferred and passively received; as transcending good for humans; as theocentric love. Nowhere, however, does he articulate what friendship is. Friendship (at least of the kind Reinders advocates) is simply taken to be any encounter that fits the requirement of the transcending concept inclusion-without-immanent-nature. There is no attempt to establish how, or even whether this relates to friendship as such; so long as it solves the problem extrinsically, passively and universally, then it is deemed to be friendship.

From a Christian perspective, this becomes a task of finding a way of placing Jesus of Nazareth—the incarnation of God's love—within the notion of friendship so envisaged, rather than drawing the meaning of friendship from how it comes to be incarnated in Jesus. Reinders does precisely this in his reading of John 9. He never asks what made the encounter of Jesus with the blind man a friendship in the first place. Instead, he assumes that the encounter was a friendship—"God always has been a friend of us, and his friendship precedes any of our actions"[62]—and takes it from there. The basis for this assumption is said to be "the unique relationship that the triune God maintains with humanity through the economy of salvation . . . grounded in God's act of self-giving."[63] Nowhere, however, is this relationship explained in terms of friendship as a real relationship. What makes friendship "friendship" is never asked. "Friendship" becomes nothing more than a word to denote the unconditional love that God has for us all, including the profoundly disabled.

---

62. Ibid., 297

63. Ibid., 273–74. Reinders derives this claim from John Zizioulas' relational theology of Trinitarian communion: universal humanity is theologically grounded in the relationship God initiates and maintains unconditionally with every human being (ibid., 252ff.).

This lacuna helps clarify why the epistemological move becomes paramount to Reinders' approach. Describing what friendship is would mean opening up the possibility of having to address the ontological issues that are laid aside from the start because of the inclusion-without-nature commitment. The commitment is treated as axiomatic—How else can the humanity of the profoundly disabled be secured?—with the result that friendship as such (what it is) is never dealt with. There is no need, therefore, to learn anything about friendship from the way Jesus of Nazareth went about befriending others. Reinders places his theocentric friendship at the center of his project to include the profoundly disabled in a common humanity, but fails to provide a corresponding and supporting account of what friendship is. Thus there appears to be nothing in Reinders' structure that might provide a way out of this debilitating problem.

From the perspective of Christian anthropology, perhaps the closest Hans Reinders gets to a definition of friendship is this:

> [F]rom the point of view of biblical faith . . . [w]e do not choose our friends for their virtue, that is, in order to extend acts of good will to them—particularly not when these friends are despised in the eyes of the world. We are called to be their friends. . . . Friendship is our vocation because of what we have heard about the love of God, the forgiving Father.[64]

Of course, asserting that friendship has a vocational characteristic, implying that befriending is our anthropological calling, does not provide the theological analysis of friendship missing from *Receiving the Gift of Friendship*. It does not tell us, for example, anything about what kind of relationship is involved when befriending, nor how it differs from other kinds of human love, and why. Nevertheless, his reasoning for this vocational move is instructive because it reminds us once more of the transcendent conceptualization within which he has couched his understanding of friendship—namely, the unconditional love that God has chosen to confer on us all, thereby securing our humanity. It is the theocentric choosing-ness of befriending, so to speak, that Reinders prizes most of all. Friendship—or more specifically, befriending others—is our calling, our purpose in life, precisely because we have been chosen as a friend by God and he has made this known to us.

---

64. Ibid., 365–66.

Reinders is not wrong in making a vocational association. From a theological context, we may say that the purpose of all things, including human friendship, originates in God the Creator of all things. Such a general assertion tells us nothing about how friendship thereby exhibits its divinely given purpose—its vocation—in human beings and for human life. The one thing that Reinders' vocational move does tell us about his theological take on friendship is that he treats it as an epistemic commitment to the way in which God loves. Knowing, in faith, that other human beings are loved by God, and knowing, in faith, that we are similarly loved by God, thereby gives the only reason needed by us to love others. As such, it tells us nothing of the anthropological reality of friendship, of what "being a friend" means for being human, raising the question about how friendship is supposed to secure the humanity of anyone, let alone the profoundly impaired.

Reinders himself admits as much: it is not because of who someone is ("for their virtue") that we might choose him as a friend, but because choosing him as a friend is an imperative ("we are called") given by God and known to us ("what we have heard"). There is no need of a subject—no need of an anthropological other—who might elicit in us our friendship; there is only our subjective commitment to God's "unmotivated" way of loving (to recall the language of Nygren and the meaning he gives to it). For Reinders, we befriend another not because he or she is a human being or even because of who he or she is as a human being, but because of a commitment to how God loves human beings.

Yet, if a theological understanding of friendship is to play its part in securing the humanity of the profoundly impaired, then what is needed is an argument centered on the anthropological reality of friendship, and not on an epistemic commitment to it. Where are we to turn to find such an understanding and can it provide the grounding required anyway? For a start we may turn to John 15, where Jesus speaks directly about friendship and where the vocational dimensions of friendship are evident. What theological insights might be drawn from a more detailed examination of this text? Might it offer a different meaning to friendship from the epistemological one that Reinders has given to it? Even if it does, will this provide reasons for affirming that friendship can carry the anthropological load it is being asked to bear? These are some of the questions that now arise, having exposed the nature of the flaws in Reinders' project to secure the humanity of the profoundly disabled (not in the question he asks, but in the response he offers). It is in this context that the notion of friendship as vocation can be questioned as well. How is it that being called as a friend opens us to call others? And if friendship is transitive in this way, why does this not undermine the insistence that the profoundly impaired are human simply by being called?

Before turning to these various questions, it will be helpful to have before us some appreciation of where the question of friendship currently sits in contemporary Christian theology. This may be fruitfully done by considering the extent to which contemporary theological reflection on friendship has taken up the anthropological question, and by seeing what else is being said about the profoundly impaired in the context of friendship. Both of these tasks may be viewed also with an eye to the Johannine text.

3

A THOROUGHLY HUMAN ENTERPRISE
The Place of Friendship in a Christian Anthropology

A Human Enterprise

FRIENDSHIP HAS ALWAYS HAD a privileged place in a Christian understanding of love, drawing on both biblical and classical insights for its theological grounding.[1] The word "friendship" has come into contemporary Christian theology from both classical and Christian antiquity (roughly translating the Greek *philia* and the Latin *amicitia*). In its theological context, it has tended to find a close and abiding association with that specifically Christian form of love, most commonly referred to as "charity" (*agape/caritas*), grounded in the life, death, and resurrection of Jesus of Nazareth. Saint Thomas Aquinas summed up the Christian tradition of associating friendship with charity by stating: "charity is the friendship of man for God" (*ST* II-II.23.1.*resp*).[2] Significantly, Aquinas refers to John 15:15 to make his argument: "the Lord's words . . . can be explained only in terms of charity, which, therefore, is friendship" (23.1.sed contra).

Reinders himself refers to this question in Aquinas' *Summa* to bring to the fore the anthropological significance—the human dimension—of

---

1. For a detailed survey of the provenance of friendship-love in Christian theology, see Carmichael, *Friendship*.

2. This is the author's translation of the Latin original: *Unde manifestum est quod caritas amicitia quaedam est hominis ad Deum*, which the Blackfriars edition (incorrectly) translates as "charity is a friendship of man and God."

friendship. As would be expected, however, he rejects the way he sees Aquinas then associating friendship with an immanent conception of human nature, claiming it throws doubt on "the universality of being human from the perspective of the supernatural end."[3] We do not need to rehearse again Reinders' reasoning for this rejection; it is simply worth noting that his own position is a reaction to the elements of the tradition that have come down to present times.

For the English Dominican Herbert McCabe, understanding the human dimension of friendship was a task of recognizing its thoroughly mundane reality:

> We have, then, a special name for *human* living with each other: we call it friendship. . . . Now, if the purpose of human living is to live with each other, and if this involves living in friendship . . . [then] this is *not* something that we have resolved upon, not a decision or option we have come to, not even a fundamental option. It is something that belongs to us because of the kind of animal we are . . . We are born as players of this game; we do not *decide* what shall be its aim and purpose. We *discover* these things.[4]

While friendship might be a "special name" for the living of the human life, the living itself reveals friendship to be an utterly ordinary feature of human beings. In this sense, the recognition that someone is a human being is made in the discovery that he or she is befriendable. So strongly did McCabe make this point that he argued that the concept of friendship can only apply to God economically, and not immanently: "Those who love *seek* to be *of* one mind and heart. The Father and the Son *are* quite simply one mind and one heart."[5] God can befriend and can be befriended only because Jesus of Nazareth is the unique incarnation of the Son who, precisely as a distinct individual human being, shares in the love of God. The lesson that McCabe wanted to stress is this: if we want to understand friendship, then we need to keep it human, because "befriending" simply is "living well a human kind of life."

Friendship is thoroughly ordinary for human beings because it is a thoroughly human enterprise; it is so peculiarly human that human

---

3. Reinders, *Receiving the Gift of Friendship*, 116 n68. He is referring to ST II-II.23.1.*ad*1.

4. McCabe, *On Aquinas*, 54–55.

5. McCabe, *God, Christ and Us*, 51.

existence depends on it.⁶ Yet immediately we may ask: Precisely what kind of human enterprise is it? This is, of course, the underlying question that has arisen following the discussion of Reinders' project attempting to make a transcending conception of friendship central to the humanity of the profoundly disabled. McCabe has offered his own insight into the question in the following terms:

> [Friendship] is a way of being with another, of sharing life with another.... Friendship is a quest for unity..... Friendship is finding the *sharing* of life more important than carrying on the individual life.... Friendship is always *with*. It is always reciprocal.⁷

As brief a statement as this is—and he does not flesh it out any further—it does imply a number of features pertaining to friendship: it is a particular kind of relating; it answers to concepts of sharing, of the common life or community, and of being with; it has something to do with what is good and important for human living; it reveals something of the distinctive nature and purpose of being human. The quotation occurs within a discussion on the sanctity of Jesus, which McCabe defines as "a human being with whom God is in love, with whom God shares his own divine life."⁸ This sanctifying relationship he then identifies with friendship. It is because of the incarnate human being, Jesus of Nazareth, in accordance with his human nature, that it can be said of the Son and the Father that they are truly friends. In other words, McCabe places the sanctifying nature of the relationship between God and Jesus—their friendship—at the heart of what it means for Jesus to be human. From a theological point of view, it is noteworthy that McCabe supports his claim, at least in part, by pointing to John 15, where Jesus calls his disciples his friends, and to what might be called the ultimate reach of friendship, its "no greater love" dimension.

> We are not abiding in friendship if we prefer something else, if we opt for anything else, even life itself, at the expense of unity with our friends. That is why Jesus goes on to say: "No one has greater love than this, to lay down one's life for one's friends" (John 15:13). Friendship is finding the *sharing* of life more important than carrying on the individual life.⁹

---

6. McCabe, *On Aquinas*, 57.
7. McCabe, *God, Christ and Us*, 48–49.
8. Ibid., 48.
9. Ibid., 48–49.

McCabe's brief remarks on friendship have the advantage of suggesting two lessons to be kept in mind as we now take up the question of what kind of human enterprise friendship is. First, the thoroughly human nature of friendship, its utter mundaneness, is central to understanding the role of friendship for human beings. This is a direct challenge to Reinders' transcendent conceptualisation of friendship. It is also a reminder of the ever-present risk of an overly elevated anthropology; if friendship is thoroughly human then it must be able to say something to any human being something about how it involves them in living well a human life. The second, related lesson can be drawn from the christological infusion McCabe gives to friendship. By offering the friendships of Jesus of Nazareth as the paradigm of human friendship, he has reminded Christian theology that its own insights into friendship must be scripturally supportable. Otherwise, it has nothing unique to say.

Given these lessons, the question we are faced with is this: Is there a theological way of understanding friendship that is mindful of the profoundly impaired, attentive to an evangelical foundation (especially John 15), yet does not undermine its anthropological integrity? We may begin this task by looking at how the question of friendship has been approached by another of those theologians who have sought to reimagine theologically the humanity of people living with a profound cognitive impairment, the Scottish theologian John Swinton.

"Radical Friendship"

John Swinton has made a Christian perspective on friendship central to his concern for people suffering from severe mental illnesses.[10] Swinton is interested in recovering what he calls "radical friendship," a particular kind of friendship that he identifies with the life and actions of Jesus Christ, "friend and protector of the poor, the outcast, and the stranger," and that is to be practiced, in turn, by the Christian community.[11] Swinton's interest in radical friendship is motivated by the way in which people with mental health problems can cease to be persons, as he puts it, in the eyes of many because they have come to be identified in the essential terms of their pathologies (e.g., "schizophrenic"; "manic depressive"). The task he sets himself is to "explore ways of conceptually and

10. Swinton, *Resurrecting the Person*.
11. Ibid., 9.

practically separating [such] people from their illnesses, and, in so doing, help enable the 'resurrection of the person.'"[12] Radical friendship, modeled on the personal relationships Jesus of Nazareth pursued, especially with the poor, marginalized and outcast, is his response to this task.

Swinton's project is similar to Reinders' in as much as he is concerned with the meaning and place of friendship in the lives of those who are profoundly impaired in one way or another.[13] Both have a concern for people who, because of their impairments, have been excluded from human society and all that that entails for human flourishing; both seek to establish a notion of humanity that is inclusive of them; and both suggest that the Christian understanding of friendship is central to this goal. In other words, while they have adopted different language and methods, both Reinders and Swinton propose a conceptual re-visioning of the humanity of profoundly impaired people in terms of inclusion through a theocentric understanding of friendship.

Swinton begins his analysis of radical friendship by describing two different narratives that are told about the care of people with mental health problems.[14] The predominant narrative is told in terms of a medical model of care, wherein someone with a mental illness is viewed through the prism of the pathology of his or her condition. In such a narrative the focus is on the illness, and its language is that of eradication, minimization and management. Such a narrative "tells us nothing of what it means to be human and to live humanly even in the midst of our particular difficulties."[15] Consequently, what is required is "a liberating counter-understanding" that shifts the focus from the illness to the individual, including the social environment in which he or she is situated.[16] This alternative narrative cannot be understood biologically, but requires a language of personhood and personal relationships.

> What one has here is a clash of interpretations and priorities and a fundamental difference in situational definition—two narratives revolving around the same situation, one focusing on the person-as-illness, the other focusing on the person-as-person,

---

12. Ibid., 10.

13. Ibid., 11. Unlike Reinders, Swinton is especially interested in the implications radical friendship has for practical theology.

14. Ibid.

15. Ibid., 33.

16. Ibid., 34.

and both coming to significantly different conclusions as to priorities and life expectations.[17]

These two narratives are meant to be understood as distinct and competing narratives. There is to be a choosing between them, with the latter being seen as better than the former in overcoming the ostracizing that people with mental illnesses often experience. The Christian community, through the conduit of radical friendship, has a particular contribution to make in this choice "because the priority of friends is the personhood of the other and not the illness."[18] In making this claim, Swinton suggests an initial definition for friendship: it is "a deeply intimate and committed relationship that encompasses people in all their fullness." The emphasis on intimacy and commitment is meant to convey that radical friendship is a "distinctly Christian gift that the church offers to marginalized people," a distinct kind of friendship.[19] This is borne out by Swinton's claim that Christian friendship is messianic in character, by which he means: it is configured to the kind of relationships that Jesus of Nazareth lived and modeled. The particular character of this kind of friendship is one of self-giving that leads to the liberation of the befriended:

> The form of friendship here is radical in that it transcends the relational boundaries that are constructed by contemporary tendencies to associate with others on the basis of likeness, utility or social exchange. It is radical also in that its primary dynamic is toward the outcast and the stranger . . . It is a profoundly humanizing relationship that reveals something of the coming kingdom of God as revealed in the person of Christ . . .[20]

Radical friendship moves beyond—transcends—the usual characteristics associated with friendship, and becomes a new way of loving which "images the messiah."[21] Swinton is proposing a highly qualified notion of friendship to do the work of inclusion for the mentally ill, and through this narrowing arrives at a much more pronounced choice

17. Ibid., 35.
18. Ibid., 37.
19. Ibid., 38.
20. Ibid., 39.
21. Ibid., 43. He marks this move by adopting language like "special quality"; "specific focus"; "solidarity with the poor and marginalized"; "total commitment to others, even to death"; "sacrificial"; "pattern of discipleship"; "faithful living."

between narratives. Nonetheless, Swinton draws on Aristotle's classical threefold distinction of utility, pleasure, and goodness to make his comparison of Christian friendship with other kinds of friendship. Aristotle's notion of true friendship, the virtuous friendship between equals, is deemed to be the issue that makes the distinction.[22] Swinton argues that there is no mention of equality in the Christian specification of friendship. Equality suggests a mutual self-recognition that demands a one-to-one exclusivity, and this is "the antithesis of the friendship revealed in the life and death of Christ."[23]

Christian friendship, on the other hand, is essentially unequal friendship; it is about befriending the other-as-different, the outcast, and so on. It includes, where other friendships exclude. Christ's way of being a friend, therefore, becomes Swinton's true friendship (noting his reference to John 15 in the following quotation):

> Jesus flattens the relational hierarchy of the Aristotelian model of friendship and presents a new and radically open understanding of friendship—a friendship that is open to . . . those who are in many respects radically unlike himself. More than that, by moving the status of his disciples from servants to friends, and by suggesting that true friendship demands commitment even unto death, Jesus presents a model of committed friendship that more than transcends the boundaries of utility and pleasure.[24]

The shift from the Aristotelian to the Christian framework highlights the sharpness of the distinction being drawn between radical friendship and other kinds of friendship. Friendships of utility and pleasure point to an underlying requirement that there be something about the one befriended—certain properties or characteristics or features that he or she has—that makes the difference. These properties, possessed by an individual either essentially or accidentally, become the prerequisite for the very possibility of friendship. It is the presence of the properties themselves, which will vary from friendship to friendship, and not the person who has them, that makes the friendship; it is not "the person" who is befriendable, but "the person with." These kinds of friendship,

---

22. Reinders also takes up Aristotle over the same issue, and for the same reasons. *Receiving the Gift of Friendship*, 358-67.

23. Swinton, *Resurrecting the Person*, 45.

24. Ibid., 47.

therefore, are conditional on the presence in the one to be befriended of what is desirable to the one who is befriending.

It should be clear where this is leading for people with mental health problems. Because of their illnesses they do not have what is desirable in terms of utility or pleasure or, for that matter, equal regard; therefore, they do not have what is required for friendships of these kinds to come about. Consequently, they are excluded from them. In terms of Swinton's two narratives, "mental illness" is the property that limits the possibility of friendship for those who have mental health problems, so any narrative that makes the illness central is unable to include in the ambit of friendship the person who suffers from it. In other words, the person-as-illness narrative will always view friendship through a property-based prism.

True Christian friendship, on the other hand, the kind of friendship that is said to locate itself within a person-as-person narrative, does not require anything other than a particular someone to befriend. Nor is it influenced by changes in circumstances. True friendship is, according to Swinton, identical with "the radical *agape* love of God for human beings" in which God bestows his sacrificial love, irrespective of what the befriended has (or does not have) to bring to the creating of this friendship.[25] It is this characteristic of unconditional bestowal upon the individual as such, rather than the conditional appraisal of the properties of the person, that is the unique feature of "agapic personal love."[26] Christian friendship is universal in character and everyone can be a recipient of it, for it is "[a solicitude] that is grounded in the reality of God's unending and unconditional love of the individual—a love that bestows worth and dignity upon the individual irrespective of context, situation, or any radical change that may occur within particular properties. This kind of solicitude offers a 'non-appraisive attitude of radical equality' underpinned by an ethic and an attitude that adopts a position of moral solidarity with the other, irrespective of circumstance."[27]

In "Bare Particular" Country: The Turn to Personhood

Having now outlined his notion of radical friendship, it is not entirely clear why Swinton believes it brings about an "attitude of radical equality."

25. Ibid., 48.
26. Ibid., 38.
27. Ibid., 49.

Presumably, he does not mean that the friends of God, by being loved in this way, are deemed equal with God's divinity. Is it, then, because the one who befriends in this *agape* way adopts a stance towards the one to be befriended such that he brackets out any reliance on relative merit in the one being befriended? What makes such a reading plausible is that the word "attitude" suggests making a choice in favor of one option over and against another. In this case, it would be a choice in favor of the person-as-person narrative over and against the person-as-illness narrative. What makes this a reasonable reading is the sense in which the attitude itself seems groundless. Is Swinton reluctant to suggest grounds for this attitude or is he simply unable to offer a reason? There seems to be nothing available in his argument to answer this question. The lacuna, however, remains.

Be that as it may, the upshot of Swinton's attitude of radical equality is that the person who lives in accordance with the person-as-person narrative is someone who has adopted an attitude of bestowal over appraisal when it comes to establishing friendships, with Christ being the exemplar *par excellence*. This is evidently an epistemological move: a prior commitment is taken and then applied to the way in which befriending takes place. In this sense, equality is chosen, not intrinsically determined. Perhaps this is why Swinton considers it radical: not in the sense of uncovering the deep-seated roots of equality, but in the sense of going beyond—transcending—the limitations of equality. We have, therefore, a different kind of equality to match a different kind of friendship that is about including everyone. (All of this, it might be noted, is reminiscent of Reinders' pursuit of inclusion through a transcending conception of friendship grounding a common humanity.)

It is only by focussing in on the personhood of those who suffer from mental health problems that friendships of radical equality are made possible with them. This is a task of re-conception. Swinton's way of making this move is to "separate the person from the illness"; it is a matter of "think[ing] in terms of the individual as a *person* who also has a disorder, rather than a person who *is* a disorder."[28] A life marked by demoralization and exclusion in the person-is-disorder mode, is reframed in terms of hope and inclusion through the person-with-disorder mode.[29] This is how the book's title comes into play: Christians are to "resurrect

---

28. Ibid., 134.
29. Ibid., 137, 138.

persons" by offering those with mental illnesses a personal relationship of love that is catalytic in character ("being someone for them"), rather than remaining within the framework of instrumental friendship ("doing something for them").[30] Without saying so explicitly, Swinton seems to be claiming that the person is the individual human being apart from his or her illness, or, for that matter, apart from any other aspect or property or characteristic or condition of the individual that might hinder equal regard. Something of this "pure personhood" is captured in the following remark:

> This type of committed caring that focuses on the person behind the diagnosis is very much in line with the kind of relationally based, committed caring that is revealed in the life of Jesus and in his friendships.[31]

The notion of personhood that emerges is one whereby "the person" is a deeper, higher, more aboriginal grounding of the individual who is mentally ill, or any of the myriad of descriptions under which human beings come to be characterised, either essentially or accidentally. It is about reconceiving humanity, about changing the way of knowing people who are profoundly impaired. The issue here is that the human condition comes to play no essential part; and this is claimed to be the case for theological reasons. True friendship looks behind all the properties of the individual, so to speak, in order to locate the person that transcends those properties. Thus, Jesus is said to have "reached beyond social expectations to reclaim the personhood of the other."[32]

It is worth pausing here to consider how Swinton compares with Reinders. Swinton's aim is to develop a narrative around the life of a person that bypasses the properties characteristic of that individual. This is because some properties (e.g., mental illness) are conceived of as limiting and marginalizing for human beings. Instead, he is looking for a way of conceiving human life such that it transcends the quiddity of human existence. Reinders, on his part, aims for a transcending concept that renders irrelevant any reliance on an intrinsic account of human beings. This is

---

30. Ibid., 143. "Instrumental" should not be seen as "opposite to categorical." Swinton holds that the radical friendship of Jesus—the true opposite of an instrumental friendship—was not simply friendship for its own sake; rather, it was "primarily aimed at regaining the dignity and personhood of those whom society had rejected and depersonalized" (142).

31. Ibid., 142.

32. Ibid., 143.

because such an account is dependent on the presence of certain features (e.g., agency) the absence of which excludes some people from participation in the human community. Instead, he looks for a way of conceiving human life such that it is extrinsic to the quiddity of human existence. Both, in other words, are looking for the subject that lies behind, or is at a deeper or higher level than the concrete individual who stands before the one who is offering friendship.

What is to be made of this? To borrow Elizabeth Anscombe's rather tart declaration: "Here we [are] in 'bare particular' country: *what* is the subject, which has all these predicates?"[33] Anscombe's point is that it is a mistake to go looking for a subject behind or beyond or transcendent of the individual standing before me who answers to a certain set of predicates that uniquely marks him or her out as the object of my attention. The predicates go with the subject, necessarily. Both Swinton and Reinders, however, go in search of the subject behind the predicates, as if they play no part in affirming the subject in view, rather than determining the subject who comes under the description of his or her predicates. Both are positing a subject that is beyond, deeper, transcendent of the concrete individual who stands before me, longing for friendship. So the question arises: What manner of thing is it that I would be able to show friendship to? This is the question to arise because there seems to be no "who" left upon which to get a handle; it, too, has entered into the land of bare particulars.

The tendency towards viewing the human subject as above or apart from the human condition has come to dominate anthropological and ethical questions. It is often associated with the Cartesian turn to the psychological self, but it is also said to have its roots in the nominalist turn of late medieval thinking.[34] This turn has found its way into Christian theology, which is "imbued with this idea that the self is a separate and separable reality somehow existing beyond space and time."[35] What is noteworthy about this turn is how the emergent, non-predicated human

---

33. Anscombe, "Under a Description," 209.

34. For an account of the Cartesian turn, see Kerr, *Theology after Wittgenstein*, ch. 8. Pinckaers, in *The Sources of Christian Ethics*, ch. 10, locates its provenance in the rise of nominalism in the late Middle Ages. Others locate it in the Lockean shift from the metaphysical to the psychological understanding of "person."

35. Johnstone, "The Self as Receiver and Giver: A Critique of the Modern and Post-Modern Self." Johnstone names in particular the works of Timothy O'Connell, Richard Gula, and Germain Grisez. Johnstone traces the theological seed to John Duns Scotus and Franciscus Suarez.

subject comes with a concomitant loosening of the connections with human nature. Separating out the unlimited, infinite, incorrupt, immortal longings of our humanity from the limited, finite, corrupt and mortal conditioning of our humanity leads to a shift in the understanding of what is involved in coming to live a flourishing human life. Finite human nature is no longer the basis for our transcending human tendencies. For some time now, however, theologians from a variety of traditions have been highlighting the troubling aspects of this turn.[36] The common element they each seek to communicate is how any tendency to separate out the elements of our enduringly paradoxical being not only changes the understanding of what it is to be human, but risks diminishing—even undermining—our human lives.

This seems to be the case with both Reinders and Swinton. They each lean towards advocating a transcendent human subject who is separately conceived from the human condition. The effect, however, is to render this subject, who is taken to be the object of true friendship, impenetrable to others. Swinton's "person" is perhaps more Cartesian in style: as all other things are stripped away, there is left the subject to be befriended. Reinders' "humanity" is more stridently Kantian (though without the emphasis on autonomy): a universalized, timeless, categorical subject that is unencumbered by all that is intrinsic and limiting and contingent. The difficulty is more pronounced in Reinders, where it would seem he has taken a theological distinction—namely, the nature/grace distinction key to the Reformed tradition from which he comes—and turned it into a sharp anthropological separation. Both, nonetheless, aspire to a transcendent subject that is unencumbered by mundane moorings.

To be sure, Swinton and Reinders are dealing with the theological question of friendship, and not the more philosophical question of the human subject as such. Their common concern is to discover something of the living relationship between God and his human creation, and how this informs the meaning of human friendship. Nevertheless, they have framed their theological anthropologies in ways that ensure that mundane human life carries with it no essential message for human flourishing. Because they both separate out all that is transcendent about being human from the reality of the human condition, they dissolve the enduring tension between transcendence and immanence so characteristic of

---

36. See, for example, the Melkite theologian Jean Corbon, *The Wellspring of Worship*, translated from *Liturgie de Source*, 91; and the broadly Western Protestant position found in Rowan Williams, "Interiority and Epiphany," 29.

human life. For the sake of inclusion, the unlimited, infinite, incorrupt, immortal longings of human life are conceptually removed from all possible sources of exclusion, those being the limited, finite, corrupt, and mortal conditions of human life. The outcome, however, is the opposite of what is intended: instead of affirming the humanity of the profoundly disabled or the mentally ill, their personal presence before the world, whereby they become possible objects of friendship, is diminished to the point of invisibility. The Scottish Dominican Fergus Kerr has called this way of thinking "aspiring to become non-human":

> The characteristic temptation of religion, it may be said, emerges when the difference between human finitude and the unlimited has been established, in the thought that there is this other form of existence in which unlimitedness is a possibility.[37]

Despite these signs of similarity between Swinton and Reinders, there is one key difference between them at an anthropological level that makes a real difference to how Swinton's notion of radical friendship plays out in the lives of the profoundly impaired. For Swinton, friendship is a consequence of, as well as a response to, a meeting of persons (albeit stripped down to a phantom-like "bare particular"). Each time Jesus offered his love it was because there was someone who was poor, marginalized, outcast standing before him. Therefore, it is the personal presence of the individual that brings about the offer of friendship. This ordering is significant for it places the life of the individual, in the midst of his afflictions, at the center of attention, thereby making his life the reason for the offer. It is the person so conditioned who puts forward the claim for friendship, and not the condition itself. At least this seems to be the sense in which Swinton intends his person-as-person narrative to be read: befriending is ordered to a conditioned person, and not to a subject apart from being conditioned. This suggests that Swinton's ordering of friendship is structurally different from Reinders', even though it retains a similar ontological insubstantiality.

Friendship and Jesus of Nazareth: Swinton's Biblical Evidence

It is time to consider how Swinton applies the evangelical imperative to friendship. In this regard, he has a particular description of friendship in mind when it comes to the way Jesus of Nazareth befriended others:

37. Kerr, *Theology after Wittgenstein*, 206.

> His relationships were marked by such things as unconditional acceptance (Jn 4.5), solidarity with the poor and the marginalized (Mt 9.10), and a total commitment to others, even unto death (Jn 15.13). The name he and other gospel writers gave to this form of committed relationship was *friendship*. It would not be unreasonable to define discipleship as friendship with Jesus.[38]

While identifying friendship as sacrificial, the defining phrase in the quotation is "committed relationship." Jesus had committed relationships with others that were characterized by acceptance, solidarity and sacrifice, and these characteristics were to be the hallmarks of discipleship, which is nothing more than friendship from the perspective of the person befriended. This differs from so-called ordinary friendship on two counts: unlike other friendships (and read here Aristotelian categories of friendship), the committed relationships of Jesus are said to be radically inclusive and radically unequal:

> Thus, in the friendships of Jesus we find a model of friendship, not as a closed relationship with a single like-minded individual, but as an open relationship focused on "the outsider."[39]

It is the committed relationships of Jesus with others that is the standout feature of Swinton's description of radical friendship. He lists a number of encounters during Jesus' public life as examples: the encounter with the Samaritan woman at the well (John 4); the healing of the possessed Gerasene man (Luke 8); the calling of Zaccheus (Luke 19); dining with the tax collectors and sinners (Matt 9); the Last Supper with his disciples (Matt 26). Clearly, the relational emphasis in each of these examples is different, something of which Swinton is mindful: "Friendship . . . is context dependent—that is, the word 'friendship' does not have a universal meaning."[40] We may view these examples, therefore, as exhibiting a certain family resemblance, and taken together they suggest a shared meaning that cannot be understood entirely free from context.

What can be learned from them in terms of the anthropological reality of friendship? To begin with, it would appear that what constitutes a "committed relationship" is determined from the perspective of Jesus alone: perhaps the tax collectors and sinners who dined with Jesus

---

38. Swinton, *Resurrecting the Person*, 43.
39. Ibid., 47.
40. Ibid., 50.

were there simply to enjoy a pleasant diversion with a man whose words and deeds had made him a *cause célèbre*? In other words, the relational commitment is taken to be of Jesus' doing; it is what he brings to the encounter. This being the case, "commitment" is an act of Jesus; either he is responding to an approach (as with Zaccheus) or he goes looking for a response (as with the Samaritan woman). Swinton is presenting the five examples as properly personal relationships, but as they are constituted from the perspective of Jesus and connected to the gospel love of *agape*.

Presumably this is why Swinton would compare without contrast the encounter of Jesus with the tax collectors and sinners and his final meal with his disciples. They are hardly alike in any way other than that a meal was involved. This emphasis given to personal commitment seems designed to answer the question as to why Jesus pursued such relationships: he could not do otherwise. Consequently, any and every personal encounter of Jesus with someone else is considered a friendship because any and every encounter entered into by Jesus involves a commitment of *agape* love. What Swinton presents by way of examples of friendship is not determined to be so by reference to a notion of friendship but by reference to an agapeic notion of a loving relationship. This is tantamount to saying that every time Jesus involved himself in a loving relationship, then it must have been a radical-friendship kind of relationship.

It is telling that at no time does Jesus use the language of friendship in terms of the five personal encounters Swinton presents as examples of Jesus befriending. This fact might be dismissed on the grounds that friends do not habitually describe their meetings using friendship language, and there is no reason to expect it would be any different with Jesus. Perhaps the encounters Jesus had with the Samaritan woman or the Gerasene man or Zaccheus could be read as friendships without the corresponding language? The response to this is to look to how Jesus spoke of his love for God's people outside the actual encounters mentioned and to see if the language or image of friendship is present. In other words, does the language of friendship enter into Jesus' lexicon elsewhere in the gospels or does he ever describe his love for others using images of friendship?

There are only two occasions when Jesus uses the language of friendship. The first is at Matthew 11, when he remarks on comments made about him by others: "The Son of man came, eating and drinking, and they say, 'Look, a glutton and a drunkard, a friend of tax collectors and sinners'" (Matt 11:19). It is not, however, an example of Jesus himself making use of the language of friendship but a moment when he is pointing out how misplaced his detractors were in their interpretation of what he was on about. For this reason, the Matthean reference does not support Swinton's claims. The second use occurs in the Johannine context we have been alluding to, but now need to deal with more directly, namely: the Last Supper Discourse of John 15: "No one has greater love than this, to lay down one's life for one's friends. . . . I do not call you servants any longer . . . I have called you friends" (John 15:13, 15).

Significantly, Jesus uses the language and image of friendship here to draw a line of demarcation. He calls his disciples friends at this stage of their relationship so as to distinguish it from the way he had, until then, related to them. It was an explicit change in the way he would relate to them. Most tellingly for Swinton's claims, the use of friendship language in this example strongly suggests that Jesus himself saw his committed relationship to the disciples as taking on different forms at different times and circumstances. Jesus does not see it as any less a personal relationship of love ("I chose you"—v. 16), but clearly not all such relationships were friendships for him, nor were they friendships at all stages in the relationship.

Yet, precisely at the place where Jesus demarcates, Swinton conflates. At the heart of John 15 Jesus pronounces what might be called friendship's ultimate reach: in the moment of offering his disciples friendship, Jesus offers them his life. It is important to note that Jesus does not say that this ultimate reach, made by him out of friendship, is a requirement or condition of friendship. In his reference to John 15, however, Swinton notes the sacrificial aspect of this moment, but then makes it the defining feature: "Sacrificial friendship is the definition of love."[41] The ultimate reach of friendship becomes a requirement of true Christian friendship, demanding a total commitment to others, even unto death. The notion of self-sacrificing love is identified exclusively with the notion of friendship. The problem with this, of course, is that every relationship of sacrificial love is now deemed to be a friendship by virtue of its sacrificial character alone. We need only consider the sacrificial character of much parental love to see the problem with this. Love does not have to be friendship for it to be sacrificial, and friendship does not have to be sacrificial for it to be Christ-like in love. The conflation of "friendship" and "sacrificial love"

---

41. Ibid., 43.

has the undermining effect of casting the scope of friendship so widely as to include any sacrificial relationship.

One further aspect of friendship implied in John 15, but not significant for Swinton's five examples of friendship, is the question of how friendship unfolds and is sustained over time. Swinton draws attention to the temporality of friendship: "people need to meet one another before they can become friends."[42] Jesus too implies this had been the case for him as he speaks with his disciples about his friendship for them: "I call you friends because I have made known to you everything I have learned from my Father" (John 15:15). This sense of a friendship unfolding and developing over time is not, however, readily evident in most of the other examples of friendship Swinton relies on. It is at least questionable if there was enough time for friendship to emerge for the Gerasene man's brief encounter with Jesus, for example. This is not to question the love of Jesus for the man, nor to doubt that Jesus had committed himself to him sacrificially in their turbulent encounter. Rather, it is to raise a reasonable doubt as to whether or not the processes for a friendship to develop could have had the time to unfold. It is telling that in the one place in the gospels where Jesus uses the language of friendship, it throws up a crucial aspect about friendship that is not evident in most of the other examples upon which Swinton relies.

On the one significant occasion when Jesus uses friendship language he makes a point of differentiating friendship from other forms of personal relationship. How, then, does he tend to characterise his other relationships (including the relationships evident in Swinton's five examples)? Two relational metaphors used by Jesus of himself are striking in this regard: the mothering image from the Synoptics: "How often have I longed to gather [Jerusalem's] children together, as a hen gathers her brood" (Luke 13:34; Matt 23:37); and the Johannine Good Shepherd image: "I am the good shepherd; I know my own and my own know me" (John 10:14). In the synoptic simile, Jesus unambiguously associates his love with that of the parent/child relationship. The protective characterization is reminiscent of the sacrificial aspect of love. In this example, therefore, we have sacrifice and parental love being linked by Jesus, with no indication of friendship being thought of. The protective, parental analogy is being drawn on in the shepherding metaphor as well, albeit not as explicitly. It comes via the claim of ownership: Jesus claims

---

42. Ibid., 146.

as his own the people that he then loves and cares for. Neither of these images are readily associated with notions of friendship; rather, they both strongly point to familial relationships that are associated with notions of sacrificial love. Consequently, we are left with the demarcating passage of John 15 as the only significant occurrence of Jesus using friendship language and meaning.

More will need to be said about the Johannine insight into friendship in order to draw out its implications for a Christian anthropology of friendship. For the moment, however, this initial consideration of the Johannine insight suggests that Swinton has over-reached in his understanding of friendship and, therefore, has undermined the work he needs it to do. "Friendship" has been made to incorporate a whole series of relationships that might not readily come under the description of friendship. Like Reinders' theocentric alternative, Swinton's radical friendship extends its reach well beyond some basic features of friendship, turning it into a synonym for divine-human relationality. What we are left with are problematic questions about whether or not Swinton's radical friendship can do the anthropological work that it is supposed to be doing for the profoundly impaired.

"No Greater Love": Friendship's Ultimate Reach

For both Reinders and Swinton the concept of friendship is significant because of its supposed power to include the profoundly impaired. Yet, they see friendship as operating in markedly different ways: for Reinders, it is principally a good received; for Swinton, it is principally a love given. If this is what results from two serious attempts at grappling with the anthropological dimensions of friendship, is there anything that can be said about it that is of sustainable value for the humanity of the profoundly impaired? At its heart this is a question about whether or not friendship is, in fact, key to discovering the personal presence of each and every human life, including the profoundly impaired. McCabe said it is, and he pointed to John 15 as the evangelical warrant for his claim. Reinders' transcending concept is unable to grapple with John 15, and Swinton seems not to have taken the Johannine insight to heart. It is now time to see what we may make of it.

On the night before his passion, while at table with those he loved, Jesus said to them:

> This is my commandment, that you love one another as I have loved you. No one has greater love than this, to lay down one's life for one's friends. You are my friends if you do what I command you. I do not call you servants any longer, because the servant does not know what the master is doing; but I have called you friends, because I have made known to you everything that I have heard from my Father. You did not choose me but I chose you. And I appointed you to go and bear fruit, fruit that will last, so that the Father will give you whatever you ask him in my name. I am giving you these commands so that you may love one another. (John 15:12–17)[43]

"No greater love . . ." is certainly a declaration known and quoted far beyond its biblical setting and Christian significance, and often without awareness of its source.[44] It has come to evoke deep resonances in human lives and, more broadly, human cultures. Even so, what can the biblical account of friendship's ultimate reach tell us about the nature of friendship itself? In designating his disciples as friends by offering up his life for them, Jesus made no move towards abandoning their teacher/disciple relationship. Discipleship would remain a constitutive feature of the relationship he would continue to have with them (John 20:16). This particular kind of relationship, however, is different from other kinds of relationship, such as comradeship, familial relations, or companionship. While two of these four kinds of relationship are based on equality (comrades, companions), the other two are not; one is a biological relationship (family), unlike the others. Yet all four have incorporated into them the possibility of the same qualitative indicator of friendship's ultimate reach. Conforming to a fixed context or a specific kind of relationship, therefore, does not explain the meaning of "no greater love . . ." In any event, this does not need to be the case.

What then is needed? A place to begin addressing this question is to consider what it is about friendship that makes it significant in terms of a love that is capable of reaching out towards self-sacrifice. The sacrificial love that Jesus was offering requires an appropriate object towards which it can be directed. Jesus indicates that mere association would not count as such an object: *I do not call you servants any longer*. What makes

---

43. For a well-regarded biblical commentary on this passage, see Keener, *The Gospel of John*.

44. Many war memorials quote these words without reference to their biblical source.

servanthood a mere association? A servant is to be busy about his master's business, so to speak, but he is not thereby incorporated into the unfolding of his master's life. A servant is someone who may stand alongside the master as his life unfolds, who may even occupy a significant place in the unfolding events of the master's life. However, in virtue of being a servant, he is not essential to that unfolding; the master does not live for the sake of his servant, *qua* servanthood. As Jesus said: *the servant does not know what the master is doing.* May not a master lay down his life for a servant, nonetheless? Of course he may, but all this does is indicate that when the master does lay down his life for the servant this makes the servant something more than an associate. It is the individual subject, incorporated into the life of the one offering love, who is significant in terms of establishing a proper object for that love.

In John 15, Jesus designates friendship as the kind of relationship towards which he may appropriately direct his sacrificial love. However, a servant is an inadequate object towards which this friendship may be properly directed because that individual's life is not, *qua* servanthood, incorporated into the life of the subject. What then makes a friend an individual who has been incorporated into the life of the subject? Jesus answers this by explaining to his disciples how they have come to participate in a personal way in the unfolding of his life: *because I have made known to you everything that I have heard from my Father.* Jesus no longer saw his disciples as mere associates in his work; they had become friends because Jesus now includes them in the unfolding of his life. It is noteworthy that John 15:12–17 is structurally situated within a broader, unified passage that considers the metaphor of the vine and branches (cf. John 15:1–17). Friendship reveals itself as a kind of grafting of one life onto another. To say that Jesus' disciples are now grafted onto him is a metaphorical way of saying that they have come to belong with him, that they have been incorporated into his life. They no longer merely associate with him. None of this is said appropriately of servants (*qua* servanthood), but it can be said of friends.

It is also true that the basis of friendship is not simply about being in possession of knowledge concerning another. Rather, what is important is the role that that knowledge comes to play in the relationship. In designating his disciples as his friends, Jesus commits himself to living for them and not in association with them: *You did not choose me but I chose you.* They have become involved in his life in such a way that he invites them to participate with him in the living out of his life. It is not because the disciples know certain things about Jesus that makes them his friends. Someone might know very little about another, yet become friends. (Conversely, they may know a great deal about each other and not become friends.) In fact, coming to know a friend better is a delight that is itself dependent upon there being a friendship in the first place. This does not mean, however, that a friendship can exist where there is nothing held in common. To be a friend is to know the one to whom friendship is offered, but simply to know someone else is not enough. Commonality is also called for. Therefore, what matters is the way in which the disciples come to hold in common the life of Jesus, along with the things they know about Jesus.

It might be claimed that a clinical psychologist will come to know her patient through and through, and that thereby she will hold in common the life of her patient. That does not mean, however, that the therapeutic relationship, by virtue of this shared knowledge, is a friendship.[45] The issue is about who is involved. Friendship pertains to a personal subject, and individual human being, and not to some description—patient, lover, comrade, family member, colleague—under which someone is present in a relationship. It is because Jesus has chosen to include his disciples in the way things have unfolded in his own life—has allowed them to share in common with him his own life—that he now considers them his friends. Of course, what friends share in common will vary from friendship to friendship. This is why the context in which "No greater love . . ." was originally spoken is not crucial for its use elsewhere: the disciples have in common what Jesus had passed onto them, each has their work and commitments, and families have their blood ties and history. What matters is that the disciples *qua* friendship have been invited to share in common with Jesus the living of his life.

This is why the term "incorporation" (or the biblical "grafting") is well suited to the notion of friendship. It is suggestive of the fact that friendship is defined by an open-ended act of inclusion, a choosing or allowing of others to be a friend, rather than an act of exclusion. (An obvious example here is spouses: "to the exclusion of all others"). The

---

45. The way in which therapeutic relationships operate also highlights the reason why a patient can quite easily mistake it for a friendship. By intentionally involving herself in the life of the patient, the psychologist is mimicking the role of a friend. What differs between the real thing and the mimicking is that the psychologist intentionally remains abstracted from the person who is the patient. In a similar way, allied nation-states can adopt the language of friendship about each other because they relate to one another in a friendlike manner.

emphasis on action is deliberate; the claim to inclusion should not be read as meaning that friendship can be any human occurrence of an inclusive nature. Being included in the class of people with ginger hair does not make all redheads friends. Similarly, not all followers of Jesus were his friends. The circumstances around which a friendship comes into existence might be accidental, but friends are never "by accident." A friend is someone who has been welcomed by another into the personal dimensions of his or her life so that together they may share in it: *You are my friends if you do what I command you.* To be included in the unfolding of someone's life means being in an ongoing state of welcome—of reception—as a friend. Again, it is not what is shared that matters for friendship; it is the manner in which the sharing happens. Hence, incorporation; not association.

The Characteristics of Friendship

The "if" clause at John 15:14 (*if you do what I command you*) and the "because" clause at John 15:15 (*because I have made known to you*) are crucial to creating the structure that distinguishes friendship from other kinds of incorporation. For the disciples to be included in the ambit of friendship with Jesus it meant they had to become involved in the life of Jesus ("because") as well as being drawn into the dimensions of that life to be held in common ("if"). These are the steps that lead to incorporation into Jesus' life; they create the sharing of his life in common with him. This incorporation is to be understood as operating in the active tense. In other words, an act of reception needs to take place for an actual friendship to come about. Again, the emphasis on acting is deliberate: friendship involves doing, both on the part of the one offering and the one receiving. Friendship, therefore, acts precisely as a gift: it can be offered; it is grounded in something that appropriately can be given (i.e., a relationship of love); and it can be received. In gift giving, there is implied the concept of responsibility: those who receive a gift have a responsibility both to the gift and the giver.

The importance of the "if" and the "because" is further highlighted when certain characteristic phenomena of friendship are recalled: friendships can exhibit both amazing durability and astonishing fragility. A friendship can last over great distances of time, location, and circumstance. What seems to make this durability possible is that the "because" remains in force. What friends hold in common about each other will endure even when no contact is made for great lengths of time. Admittedly, there is always the possibility that that which was once held in common may no longer hold up to the scrutiny of changed life-circumstances. Yet, the phenomenon of durability is without question.

On the other hand, friendships can be broken in an instant if the "if," that which keeps friends holding the lives of each other in common, is ruptured. Perhaps this accounts for why Jesus so strongly exhorted his disciples to "abide" in his love (see the broader context of John 15:1–17): he desired the durability of friendship but recognized the fragility of it. This is not to suggest that a particular friendship cannot be unconditional in character, or that all friendships are essentially fragile. A commitment to a friendship can be unconditionally made—an analogy can be made here to a married couple who have committed themselves to each other "till death us do part"—so long as the framing conditions for such a relationship have been delineated. The "if" clause that Jesus spoke is precisely such a framing condition, which results in his unconditional friendship unto death.

In the final analysis, friendship is more than the notion of a loving relationship, even though it is that as well. Sexual attraction, familial relations, companionship, collegiality, discipleship, patronage, benevolent care and social concern are all examples that can readily come under the description of a relationship of love. Friendship also has the structure of a loving relationship, and uncomplicatedly so: "We are friends; nothing more, nothing less." Therefore it is not simply something that supervenes on other structures of love. It is not "better than" in the sense of being a more highly developed form of love. In fact, certain loving relations do not readily lend themselves to being friendships.[46] Yet, friendship can accompany each of the examples mentioned above. Therefore, neither is friendship simply one more form of love among others. Because it is not bound to any particular relational structure, it is possible to say that friendship transcends other relationships of love (though not in the sense in which Reinders uses the word!). Indeed, it is a love of—or better, love with—the other for its own sake and not dependent on another reason, as the other loves do. Friends can recognize the distinctions that exist in any particular relationship—desire, companionship, a shared political or religious outlook—without being bound to or limited by those distinctions.

---

46. For example, the relationship between a young, pre-pubescent child and an adult.

The love friends have for one another can stand on its own without further justification; though again, that does not mean friends do not have a reason for their friendship to exist in the first place.

Thus, when Jesus said: *No one has greater love than this*, the "greater than" is better read in terms of how friendship-love structurally transcends other forms of love than in terms of it being the best or highest intensity of love.[47] What makes Jesus' love for his disciples so intense is that friendship is the kind of relationship that allows for the possibility of love's ultimate reach. This claim can easily be tested by recalling the nature of most schoolyard mateships. The relationship between two mates would readily come under the description of friendship, yet it would hardly be considered the greatest expression of love (while not precluding the possibility of it becoming so). The transcending paradox of friendship is that it is mostly an ordinary, unremarkable thing; yet it is free to become the most exceptional expression of love. Jesus was prepared to lay down his life for his friends because the very ordinary, unremarkable structure of friendship was adequate for the task.

This is rightly so because the commitment of Jesus to his disciples reveals not so much a religious justification as an anthropological recognition. If anything is to be said of the foregoing analysis of John 15:12–17, it is that Jesus was communicating something about what is proper to being human. For a human being to love in the way that Jesus offered to love his disciples is for him or her to love as a friend. Captured in the commitment of Jesus is the realization—the discovery, to recall McCabe's word—that human beings are made for friendship; human beings are created for this end. We are "fit for purpose." Jesus was taking up the full mantle of his humanity when he chose to love his disciples to the end by making them his friends. Of course, this does not mean that all those whom Jesus loved thereby had to be his friends; like every other human being, he was free to befriend whomsoever he chose to chance the hand of friendship. Instead, it is to say that Jesus, quite ordinarily, made friends because he was, quite ordinarily, a human being, and friendship is that

---

47. A question might arise here about the kind of love Jesus was commending to his disciples. Debate has centered on whether or not Jesus proposed a new kind of love, one that is both distinct from, and better than other kinds of love. There are two kinds of love alluded to by Jesus in the passage we have been considering: *phileo* and *agapao*. C. S. Keener notes, however, that *phileo* and *agapao* are "more or less interchangeable semantically" (1004n159), and that there was no real distinction between the sense of the words until it was proposed by a group of British biblicists in the nineteenth century, an argument that has since been discarded by scholars (1235).

peculiarly mundane way of loving at the heart of being human. Therefore, to pursue friendship's ultimate reach is nothing more (and nothing less) than to be human, and for someone not to pursue friendship is for him or her to exhibit a reluctance for being human.

4

FRIENDSHIP-MADE

Friendship, Humanity, and the Profoundly Impaired

Recent Theological Accounts of Friendship

THE QUESTION AT THE heart of the previous chapter—Is there a way of understanding friendship that is mindful of the profoundly impaired, attentive to an evangelical foundation, yet does not undermine its anthropological integrity?—has at least been partially addressed. We now have reasons for saying that the pursuit of friendship in the way of Jesus is the pursuit of a thoroughly human enterprise: McCabe's mundane claim is borne out in the Johannine context, and Swinton's radical friendship, while fatally undermined in a number of ways, nonetheless is firmly rooted in the humanity of Jesus. Yet, we still do not have an account of how this enterprise is undertaken, nor the implications of it for the profoundly impaired. We have yet to bridge the gap from an evangelical orientation for friendship to a theological understanding of it; and we have yet to determine if friendship is a bridge too far when it comes to the profoundly impaired. This will be the task of this chapter.

There is an oddity about recent theological reflection on friendship: there is surprisingly little of it. This is not to say that it goes unmentioned; far from it. Since the re-awakening in the 1930s of love as a theme for theological and ethical reflection, instigated by Anders Nygren's *Agape and Eros*, friendship is now regularly and familiarly spoken of.[1] In

---

1. Liz Carmichael, in *Friendship*, provides a very helpful survey of the thread of friendship through theological circles since Nygren. The American Lutheran, Gilbert

much contemporary theology, and across the denominational divides, it is commonplace to speak of: friendship with God; fellowship among people; human solidarity; communion and community; and ethical friendships.[2] All of these are regularly taken to pertain to friendship in one way or another, with the result that the word "friendship" now acts mostly like a holding term for these and similar notions. Mention of friendship goes hand in hand with any theological emphasis on relationality. This, however, is precisely the point: friendship is often used to cover a multitude of sins, as it were, but in so doing it has been neglected as a point of theological concern in itself. As McCabe's observation suggests, it is the anthropological reality of friendship—its humanness—that has mostly suffered in this regard. It is not so much a neglect of the place that friendship has in human living as a neglect of the kind of human love that friendship is and how this particular kind of love then pertains to being human.

As a result, friendship, while open to an anthropological reality, has become little more than a euphemism for the relationality of human beings generally, either between humans or with God. The differences that might be noted between the ancient specifications of *agape*, *eros* and *philia* seem unnecessary, with "friendship" acting as a cover-all term; it is an (unintentional?) disengagement from the classical connections resourced by Nygen and others in the mid twentieth century.[3] To stress, this is not to accuse contemporary moral theologians of being neglectful of friendship; evidently, it now plays no small part in aiding theologians to explain what it means to live a fulfilling human life.[4] The difficulty is

---

Meilaender, is another who has written at length on friendship as a topic for theological reflection. See, for example, Meilaender, *Friendship*. From a Catholic perspective, the Irish philosopher James McEvoy wrote extensively on the love of friendship in terms of its ancient and Medieval roots. See, for example, McEvoy, "Friendship and Love," and the festschrift to McEvoy, *Amor amicitiae*.

2. Werner Jeanrond, for example, has written of friendship in terms of politics in *A Theology of Love*, while Steve Summers has written about it from an ecclesiological perspective: Summers, *Friendship*.

3. See D'Arcy, *The Mind and Heart of Love: Lion and Unicorn*, who is especially noteworthy for his critical response to Nygren from a Catholic perspective. D'Arcy has a chapter on friendship (ch. 4), in which he offers both an historical sweep of friendship and a commentary on the phenomenology of friendship, especially as this relates to the "I-Thou" relationship.

4. From a Catholic theological perspective, see such influential and diverse moral theologians as the Thomist Servais Pinckaers, *The Sources of Christian Ethics*, chapter 17; the New Natural Law theorist Germain Grisez, *The Way of the Lord Jesus*,

that these same theologies fail to distinguish friendship from other loves, to mark out how this kind of love—precisely as the kind of love that it is—makes a real difference in people's lives. It may be added that there seems little interest in drawing on any Johannine insight into friendship to guide their thinking at the points where they establish the good of friendship for the flourishing of human lives.[5]

These brief remarks suggest to us the thesis that friendship, in and of itself, has been somewhat neglected in theological circles (notably Catholic) even as friendship has become very widely referenced, especially within a moral framework.[6] This is not to conclude that friendship does not have anything distinctive to contribute, only that some well-regarded and influential theological accounts of it seem not to have made anything of its anthropological distinctiveness. They do not neglect a place for friendship in human living, but they seem to have neglected the question of how it pertains to being human precisely as friendship. This lacuna becomes acute when the profoundly impaired are reinserted into the discussion, their personal presence having been rendered silent by the somewhat elevated anthropologies of much contemporary moral theology. Consequently, clarifying how friendship is a distinctive kind of loving relationship for the good of human beings will be crucial to grasping the depth of meaning that friendship might have for being human. This particular question is nothing more than a way of returning once more to our overriding question: whether or not friendship can carry the weight of securing the humanity of the profoundly impaired.

Returning to the Sources on Friendship

It is striking that the neglect of the anthropological underpinnings of friendship coincides with a perceived general neglect of it among

---

vol. 1, *Christian Moral Principles*, chapter 5; and the Proportionalist Edward Vacek, *Love, Human and Divine*.

5. Joseph Kotva offers a well-regarded Catholic contribution to the discussion on friendship from a virtues perspective, lamenting that "the moral role of friendship is seldom mentioned in Christian ethics and receives sparse attention in theological, biblical, or liturgical reflection," yet bizarrely makes no reference at all to John 15 and barely touches on the place of friendship in Sacred Scripture. See Kotva, *Christian Case for Virtue Ethics*, 172.

6. A counterexample is Stanley Hauerwas and Charles Pinches, *Christians Among the Virtues*. They reflect on friendship as a virtue and as a method for doing ethics.

Christian thinkers of the latter part of the twentieth century. C. S. Lewis, one of the truly great Christian apologists of the last century, lamented in his famous book on love, "To the Ancients, Friendship seemed to be the happiest and most fully human of all loves.... The modern world, in comparison, ignores it."[7] Meanwhile, Josef Pieper, the German Catholic philosopher, in his seminal monograph on the same theme, noted: "friendship or, more exactly, the love of friends... is, in fact, a special form of love, though one that nowadays, oddly enough, comes in for little praise."[8] Both Lewis and Pieper point to the peculiarity of friendship as a key reason for this. In particular, they highlight two aspects to this peculiarity: the unique form of love that friendship takes, and the way this is masked by the ordinariness of friendship in human affairs. This combination of the unique and the ordinary in the peculiarity of friendship offers a helpful point of departure for the discussion at hand, and given their identification of these issues, Lewis and Pieper will prove useful guides.[9]

Lewis associates the neglect of friendship with it being uniquely the love that is freely chosen:

> Friendship is—in a sense not at all derogatory to it—the least *natural* of loves; the least instinctive, organic, biological, gregarious and necessary... Without Eros none of us would have been begotten and without Affection none of us would have been raised; but we can live and breed without Friendship. The species, biologically considered, has no need of it.[10]

---

7. Lewis, *Four Loves*, originally published in 1960, in the *C. S. Lewis Signature Classics Edition*, 69.

8. Pieper, *On Love*, originally published as *Uber dei Liebe* in 1972, in *Faith, Hope, Love*, 272.

9. Lewis is an obvious choice, given the close attention he gives to friendship in *The Four Loves*, and given the wide renown the book continues to have. Gilbert Meilaender, for example, has written extensively on Lewis' contribution to understanding friendship. See Meilaender, *The Taste for the Other* and *Friendship*. Carmichael, however, is curiously and, it might be suggested, unfairly dismissive of Lewis on friendship: "This is a quite personal essay rooted in the kind of donnish companionship, redolent of pubs, pipe-smoke and walking holidays, that he himself enjoyed." Carmichael, *Friendship*, 155. While Pieper's *On Love* is a work of philosophy and remains relatively unknown in the Anglophone world, it is full of hints and insights into how the theological rubs up against the philosophical. Furthermore, and apart from ancient and medieval sources, Lewis is the author Pieper refers to most frequently throughout his essay (23 times), and always to illuminate his own argument.

10. Lewis, *Four Loves*, 70 (original *italics*).

Almost all animals exhibit some sign of attraction, even if only minimally so, and many higher order animals exhibit complex nurturing tendencies, but only human beings befriend. While friendship is of the human species, it is the form of love by which human beings stand and face their essential animality, so to speak; it is the love that most explicitly reveals what it is to be human. Other forms of love are more evidently bound up with human animality. Friends are "drawn apart together from the herd," as Lewis puts it; in their befriending they witness to the uniqueness of being human.[11] This marks out befriending as a discriminating form of love, in the sense that to enter into a friendship is to mark out someone individually, personally, from all others. "[I]t is a relationship between men at their highest level of individuality. It withdraws men from collective 'togetherness.'"[12]

The individuality of friendship being referred to here is of a particular kind. It is the "you, personally"—the unqualified individual—who matters in the arising of friendship; not one's quiddity, but one's haecceity. It is "Mary" and "Jane" who befriend each other, not merely two individual females of the human race, even though they are that by biological classification. When Jesus said, "I chose you," it was a choice of Peter and James and John individually, and not a mere selection of individual examples instantiating a predilection of Jesus for friendship.[13] To befriend someone is to choose him out over and against others; it is not to select him from amongst others. Friendship is by choice, in a way that falling in love is not. It does not admit of necessity and it is free of requirement.[14] This sense in which friendship is by choice is itself particular, for we choose our friends by chancing on friendship. Parents do not chance their love in choosing to love their child. Friends, on the other hand, do chance their love, and the friendship is dependent upon the chance being taken up and reciprocated.

---

11. Ibid.

12. Ibid., 72.

13. I am using "predilection" (from the Latin *dilectio*) in its formal meaning of electing or selecting. See Pieper, *On Love*, 153.

14. Reinders says something similar: "Friendship is of a particular value precisely because it is constituted by appreciation. Nobody has to be my friend because of some sort of obligation or role responsibility. No one can be blamed for not being my friend; nor can anyone be questioned about not taking an interest in me. Friendship is special because it is freely chosen." See *Receiving the Gift of Friendship*, 5.

This is why Lewis insists that the forming of a friendship involves more than just an exclusionary act of drawing apart, but a "drawing apart together" instead. This is not an exclusion of type or kind, however; friendship does not exclude by way of classification or status or condition, such as by gender or kinship (or by impairment). Rather, the exclusionary feature is tied directly to the individuality feature, in that friendship comes about via an act of recognition of a kindred spirit:

> It is when two such persons discover one another, when ... they share their vision—it is then that Friendship is born. And instantly they stand together in an immense solitude.[15]

Friends draw apart from the collective of mutual respect and cooperation into an exclusive relationship together when they recognize in each other, individually, something shared by them, individually.

While the possibility of friendship is dependent on the existence of this individual distinction that is also held by another, this is not to say that what is held in common is the basis of the friendship. It would seem that the distinction could be anything and is unimportant in itself: a particular interest, a certain taste, a dawning insight. Its role is as a catalyst and trigger for the possibility of friendship. Friends have to share something in common, whatever it happens to be, but it is not what makes the friendship. Rather, what matters is the discovery and acknowledgment of the individual with whom the distinction is shared, over and against all others who may or may not share it. It is the unique "someone with" who is befriended, and not just "anyone with"; it is this someone, and not another, who makes all the difference. Hence, the exclusivity of friendship and the shared solitude it creates. Friends draw apart together.

The exclusivity of friendship, moreover, is marked by its own peculiarity. It eschews restriction and limitation, and is fundamentally egalitarian and expansive. Only one other can be my lover at any one time (moral turpitude aside); any number of others can be my friend at one and the same time. Lewis brings out the significance of this point with an illuminating example:

> In each of my friends there is something that only some other friend can fully bring out. By myself I am not large enough to call the whole man into activity; I want other lights than my own to show all his facets. Now that Charles is dead, I shall never again see Ronald's reaction to a specifically Caroline joke. Far

---

15. Lewis, *Four Loves*, 78–79.

from having more of Ronald, having him "to myself" now that Charles is away, I have less of Ronald. Hence true Friendship is the least jealous of loves.[16]

Again, looming large is the individuality of friendship. My befriending of (say) Harry strikes out precisely for a point in him that marks out me as me. It may be said that in this way I am loving egoistically: I come to befriend Harry because of something in him I see in myself. Yet, I do not thereby love him egoistically because it is Harry that I befriended, not the mere reflection of me in Harry. As Lewis is arguing, the full revelation of Harry to me is not going to be found in what he shares in common with me. I need others to draw out for me more of Harry. Conversely, more of me—more of who I am—is drawn out through the friendships I have. The good of friendship for me is the way in which the good of being the human being that I am is revealed.

Recalling how Swinton described Jesus' way of friendship as being inclusively open, we may now adjust that to say all true friendship is really exclusively open. The difference is important because it goes to the heart of how friendships come about; namely, the point of commonality that creates the possibility of friendship cannot be dispensed with even though it is not what makes friends friends. In Swinton's defense it may be said that at least he has Jesus pursuing certain features in the people he is said to want to befriend: marginalization, ejection, poverty, sinfulness (and we might add "faith"). The difficulty is then to see how Jesus saw himself as himself precisely in these characteristics, the one requirement for the creating of friendship. The same criticism is far more devastating when it is directed towards Reinders' thesis. To recall, there are to be no points of individual commonality by which the profoundly disabled are to be befriended. Rather, they are to be accepted as friends by way of an unconditional loving commitment in terms of their common humanity with us. For Reinders, there is to be no place for the exclusivity of individuality, for discovering someone-with. As Reinders would have it: "the one crucial good that disabled people long for [is]: being chosen as a friend."[17] To this Lewis retorts, "The very condition of having Friends is that we should want something else besides Friends. . . . Friendship must

---

16. Ibid., 74.
17. Reinders, *Receiving the Gift of Friendship*, 5.

be about something."[18] Pieper concurs, saying, "People who simply wish for 'a friend' will with fair certainty not find any."[19]

Friendship and the Profoundly Impaired

What, then, are we to make of the possibility of friendship for, and with, the profoundly disabled if it is so thoroughly imbued with individuality, expressed in its exclusive openness? For the one thing friendship is dependent on is that there be something held in common—something that pertains to me as me and you as you—to trigger the relational shift. We would do well to recall here the words of Jesus to Peter in John's account of the Last Supper: "If I do not wash you, you have no share with me [nothing in common with me; no part in me]" (John 13:8).[20] When Jesus washed the disciples' feet he did it for a reason beyond a simple act of cleansing, as he explained to them immediately afterwards. Yet, that explanation, couched in the language of command and of giving example ("For I have set you an example, that you also should do as I have done to you" [John 13:15]), gave to the act its individuality, its particularity. It was this particular act that created, as it were, the recognizable point of commonality that subsequently led to Jesus' verbal acknowledgment of friendship (John 15:14). The act and the acknowledgment were linked by their commonly held meaning: the washing of the feet was, indeed, one of the Johannine signs of Jesus' redemptive work. This is not to say that the friendship between Jesus and his closest disciples had not been germinating over the years they had been together. The disciples had not become friends with Jesus because of—as a causal result of—him having washed their feet. It is to say, rather, that the "I chose you" needed the sign value of an "If I do not wash you" for the disciples to recognize that the shift from teacher to friend has occurred. Peter and James and John had discovered they each had something in common with Jesus individually that would make all the difference, but it took the act of washing to make it happen.

18. Lewis, *Four Loves*, 80.

19. Pieper, *On Love*, 272.

20. The bracketed alternative translations are from the JBV and the RSV, respectively.

Of course, such an easily recognizable marker does not always present itself to two people as a trigger for friendship.[21] It would be quite wrong to suggest that the brute washing of the feet pin-points the required "shared something" that made possible Jesus' friendship with his disciples. One important point the example does highlight, however, is that the emphasis on individuality ought not to be read as being special or highly qualified. What friends share individually might be very simple or highly complex, but this in itself does not matter. What matters as a trigger for friendship—and only this seems to matter—is the "something" and the "sharing" individually. It is not "what it is" that matters, but that there is something of which it can be said: "this is it." The only question to ask, therefore, is this: Is there something shared individually?[22]

This does seem to be answerable in the affirmative for a person seeking to befriend someone who is profoundly impaired. The routine ritual of bathing someone in Jesus' actions, for example, or the regular sharing of a meal together (more mundane) are adequate triggers for the possibility of friendship. They are examples of something shared individually between two people, one of whom happens to be profoundly impaired. This does not mean that friendship has been established; the same actions involving a healthcare professional would not normally be viewed as acts of friendship because the washing in this case is not a sign by which something else is signified. Yet, neither does this preclude the possibility of actions like washing and bathing to be adequate triggers, nonetheless, to the possibility of friendship for the profoundly impaired.

There is, however, an aspect of chancing on the unique individual that friendship goes in search of which is far more problematic for the profoundly impaired. It is this: friendship seems to require mutuality. To return to the Johannine Last Supper, it is clear from the context that Jesus washed the feet of Judas (John 13:10). So, the trigger for the offer of friendship included him. It was between the trigger and the acknowledgment that Judas chose against taking up the friendship. Did a friendship come about? There is at least a doubt that it did. The something shared

21. As Lewis puts it, "Whether with immense difficulties and semi-articulate fumblings or with what would seem to us amazing and elliptical speed" (*Four Loves*, 79).

22. A possible caveat may be put on this requirement: What if the trigger is something evil? Can an evil shared in common be a catalyst for friendship, or will it pervert friendship at its core? (Can a shared interest in the sexual perversion of children be the basis for a true friendship? This is a provocative question and ought to create anxiety within us. Moreover, it shows how important it is to give a thoroughgoing account of 'friendship' without reduction to mere shared interests, desires, or perversions.)

individually seems to call for a mutual acknowledgment of it as the trigger for friendship, along with the individual making the offer. The crucial factor that drives this requirement is the choosing/chancing. Jesus chanced, but Judas did not. There was a trigger offered on Jesus' part, but not the subsequent acknowledgment of it on Judas' part as being of shared importance. Judas was looking for something else and so rejected the washing of the feet as the trigger. Here, intriguingly, the "what it is" does seem to matter, or at least it matters in terms of what is valued about the other for friendship's sake; this, but not that.

Herein lies the difficulty for the profoundly impaired: they cannot choose by chancing; they do not have the capacity to acknowledge the other's offer; they are unable to make an assessment of this over that. Consequently, it seems that they cannot enter into a friendship because of an inadequacy of response to a befriending trigger. Can friendship be offered—is it even friendship that is being offered—when it cannot be acknowledged? One need not labor the point to see how devastating this looks for Reinders' project. This requirement for mutuality—of mutual giving and of mutual receiving—should not be pushed too far. Friendship is so utterly mundane, as we have been saying, so thoroughly embedded in human life that its explicit acknowledgment by friends can easily be missed.

Consider this example: "*Now that you mention it, I suppose we would call each other friends.*" There seems to be no need of a prerequisite mutual acknowledgment in this common enough scenario, no prior explicit awareness of a friendship. Yet we would not question that the friendship exists. This suggests that there does not need to be an explicit realization of a friendship existing for it to exist nonetheless. Perhaps, therefore, the existence of a friendship ought to be given the benefit of the doubt until or unless otherwise rejected by choice (and not chance). If this is the case then the requirement of mutual acknowledgment—of explicit giving and of explicit receiving—seems less pressing, and an opening into friendship could be imagined for the profoundly impaired. Therefore, perhaps all that may be concluded is that the mutual acknowledgment in friendship for and with the profoundly impaired poses a real challenge.

Nevertheless, some immediate light can be shed on the issue by the way in which friendships exist without the need for explicit acknowledgment of their existence. Returning to Lewis, he offers an insight into friendship by drawing attention to how it presents or manifests itself in the midst of human life: "we picture lovers face to face but Friends side by side; their eyes look ahead."[23] As with any metaphor, we need to ask what it is drawing attention to. In this case, it seems that the side-by-side image presents something of the unique way in which friendship is a love that does not need to be spoken to the one befriended. Friends do not say "I love you" as a parent might regularly say to a child; friends do not need to express their love for each other verbally as married couples do. In fact, friends rarely speak the language of love/friendship to one another.

This characteristic of friendship draws attention to the notion that friends do not have themselves as their point of focus; instead, their focus lies elsewhere. Where specifically? Pieper suggests the following: "Friends do not gaze at each other . . . Their gaze is fixed upon the things in which they take a common interest."[24] We are back, therefore, with the triggers of friendship, the things that are shared individually between friends, while noting that it is the gaze of friends that is so directed, and not the love. In other words, friendship is not the love of things held in common, it is the love between those individuals who hold things in common.

This provides a clue as to why a friendship can remain unacknowledged. When the focus is directed elsewhere, the love it triggers appears to be a consequence of the trigger and, therefore, of secondary importance. It is the things of the friendship that are talked about, shared upon, referenced incessantly. (Consider two friends who are supporters of a sporting team.) Meanwhile, the love that sustains the point of focus remains hidden. The love that is the friendship does not need to be referred to, so it may appear as inconsequential. Nonetheless, what appears to be the case is, in fact, the reverse. The point of focus in a friendship remains so only because of the love between the two individuals sustains it as a chosen focus. My love for my friend is what makes our shared interest important to us; we freely befriend each other, not our interests. (There are 9,999 other supporters of our team in the stadium but they are not my friends.) Consequently, the trigger for friendship is not what sustains friendship, even though it appears as if this is the case.

This means three things at least. First, a friendship needs a point of focus, other than the friends themselves, to be a friendship kind of love. Secondly, this point of focus in a friendship is not intrinsic to the friendship; it can evolve, be discarded for something else, or take on a greater significance. Thirdly, there needs to be some sense in which the sharing

---

23. Lewis, *Four Loves*, 80.
24. Pieper, *On Love*, 272.

together is free of coercion. Friendship is a love between two people with a shared set of interests, not a love of two people for a shared set of interests. The difference is important because it seems to ease the pressure on making an explicit choice a requirement for friendship, without removing choice altogether. It is a reminder that friendships can happen in the most ordinary of ways and circumstances. All sorts of people enter into friendships, and all sorts of people can be befriended; and there is not even a need for explicit acknowledgment for a friendship to exist.

It was suggested earlier that the sharing of a routine meal might be a trigger for befriending someone with a profound impairment. The presumption in this example is that there can be no explicit acknowledgment on the part of the impaired person that a friendship exists, and the suggestion is that neither need there be any explicit acknowledgment on the part of the unimpaired person. Perhaps a third person observing their meals together—their shared point of focus—might venture to suggest that they have a lovely friendship, and the unimpaired person might then recognize it as such. (She might not.) Does a friendship exist? We might be inclined to say yes, at least *prima facie*, and until some other factor might arise that plants a seed of doubt.

One apparent candidate of such a seed, however—the supposed inequality of their relationship—does not push us into this realm of doubt because inequality between people is not, in itself, a reason for precluding friendship. A trigger—something shared individually—is all that is needed for a friendship to ignite. Thus, and with the principle of charity in mind, there can be a presumption in favor of a friendship existing, even if at a quite rudimentary level, because, sitting side-by-side at a meal table, they have recognizably drawn apart together. The discovery of the friendship does not need to have been articulated and the acknowledgment of its existence does not need to have been made explicitly. As Lewis indicates, friendship is a side-by-side kind of love; it need not be "faced" for it to exist and be sustained:

> Look, I am standing at the door, knocking. If one of you hears me calling and opens the door, I will come in to share his meal, side by side with him. (Rev 3:20 JBV)

We must hasten to add, however, that this does not grant a licence to undermine the notion we began with—namely, that friendship is the distinctively unnecessary human love because it is the love that human beings choose (by chancing). Again, a picture from Lewis will help to draw attention to this point: "Eros will have naked bodies; Friendship naked personalities."[25] Lewis is not using "personality" in the colloquial sense of someone whose distinctive character traits are appealing, as if friendship were a function of psychological attraction. Rather, "personality" is being employed in the more formal sense of the totality of someone as he is present before me. It is the individual subject—the someone—who matters. Importantly for friendship, the presentation of my friend to me, and I to him, is mediated through the shared pursuit of our common vision. It is as if we unintentionally reveal ourselves to each other over the course of time. Thus, our developing friendship is closely tied to our coming to know each other via the sharing in each other's lives. Pieper draws this point out by indicating that friendship, at its best, is self-revelatory. In effect, it reveals me in my coming to know you:

> Although, therefore, real intimacy [of eros] does not exist in friendship, a friend is perhaps the only human being in whose presence we speak with complete sincerity and "think aloud" without embarrassment.[26]

The more naked the personality, the more present the person.

"Rational" Friendship?

One lingering question pertaining to friendship, which arises even with the weak sense of choosing just highlighted, is that a rational aspect seems always to be present. Yet, the lack of a capacity for reason (and will) is at the heart of the lingering doubt about whether or not the profoundly impaired can befriend. Choosing involves knowing, and knowing is an act of reason. Those who befriend, therefore, are involved in a rational activity. Such a statement about friendship certainly requires immediate qualification. Linking friendship to rationality does not mean that friendship is conditional upon the proficient exercise of the rational faculty. Childhood friends are no less friends. Nor does it mean that the more intellectually capable friends are, the better the friendship will be. Instead, to say that friendship presents itself in a rational guise is another way of indicating how it is that friendship is a peculiarly human kind of love. Other, non-human animals may exhibit signs of nurturing and

---

25. Lewis, *Four Loves*, 85.
26. Pieper, *On Love*, 272.

affection towards one another within the context of the herd, but they do not exhibit signs of friendship, of drawing apart together from the herd. Only human beings do this, and in a way that marks them out as human. The link to rationality is not at the level of essence, but at the level of existence. Human beings cannot exist but rationally and this is borne out in the structure of friendship.

Again, a point of qualification needs to be made. In noting the existential aspect of friendship as it relates to human rationality, this does not mean the essential aspect is insignificant for friendship's sake. Some capacity for the exercise of rationality in a human way—a capacity for human agency—seems to be essential for the task of forming friendships. For example, it is an entirely unremarkable thing to say that infant children cannot form friendships until such time as a sufficient level of rational development has occurred. This is not to call into question what we would accept as equally unremarkable: that, by virtue of them being human beings, infant children are linguistic beings. Yet, we will also want to say that one key measure of rational sufficiency is coming to grasp the rudiments of language by an infant, which, in turn, is a critical factor in the moving of a child into a stage of life where he or she can begin to form friendships. Note, however, that we have shifted from talking existentially to talking essentially as we shifted from talk about infancy generally to talk about individual infants.

Oddly enough, this is precisely where Reinders takes issue with the agency-based notion of humanity. It sets up a distinction between those human beings who are rationally capable and those who are not, thereby excluding the have-nots from what it means to flourish as a human being. This is odd because the example of the infants is a case in point where agency does mark out an essential difference among human beings—some can be friends, while others cannot—but not an existential difference. Yet this place where the distinction at the essential level is so unambiguous is precisely where Reinders wants to locate his way around the agency trap, namely, in the realm of friendship. While the example of the infants shows how the essential question may legitimately be raised within a more fundamental existential grounding, Reinders places all the emphasis on essentialist manifestations of friendship and works from there.

This is also where Reinders misrepresents Aristotle. He is concerned with the kinds of friendship Aristotle articulates, and notes either the inadequacy of his classifications or their limitations in the face of the love of God, as revealed in the Christian faith. This is an entirely appropriate question to raise but it does not take into account the prior grounding upon which Aristotle makes his claims about friendship—namely, that it is human beings *simpliciter* who enter into friendships, and precisely because it is good for being human. Thus, "friendship is especially necessary for living, to the extent that no one, even though he had all other goods, would choose to live without friends."[27] It is under the description of "man" that we befriend, and not under the description of "member of the human species" or "human properties/capacities." The fact that we readily recognize that some friendships are good for the people in them and others bad, that some friendships are incredibly fragile and others remarkably durable, and that some relationships labelled as friendships are anything but, is a reminder that the kind and quality of a particular friendship, including divine/human friendship, and even its actual existence, is entirely dependent upon there first being unique individuals for whom friendship reveals to them their humanity.

In raising Aristotle to criticise Reinders, however, the discussion on friendship has shifted from talk of choice to talk of necessity. No one would choose to be without friends, says Aristotle, which may be paraphrased as: the good of human life is dependent on friendship. Yet, we have been advocating a view of friendship as freely chanced. Which is it to be? Returning to the example of the infants, we saw how a distinction can be made between being linguistic and being able to grasp language. This example neatly shows the existential/essential demarcation, and it also points out a way to differentiate friendship-as-necessity from friendship-as-choice. We might say that infants are language-made though not language-capable, and that this makes a difference for the possibility of them entering into discourse. The distinction being made here is not a matter of degree, of potentiality leading to actuality, but of kind. Human beings exist linguistically. This is not a matter of what humans beings have, awaiting activation, but a matter of how human beings are the beings that they are. It is an entirely different issue as to whether or not an individual human being can then go on to grasp a language and enter into discourse. Human beings are existentially linguistic, but essentially language speaking.

In a similar way, we may speak of human beings as being friendship-made, meaning that friendship is a given of being human, the manner

---

27. Aristotle, *Nicomachean Ethics*, Book XIII, ch. 1; 1155a5, in Thomas Aquinas, *Commentary on Aristotle's Nicomachean Ethics*, 475.

in which human beings exist as the human beings that they are. This is where the language of necessity rightly fits and where existential questions about friendship can be raised. The language of choice comes into its own when we consider whether or not an individual human being can grasp what is involved in befriending, and whether or not he or she has what is essentially important for friendship's sake. It is at this level of particularity where qualitative questions become appropriate: Is Jane capable of entering into a friendship? Is the friendship of Francis and Chiara good or bad, weak or strong? Are Jesus and Judas friends? Friendship is both an existential given and an essential choice. It is of the nature of friendship that we go about taking the chance on friends, but it is of the nature of being human that we are made for friendship.

Therefore, we may conclude: friendship is a love given to humanity as a good for human life, but which always and only finds expression—is revealed—in the love of friends, which individual people freely pursue. Such an understanding preserves the peculiar individuality at the heart of every friendship, while at the same time recognizing that friendship is intrinsically caught up in what is involved in living a human life, of being human. To recall the words of McCabe: we are born as players of this game, to which may be added: the kind of players of the game we become will depend on the choices we make (and the chances we take) in the game. Most particularly, friendship is that peculiar game of love that can only be played by being human.

Being Included in Friendship

Given that human beings are made for the game of befriending, that it is something proper to being human, it follows that friendship is primarily something to be lost, rather than something to be gained, and for that matter something lost by choice.[28] Consequently, we may say that someone who does not pursue friendship is someone who exhibits a reluctance towards being human; not to want to befriend (or not to want to be befriended) is not to want to live a human kind of life. This negatively expressed insight into the anthropology of friendship has an important implication for the profoundly impaired, because it suggests that the relationship between being befriended and being included is to

---

28. Jesus said of Judas, "Not one is lost except the one who chose to be lost" (John 17:12 JBV). The NRSV replaces "who chose" with "destined."

be understood according to a particular structure that takes inclusion to be a given of human beings (something we start with) and not a goal (something we aim for).

Inclusion-as-goal (which is, to recall, Reinders' principal motivation for securing the humanity of the profoundly disabled) is about pursuing something that is as yet unattained. It requires exercising that which will bring about this attainment but this is precisely what the profoundly disabled are unable to do: they cannot pursue inclusion as a goal because they are unable to exercise that which will bring it about. Herein lies the reason why Reinders has no option but to adopt an entirely transcendent conception of friendship. Someone extrinsic to the profoundly disabled must be made to take up the cause of the profoundly disabled on their behalf so that they may be included in the realm of humanity. So if friendship is the way to inclusion, then someone must be active for them in their friendships. Therefore, friendship for the impaired, according to this logic, is not some utterly passive conception; rather, the proper activity of friendship is simply shifted onto the transcendent other—that is, God, who acts as proxy for the profoundly impaired in gaining inclusion for them. By implication, if one were to befriend someone who is profoundly impaired, one would not be befriending that individual, but his transcendent Proxy, with the consequence that the impaired person himself fails to achieve the goal of inclusion, because he fails to achieve anything by himself.

The inclusion-as-given understanding, on the other hand, starts with the presumption that someone who is profoundly impaired is already included in the fullness of humanity; it is not something he needs to attain for and by himself. His impairment is not an obstacle to be overcome in the pursuit of inclusion because he is, with his impairment, already included. This sense of inclusion coincides with the way friendship reveals itself: the profoundly impaired are already players in the game of befriending simply by virtue of their human existence. Being friendship-made applies equally to the profoundly impaired as to people who are not. The impaired and the unimpaired are radically unalike precisely because the impaired are not choosers. They cannot make a choice against friendship; and in the same way, they cannot choose to be excluded. Yet, they come to be excluded, as is manifestly a real phenomenon for many of them; they are not befriended. How, then, can this lack of choosing ability actually be seen as good for the profoundly impaired?

The answer lies in reflecting the question back onto those who can choose not to befriend the profoundly impaired (or choose not to be befriended by them). If friendship is something to be lost by way of a decision, resulting in a loss to one's very humanity, then in the case of the loss or negation of friendship experienced by the profoundly impaired, this loss is not of their making. Therefore, it cannot be said that their loss is also a loss unto their very humanity. If they are excluded from the human community it cannot be for this reason. Such a loss lies only in the hands of someone who can choose. While the phenomenon of exclusion from the human community seems to fall on the side of the profoundly impaired, it actually falls upon those who choose against friendship. To understand inclusion as already given means recognizing inclusion to be something to be discovered (or recovered), not attained.

Inclusion in this mode of "given," therefore, is best understood as a declarative act given towards those who have lost sight of that which is already present in the profoundly impaired, although experientially hidden. It is a declaration of the discovery (or recovery) of the human person already before us, and not a future-directed means by which someone is subsequently incorporated into the realm of the human. Thus, we begin with the existential reality of human friendship, there to be recognized, and look to overcome the imposition of a decisive move towards exclusion. Those who choose to exclude others do so at the peril of a self-imposed exclusion. This is a reversal of Reinders' thinking, in that his sense of inclusion is something to be extended towards the profoundly impaired, so as to secure their humanity. As such, it sets up humanity as something to be attained, an innovation, and those who cannot achieve this goal will always be subject to exclusion.

The Downward Movement into Friendship

What implication may be drawn for the humanity of the profoundly impaired from seeing a coincidence between being friendship-made and being declaratively included? We may seek an answer to this question by turning to the anthropological imagination of Jean Vanier, that great befriender of the profoundly impaired and advocate for their humanity. Vanier, who chose to enter into the experiential world of the profoundly impaired in 1964, and who has lived his own life ever since in friendship with them in the communities of *L'Arche*, has described their life together as a sign "touching the roots" of humanity, a discovery of a way of life "other than the ladder of material success and individual accomplishment."[29] This ladder metaphor is a theme that recurs throughout Vanier's extensive spiritual and theological writings. He uses it as a kind of measure of human life, locating those persons who are most often considered weak or broken in society at the bottom of the metaphorical ladder, and calling those who are not so marked to go down the ladder to be with the marginalized and poor and thereby discover their own humanity. Vanier speaks often of how his life has been transformed by "descending the ladder," and he has come to use this metaphor in a variety of forms as a pointer to the deeper purposes of being—or, as he prefers to say, becoming—human.

Significantly for the present discussion, Vanier's various reflections on this metaphor have led him to a particular understanding of the relationship between befriending and including. Consider the following remark (incorporating a pyramidal variation on the metaphor):

> The excluded, I believe, live certain values that we all need to discover and to live ourselves before we can become truly human. It is not just a question of performing good deeds for those who are excluded but of being open and vulnerable to them in order to receive the life that they can offer; it is to become their friends. If we start to include the disadvantaged in our lives and enter into heartfelt relationships with them, they will change things in us. . . . So, the one-way street, where those on top tell those at the bottom what to do, what to think, and how to be, becomes a two-way street, where we listen to what they, the "outsiders," the "strangers," have to say and we accept what they have to give, that is, a simpler and more profound understanding of what it means to be truly human. If we start to see people at the bottom as friends, as people with gifts to bring to others, then the social pyramid, with the powerful, the knowledgeable, and the wealthy on top, becomes a place of belonging where each person finds a place and where we live in mutual trust.[30]

The first sentence of this remark highlights a difference Vanier perceives between the experiential exclusion of those at the bottom of the ladder

---

29. Vanier, *Encountering the Other*, 1. L'Arche is an international network of communities in which people who are profoundly and complexly disabled and people who are not live together in a family environment. See http://www.larche.org/home.en-gb.1.0.index.htm.

30. Vanier, *Becoming Human*, 84–85.

and the real measure of their humanity. There is no question mark about their being human; the issue is the way in which others respond to them. Vanier's anthropological commentary, therefore, is not actually about those at the bottom, but about those who are not yet located where they are. To pick up on a language used at the beginning, there is indeed something at stake for all who are on the ladder of humanity, but it is those who are higher up, and not those at the bottom, for which the stakes run higher.

It is in this context that his remark about friendship, and its link to the experientially excluded, needs to be read. For Reinders (to recall), the underlying motivation for adopting his paradigm of inclusion for the profoundly disabled is that they lack the gift of friendship.[31] For Vanier, it is not those who are at the bottom who lack friendship, at least as he understands it in terms of a relationship of vulnerability and openness; rather, it is those at the top who have chosen to place themselves outside of the sphere of friendship. For Reinders, it is the profoundly disabled who lack the good of friendship and therefore are in need of being included in its goodness. For Vanier it is the powerful who lack it, and it is they who need to go down the ladder to be included in its goodness.

Vanier's point is not that the people who are among those at the bottom of the social ladder, including the profoundly impaired, do not have a desire for the experience of friendship, but that being at the bottom has placed them in a position of appreciating friendship over power or domination or self-will. Their personal situation—embedded in the very condition of their lives—wins for them a ready-made predilection for friendship. Other people have to work for it, to choose it, to discover (recover) it. The implication is that friendship itself is something that is peculiarly located at the metaphorical bottom rung. Friendship can find a ready expression and can flourish here precisely because, at the bottom, the focus is not about those essential properties familiar to human beings, but which characterise an overly elevated anthropology. The German theologian Bernd Wannenwetsch sums up well Vanier's insight—using language and notions already significant for us—that it is the humanity

---

31. "Despite the success they have found in strengthening their status in the public sphere, people with disabilities—especially intellectual disabilities—experience loneliness and isolation is the sphere of their personal lives. This kind of observation gives shape to the main aim of this book. . . . In many cases, the lives of persons with disabilities lack the blessing of intimacy: that is, they lack friends, which is the one kind of good that rights and justice claims cannot achieve." Reinders, *Receiving the Gift of Friendship*, 6.

of those at the bottom, including the profoundly impaired, that tells us about our own humanity:

> The disabled do not automatically evoke the best in us, but their recognition as persons functions as a litmus test for our own human dignity as persons. They function as such because their existence as fellow human beings and our kin can only be genuinely recognized if, in turn, we recognize the revelatory quality of their lives for the understanding of our own humanity. It is precisely what they seem to lack that reveals the truth about our own life which, in turn, possesses the potential to heal us from the deceptive love-affair with the epochal demons of self-mastery and control.... Not in spite of her embarrassment are we to count a disabled person as one of us but precisely *because of* her embarrassment—an embarrassment that needs to be recognized as our own, as the hidden and notoriously unacknowledged fact of our own lives as *enoschim*, creatures of the dust.[32]

We may venture to draw our own conclusion from the understanding of the relationship between friendship and inclusion offered by Vanier's anthropological imagination: when it comes to friendship, the profoundly impaired are less inadequate than the rest of humanity because they are already personally present to where friendship may be more readily found. It is the profoundly impaired themselves who are a paradigm of inclusion, even in the midst of their experiential marginalization. Vanier's insight is that the drawing together in friendship involves the drawing away from the tendencies to individual power and autonomy so prevalent in the unimpaired. Instead, coming to friendship—that peculiarly human sign of our nature—involves a downward movement that is a decisive movement towards being in relationship with others. Friendship is always in the direction of self-giving, not self-making. In the light of Vanier's anthropological imagination, it is manifestly the sign of living a truly human life. It is in recognizing the humanity of the profoundly impaired that we discover the kind of persons we all are: creatures who are made for friendship.

Who Is the Creature Who Befriends?

This chapter began with a lesson to be kept close at hand: if we want to understand the role of friendship, then we need to keep it human. What

32. Wannenwetsch, "Angels with Clipped Wings," 192.

has emerged from the ensuing discussion has been an opening up onto a picture of the subject who befriends and is befriended, the one who has been made for friendship so as to chance friendship. It is a picture that reveals much about how we are made for what we are made. All along, however, one particular question has remained unanswered: Who is this unique individual made so as to draw apart together? Who is this player in the game of friendship? To date, the simple response has been to plug in "human being" wherever the question arose. That in itself tells us something significant: "Man" answers the question: "Friend?" Yet, the temptation is then to look to the questions of quiddity for answers about our humanity.

However, the picture of friendship that has emerged is such that we would do better to look to the questions of haecceity. Hence, how are we the creatures who we are, and why are we so revealed in friendship? These are questions to which human life attests, to which it bears witness. Specifically, they hold up for consideration the notion that being human is something that is a given for human beings—that human beings are begotten in their humanity, that their humanity is not self-made or self-determined—and that this is affirmed in the human good of our befriending and in our being befriended.[33] Why has God created us such that friendship affirms us? How are we the creatures that we are because we are friendship-made? As Pieper elegantly says:

> According to Genesis, God did not simply make the universe and man exist. He gave man instead a taste of the honey as well as the milk; that is, he specifically confirmed their existence and literally declared it "good, very good" . . . To so experience [this affirmation] he must, of course, think of himself and the world as *creatura*.[34]

This is a stance in need of elaboration. Our discussion of friendship has itself suggested that this is the question now to be broached. While we may conclude that friendship reveals to us that we are human beings, we may also conclude that we cannot answer the question of our humanity by means of friendship. In the human affirmation of friendship—"How good that you exist!"—we are confronted with a question that cannot be

---

33. Oliver O'Donovan has written from a bioethical perspective on the difference Christian anthropology draws between human beings "being begotten" and "being made" in O'Donovan, *Begotten or Made?*

34. Pieper, *On Love*, 176–77.

answered from within a structure of friendship.[35] Always we are led back to the question: Who? It has been the Christian tradition—expressed in the doctrine of the *imago Dei* and the language of personhood—that has offered the possibility of responding to the question of our creatureliness. It is time to return to this tradition, which Reinders rejects, and to ask the question: Who is it that we are recognizing when we recognize the creature who befriends?

---

35. This declaration, repeated over and again by Pieper throughout his work *On Love*, is the primordial act of love. At its basis, to love someone is to affirm the goodness of his or her existence.

5

BEING A CREATURE

Recovering the Human Project

Rejecting and Recovering the Doctrine of the *imago Dei*

Two anthropological claims drive Hans Reinders' project: people with profound intellectual disabilities are people like other people; and the best way to understand human beings is not to be found in the faculties of human agency, of reason and will. He turns to his leitmotif of a transcendent conception of the human good of friendship as the only sure way of supporting these claims. Having now exposed some of the flaws and confusions inherent in this move, it is time to consider precisely what it is that Reinders is rejecting as its ideological opposite. He does this at the very beginning of *Receiving the Gift of Friendship* when he rejects the doctrine of the *imago Dei*, as found throughout the Christian tradition, as a universalizing understanding of human being. He does so because he takes this doctrine to be advocating an essentialist and immanentist position centered on the human capacity for reason and will such that "the things that human faculties allow people to do or to have are what make people different."[1]

Reinders does not entirely reject a notion of human beings being made in the image of God, but he does center his own sense of this notion on the extrinsic love that God has for his human creation: "Whatever else it may mean to say that I am created in the divine image, it must surely

1. Reinders, *Receiving the Gift of Friendship*, 2.

mean that I am created in God's love."[2] However, he does not discuss the implications of this claim until the seventh chapter of *Receiving the Gift of Friendship*, and then only after first arguing for his turn to friendship. Reinders is not denying a place for the doctrine in theological anthropology; rather, he simply rejects what he thinks the Christian tradition has done with it.[3] His specific issue is this:

> What we mean by human being created in God's image is determined by what we think about God's being. This means that the logically prior task is to argue from our understanding of God to our understanding of being human.... [However,] the tradition is to a large extent dominated by the explanation of the divine image in terms of the human faculties.[4]

In other words, the tradition (with the Catholic tradition receiving particular attention) has come to hold that the rational nature of human beings—what we are, intrinsically—determines what it means to be created in the image of God.

The problem, so Reinders would have it, is that the tradition has replaced a theological logic, whereby the argument moves from an understanding of God to an understanding of humanity, with an ontological (specifically metaphysical) logic, whereby the argument moves from humanity to God. By elevating the rational nature of human beings to the point of it being the determinative marker of divine-human identity, the theological heritage has rendered the doctrine of the *imago Dei* poisonous to the humanity of the profoundly impaired. Consequently, "the Christian tradition is not alien to a hierarchy of being that marginalizes people in whom the faculties of reason and will remain underdeveloped."[5] Whatever the doctrine of the *imago Dei* is, for Reinders it must be about who God is before it can be about what human beings are, but this is precisely what he thinks the Christian, and specifically Catholic, provenance on the *imago Dei* has failed to provide.

Be that as it may, Reinders' intention to get the right theological orientation for the doctrine happens to provide a ready-made agenda for approaching its anthropological merits. To take up the notion of the *imago Dei* as the firm grounding for a fruitful understanding of what it

2. Ibid., 38.
3. Ibid., 227.
4. Ibid., 227–28.
5. Ibid., 228.

means to be human first means delving into how we may come to it as a theme of anthropological import.[6] The task this agenda sets for us is twofold: to retrieve from the Christian tradition a fruitful approach to the doctrine of the *imago Dei* from an anthropological perspective; and to consider how that may then inform our broader project of recognizing the personal presence of the profoundly impaired amongst the community of persons. It will be helpful to begin, however, with a brief survey of how the contemporary theological scene is approaching the doctrine so as to give orientation to our intended discussion of its anthropological import. As it is chiefly a Catholic perspective on the theme of the *imago Dei* that is the primary target of Reinders' rejection of its anthropological efficacy, we will likewise make it the primary focus of our own agenda, noting in passing any relevant lines of thinking from a broadly Protestant perspective.

If "it is the doctrine of the *imago Dei* that decides the destiny of all theology," as Emil Brunner would have it, then "[it] leaves open the question as to where exactly it is that the similarity between God and his image lies," as Hans Urs von Balthasar notes.[7] Both this sense of significance and of under-determination has marked recent theological thinking on the *imago Dei*. Yet, it is the recentness of it all that is the first thing to be noted. In 2004, the *International Theological Commission* (ITC) of the *Congregation for the Doctrine of the Faith* (CDF) noted how the theme of the *imago Dei* has been retrieved only recently from a lengthy period of philosophical and theological neglect.[8] While the ITC gives no indication of when the retrieval began, it seems to go back no further than the early to mid part of the twentieth century.[9] What

---

6. In the final chapter of her book *A Constructive Theology of Intellectual Disability*, Molly C. Haslam develops the theme of *imago Dei* in light of what she perceives as the shortcomings in traditional accounts from Thomas Aquinas, Augustine, and Protestant contributions such as Lutheranism, John Calvin, and ultimately argues for the construction of a stronger relational account of how the image of God is conceived in human creaturliness (92–116).

7. Brunner, quoted in Ouellet, *Divine Likeness*, 26; Balthasar, *Glory of the Lord*, 6:90.

8. International Theological Commission, *Communion and Stewardship*, §§2–4.

9. The 1922 edition of the *Dictionnaire de Théologie Catholique* makes no reference at all to the *imago Dei* in its entry on "Image," focusing only on the nature and use of religious images, the relationship between image and idol, and the debate concerning iconoclasm. See "Images (Culte Des)," *Dictionnaire de Théologie Catholique*, Tome VII/1, 766–843. The *Dictionnaire de Spiritualité* of 1971 does make reference to the doctrine, but it is silent on its theological development from the time of the Carmelite

was bequeathed to contemporary times, therefore, was a tradition that reached its peak in the Middle Ages, especially as expounded by Thomas Aquinas, with a broadly substantialist understanding that envisaged it in terms of the rational nature of human beings reflecting the Triune nature of God.[10]

This is the basic position that was picked up by the conciliar mind of the Church when it made a conscious return to the theme during the Second Vatican Council, in the anthropological section of *Gaudium et Spes*.[11] As to the nature of the theological approach adopted by the Council Fathers in making this return, the Canadian Cardinal-theologian Marc Ouellet has noted, "The analogical method [of *Gaudium et Spes*] proceeds from the bottom up, beginning with creatures and rising towards God. It presumes a balance of affirmation and negation in expressing the resemblance and difference between creature and Creator."[12] Ouellet is here highlighting the generally theistic approach adopted in *Gaudium et Spes*, and the emphasis given by it to issues of identity (and difference) in grounding the dignity of human beings in the image of God. In this regard, mention of the creaturely grounding of this dignity should not be missed. However, *Gaudium et Spes* is also noteworthy for a decisive turn made in it towards giving a christological emphasis to the orientation and fulfilment of the creaturely life of human beings. However, Ouellet has noted that while it gave a more relational, personalist emphasis to the theme of the *imago Dei*, it did not develop this emphasis into a well-integrated anthropological insight.[13]

This developmental lacuna in the Catholic teaching on the *imago Dei*, however, was decisively overcome by a series of teachings given by Pope John Paul II over several years in the 1980s, taking as his point of departure a theological reflection on the creation narrative to develop what has become known as his "theology of the body."[14] From these talks

---

reform of the sixteenth century to the Second Vatican Council, and its bibliographical citations go back no further than 1929. See Scheffczyk, "Image et ressemblance," 1402–72. Likewise, there is a complete lack of reference to the *imago Dei* in Karl Rahner's article on Theological Anthropology in his multivolumed *Sacramentum Mundi*, vol. 3, 365–70.

10. See Kerr, *Twentieth-Century Catholic Theologians*, 194–95, for a useful summary of Aquinas' theology of the *imago Dei*.

11. Vatican II, *Gaudium et Spes*: §§12–22.

12. Ouellet, *Divine Likeness*, 14.

13. Ibid., 12.

14. John Paul II, *Man and Woman He Created Them*. Pope John Paul commenced

came a new and remarkable theological notion of the nuptial meaning of the *imago Dei*, marking a departure from the "substance" tradition as it had been developed through Augustine and Aquinas, with sexual difference becoming the key to unlocking the theological understanding of human nature and destiny.[15] The theological underpinning of this papal teaching (itself a theological exposition) may be traced, in the Catholic tradition, to Hans Urs von Balthasar, who himself developed theological insights into the *imago Dei* first developed by Karl Barth and Emil Brunner.[16] Key to all of these Christian thinkers is the covenantal relationship within which God and human beings are related in an "I-Thou" mode, expressed in the bodily differences of the sexes and grounded in the history of salvation, culminating in Christ.[17]

Two complementary themes, therefore, currently hold sway, each being championed in recent Church teaching: the ITC document favoring the more traditional reading, and a 2004 document of the CDF, *On the Collaboration of Men and Women in the Church and in the World*, taking up the nuptial reading.[18] How these two competing interpretations will eventually be worked through in the future is not a question for this project. We may simply note that there is now a burgeoning field of theological research into the theme of the *imago Dei*, especially as it relates to questions of human dignity and the sanctity of human life, that take as their point of departure these two broad strands of thought.[19]

While noting this trend, we may also take a stand as to which strand will better aid our particular agenda. The nuptial meaning that John Paul

---

his weekly catechesis on human love in the divine plan on 5 September 1979, the last being delivered on 28 November 1984.

15. This is a point made by Kerr in *Twentieth-Century Catholic Theologians*, 201.

16. Von Balthasar, *The Glory of the Lord*, vol. 6, Section B: "The Image," is entirely devoted to the *imago Dei*. See Barth, *Church Dogmatics – Volume III: The Doctrine of Creation, Part One*: §41. Creation and Covenant, 2. Creation as the External Basis of the Covenant. See Emil Brunner, *Man in Revolt*: Section I. Foundations, Chapter V. The Origin: The *Imago Dei*.

17. For a dialogue between St John Paul II's theology of the body and the thought of another notable twentieth century philosopher, Emmanuel Levinas, see Nigel Zimmermann's *Facing the Other*.

18. Congregation for the Doctrine of the Faith, *Letter to the Bishops of the Catholic Church on the Collaboration of Men and Women in the Church and in the World*, 31 May 2004.

19. For a supporter of the more traditional reading, see Kerr, *After*, and *Twentieth-Century Catholic Theologians*. See Scola, *The Nuptial Mystery* for a defender of the new reading.

II has seen in the *imago Dei* is certainly concerned with what it means to be created in the image of God, but it is not "being human" as such that is the focus. Rather, his focus, and the focus of both those who anticipated the nuptial theme and those who have since developed it, is on the meaning for human beings of having been created in the image of God as male and female. This is a focus, therefore, on how the image is received in—manifested by—the creature who has it, and not about the kind of creature who is so imaged. The focus of our question, however, is about how it is that certain creatures made in God's image are distinctly human beings, and not some other being. To bring the point out concretely, it will not be in the manifestation of the maleness and femaleness of the profoundly impaired that their claim to a personal humanity may be recognized. It will be in the creaturely reality of human beings, and not in their nuptuality, that the value of the doctrine of the *imago Dei* will need to be tested.

This is not the only stance that matters to us, either; the scriptural configuration of the *imago Dei* also proposes various readings that need to be chosen between:

> The array of different types of claims about human being that are traditionally made in Christian theological anthropology have been held together by showing how they all tie into a central claim derived from Genesis 1.26a: "Then God said, 'let us make humankind in our image, according to our likeness.'"[20]

The first chapter of the book of Genesis (Gen 1:26-27) provides the passage that both establishes man's special relationship with God as his distinctive creature *par excellence* and gives the language in which that distinctiveness is expressed. It is also the principal text dealing with the anthropological consequences of the doctrine, especially that of the dignity afforded human beings by being so identified with God's image (Gen 1:28-30). This twofold step from distinctive creature to dignified being afforded by the *imago Dei* in human beings is repeated, without elaboration, in Gen 5:1 (using "likeness") and Gen 9:6. These are the only direct references to the *imago Dei* found in the Hebrew Scriptures. All other scriptural passages that explicitly refer to "image" in the context of human beings come from the Pauline corpus of the New Testament. Most importantly, these texts pertain to the one human being, Jesus Christ,

---

20. Kelsey, *Eccentric Existence*, 2:895. Kelsey's substantial work has emerged as a significant contribution to theological anthropology.

either in himself as the perfect or true image of God (1 Cor 11:7; 2 Cor 4:4; Col 1:15) or in the relationship all other human beings have to him and in him (Rom 8:29; 1 Cor 15:49; 2 Cor 3:18; Col 3:10). The one exception is 1 Cor 11:7, where Paul uses the notion of the *imago Dei* to make a distinction between males and females, which is based on a biology that has been long superseded.

We have, therefore, three broad ways in which the notion of the *imago Dei* is used in Scripture: as it pertains to the origin of human life; as it pertains to the end of human life ("in Christ"); and as it pertains to the individual life of Jesus Christ. The second and third uses we do not need to concern ourselves with, other than in passing, as it may be presumed that these uses of the *imago Dei* take the question: Human being? to have been answered positively already (the second through redemption and the third in that Christ is God-made-man). This leaves us with the question of our human origins, which is precisely concerned with the presumption itself: Who is this creature "human being" and how is it that he is the creature that he is?, and not with what may or may not happen to him as an individual human being thereafter. Creation, and the question of how we are made in the image of God, is our focus, and not what might be said about the end result of a human life lived in the image of God (noting, nonetheless, a continuity of nature and identity of each individual human being from creation to redemption).

This leaves us with Gen 1 and the relationship of the *imago Dei* to the origins of human life, which has certainly been the overriding point of departure in the renewed focus on the traditional theological understanding of the doctrine. As the ITC notes, the notion of the *imago Dei* is "the key to the biblical understanding of human nature," even to the extent that it "constitutes almost a definition of man."[21] Therefore, the theological distinctiveness of the created nature of human beings draws its meaning from the narrative of Gen 1 and the language of the *imago Dei*.

Yet, this is not where theological reflection has tended to dwell. Instead, the notion that human beings receive the dignity that they have as a result of their being made in the image of God plays a key part in much of the theological work currently being done on the doctrine. Consideration of what it means to be of a human nature in God's image is quickly passed over in favor of the implications of the doctrine for the living of

---

21. *Communion and Stewardship*: §7.

a human life, such as: human dominion in a created world;[22] creaturely communion with God in its christological and ecclesial dimensions;[23] and the status of human beings as a consequence of being finite creatures in God's image.[24] This is not to suggest that these themes (and many others), arising from consideration of the doctrine of the *imago Dei*, are unimportant; they are crucial to any fuller discussion of the doctrine and how it plays out in our lives. This is precisely the issue at hand: they all touch consequentially on the human being in the image of God, and do not remain with the question of the grounding of the creature's humanity. This is why Reinders is correct in seeking the right theological orientation for the doctrine, and why our initial task is one of asking the question about who we are (who are in the image of God), so as to retrieve a fruitful way of approaching the doctrine of the *imago Dei*. It is to this question of our creaturely existence that we must now turn.

Creaturely Existence and the Securing of the Humanity of a Human Life

Let us begin with a basic anthropological claim: at its most fundamental level human existence is a created reality, and not self-made. As the philosopher Hannah Arendt has noted, "The human artifice of the world separates human existence from all mere animal environment, but life itself is outside this artificial world, and through life man remains related to all other living organisms. . . . [M]an belongs among the children of nature."[25] By definition "man" is not the manufacturer of his own existence, but has it as a given, as begotten. Accordingly, if human existence—being a human creature—is given, in a way not of human making, any desire to escape this conditionedness will have as its terminus the cessation of human beings as "human being." To quote Arendt again: "The human

---

22. See, for example, Pannenberg, *Anthropology in Theological Perspective*, 74ff., and Fergusson, *Cosmos and the Creator*, 13ff.

23. See Zizioulas, *Communion and Otherness*, 5ff.

24. For an early example, see Niebuhr, *Nature and Destiny of Man*, 1:161ff.; also Clément, *On Human Being*, 33ff., who has written on the "tragedy" of being made in God's image. Ormerod, *Creation, Grace and Redemption*, 25ff., has reflected on human life in its evolutionary condition.

25. Arendt, *Human Condition*, 2-3.

condition comprehends more than the condition under which life has been given to man. . . . [H]uman existence is conditioned existence."[26]

We face, therefore, a practical—a moral—question whenever human existence is considered. However, the claim that human existence is a conditioned existence stops there; it makes no further claim that the human condition as it is lived out is what makes the man. In other words, the conditioned mode under which an individual exists is determinative of "human being," but the conditions under which that individual lives are not. To recognize a human being, therefore, is to acknowledge him or her in terms of being ordered to the living of a human life, but as it has been given to be lived and not as it is subsequently being lived. To speak of the created existence of human beings is already to speak of an order to that existence.[27] The Christian response, of course, falls on the side of human existence being a created reality, but the decision itself is not a faith-based one: recognizing human existence as being a fundamentally ordered existence is a common human enterprise. While this recognition does not answer the question as to how human beings are so ordered, or why it is the case, it does suggest that a theological framework will be needed to make sense of it. At the very least, a "created" anthropology proposes an accompanying "creator" theology.

We have, then, a point of departure—and the basic presupposition—from which we may approach the question: Human being? It is this: to be human is to exist as a human kind of creature.[28] What, however, does this mean? Most immediately, it is a claim that human existence is a creaturely existence, by which is meant: to be a human being is to have one's existence as a human creature, and it is to have that existence in a different way from all other creatures. Initially, this is simply to say that human beings exist as something, specifically: as living human creatures. Human beings are begotten, like the rest of living creation, and not manufactured, which is what gives creaturely shape to their existing.

The claim also says that being a human being is to be begotten in a mode of being that is distinctively human, which gives shape to a distinctiveness from the rest of living creation. A human being is always a

---

26. Ibid., 9.

27. For a reminder of this, see O'Donovan, *Resurrection and Moral Order*, 31.

28. John Swinton also has recently taken up the question of the creaturely existence of human beings to describe and understand people with dementia, drawing initially on the ideas of Robert Spaemann about personhood outlined in *Persons*. See Swinton, *Dementia*, especially chapter 7.

human creature and never any other kind of creature; a human creature can only live a human life, and all that might be implied from that subsequently. This raises for us a question to pursue: How does being a human creature shape or mark or characterise being human? It is a question that suggests that being a human creature makes a real difference to understanding what is meant by being human. It poses itself as a value-laden question about how a human kind of existence is lived, and not a descriptive question about what a human being is. This is the question that will now set our direction.

These are precisely the sorts of judgments that Reinders shies away from, in as much as they cannot open up onto a path that will lead to the grounding of the humanity of the profoundly disabled. This may present itself as somewhat odd, given that Reinders does not deny that human beings are fundamentally human creatures; he readily accepts as Christian faith that God creates and directs all human lives precisely in their humanity. What Reinders' questioning of these judgments does highlight is that the act of accepting a creaturely principle for human existence does not, in itself, reveal the manner in which it is subsequently understood. In other words, there is no logical deduction to be had about the content of a human life from the mere concept of his or her creaturely existence. Thus there is scope in questioning the way in which the principle of creaturely existence and the content of human life are linked. This is precisely what Reinders is doing when he questions the way in which the Christian tradition (meaning: Catholic teaching and theology) has come to interpret human existence through the prism of the doctrine of the *imago Dei*.

Reinders claims that an *imago Dei* rendering of the tradition is wrong because it has conflated, and thereby confused, the end or *telos* of human life with the origins or *genesis* of human existence. It has attempted to answer questions about the purpose of human life by asking questions about human nature. In so doing, says Reinders, the tradition has failed to distinguish the end from the origin, a distinction that would make the required real difference in the lives of the profoundly disabled, given that their human nature is not in question but only their "humanity properly so called" (as he constantly puts it). Thus:

> Even when questions regarding the protection of human beings like Kelly [a profoundly intellectually disabled teenager] can be effectively answered on the grounds of human descent, this does not answer the question of what it means for Kelly to

lead a human life. With regard to ethical questions concerned with human life properly so called, we not only need to identify her origin as a human being; we also need to ask how she participates in our final end as a human being. I will show that the Roman Catholic position does not provide an answer to this second question, other than to say that a human life like Kelly's is defective. That is, the tradition has no positive answer to that question. The reason why profoundly disabled human beings do not lead a human life properly so called from the perspective of our final end is that they do not develop the capacities of reason and will.[29]

The most telling point about Reinders' claim is the distinction he draws between "being of human descent" and "living a human life." It is the making of this distinction—with the implication that nothing can be inferred about the latter from the former ("this does not answer the question")—that drives Reinders' critical take on the Catholic tradition. So, what is the point he wants to make by holding such a sharp distinction? The first of two parts to an answer to this question lies in his drawing attention to the capacities of reason and will, and his associating of them entirely with the question of human nature. In Reinders' thinking, any account given of human beings from the perspective of their origins will always be undermined by qualitative constraints because the question of the nature of human beings is fundamentally a question of the capacities of human beings, and these are qualitative in nature. Some human beings will have the full set of capacities while others will not; and those who do not are defective human beings. Remember, Reinders' overriding presupposition is that the profoundly disabled—those who are not, and never will be, endowed with critical human faculties like reason and will—are people like all other people, nonetheless. Therefore, any account of human beings where some are not "like unto others"—namely, one based on human origins wherein capacity is the determining factor—cannot be a source for the securing of their humanity because it cannot break free of qualitative constraints.

Secondly, an account of human beings from the perspective of their origins is entirely and essentially a descriptive one for Reinders. It offers no evaluative or normative content. Once a creature has been established as being of human nature, the established nature has no ongoing influence on that human life. This point is brought home by the way in which

29. Reinders, *Receiving the Gift of Friendship*, 92.

Reinders associates the question of the ethical with the "human life properly so called" side of the distinction. Human nature is a necessary ("we not only need to identify her origin as a human being"), but morally neutral repository from which a human life is to be lived ("we also need to ask how she participates in our final end as a human being"). Having a human nature, therefore, makes no contribution to living a human life. Just as the former renders the profoundly disabled defective, so the latter must carry the weight of establishing their humanity. It is the human being "properly so called"—the "real" human being beyond its nature—that matters.

An Anthropology of Discontinuity

At the heart of Reinders' distinction, therefore, is a commitment on his part to an anthropology of discontinuity, whereby what it is to be a human being (understood in descriptive terms) is an entirely separate question from the one of how that being is lived out (understood in value-laden terms). In such a distinction of discontinuity, philosophy takes on the role of answering the former question (with its focus on origins and nature), while theology is the purveyor par excellence of answers to the latter (with its focus on purposes and ends). What a human being is endowed with by nature can tell us nothing of the value or purpose of that individual's human life.

> Because in some human beings there are no intrinsic qualities to build on, any anthropology and ethics that proceeds from such qualities cannot be truly universal for that very reason. By the same token, we can infer that any anthropology and ethics that claims to be truly universal in the face of profoundly disabled human beings cannot but proceed from the principle that whatever quality there is to build on must be extrinsic.[30]

Therefore, what Reinders takes to be a theological perspective on someone's humanity is only that which can be established extrinsically about his or her humanity. This is not to say that Reinders does not hold that "human being" is a *nomen dignitatis*, only that human nature is not a constituting factor in the dignity of being human. Because he is committed to understanding the humanity of the profoundly disabled in exactly the same terms as that of every other human being, he is likewise

30. Ibid., 117.

committed to locating the source of that dignity away from the descriptive, philosophical, intrinsic path of human *genesis* that will not provide such a universalisable humanity, and in a value-laden, theological, extrinsic path of human *telos*. We have seen this pattern of discontinuity before, in Reinders' thinking about friendship: transcendent over and against immanent. The same move is now simply being played out in terms of extrinsic and intrinsic. It shows up how deeply and far-reaching Reinders' commitment is to an anthropology of discontinuity. The "human" in "human being" is separated out so markedly from the "being" that no possibility is left to draw anything meaningful about the living of a human life from the nature of that life.

There are implications for this kind of commitment in terms of our current question concerning the importance of a creaturely principle to being human. Because Reinders does not understand human nature in anything other than qualitative and descriptive terms, he cannot but view positions that understand human nature to be fundamentally value-laden—positions that insist on "a principle intrinsic to our being as the indisputable ground of our dignity as persons"—as undermining the humanity of people like Kelly who lack natural qualities.[31] Consequently, he considers the Catholic tradition—with its emphasis on a creaturely, and therefore, substantial grounding of the *imago Dei* in human beings—to be fundamentally flawed. Why? Because "Roman Catholicism does not allow theological explanation to be pitched against natural reason,"[32] a reasoning which holds that "there is no distinction between the human being [Reinders' "properly so called"] and the human person [Reinders' "of human descent"]: all human beings are persons."[33]

What is truly remarkable about this conclusion is how the language of personhood—by which Christianity has communicated the uniqueness of the divine/human relationship since the time of the Council of Chalcedon—is taken to be the source of the undermining of the humanity of the profoundly disabled. This is an intentionally epistemological—and, by implication, a deeply dualist—move on Reinders' part: there is no such personal being as "man," but only a being who, from one perspective, is a person and, from another perspective, is a human ("properly so called"). These are two entirely different ways of accounting for human

---

31. Ibid., 122.
32. Ibid., 115.
33. Ibid., 117.

beings. The *genesis* and *telos* of human being are permanently separated out into two "either/or" epistemological paradigms so that a universalizing principle of human living can be attained for the profoundly disabled, unencumbered by questions of nature and condition (i.e., personhood). Any anthropology and ethics attempting to combine the two in a "both/and" ontological approach to human origin and end is wrongheaded because it will always undermine the humanity of such people by privileging capacity in the grounding of humanity. The Catholic tradition goes wrong in precisely this way by locating the good of being human in a "community of genealogy," as he calls it, instead of in a "community of teleology."[34] We have, then, two different anthropological paradigms to choose from to ground the humanity of all human beings, with each fundamentally opposed to the other. The Catholic Church has adopted the wrong one—or so claims Reinders.

Reinders' Misinterpretation of Catholic Anthropology

The preceding discussion has been directed by the possibility that asking the question: How does being a human creature shape or mark or characterize being human? is the wrong question to ask. Reinders says it is because the creaturely question, as he interprets it, assumes an anthropology of ontology, of origins, of capacity, of personhood, which can only lead to a defective, marginalized form of humanity for the profoundly disabled. We are left, then, with two questions to ask. First, is Reinders' alternative, epistemological anthropology, which eschews all focus on creaturely life, right? Secondly, is his reading of Catholic doctrine and theology, seen through the prism of discontinuity, justified? An answer to the first question will best emerge by showing that the answer to the second question is to be made in the negative.

Consider the following example of how Reinders (mis)reads the Catholic tradition concerning the intrinsic value of each and every human life, drawn from the Instruction *Donum Vitae*[35] and the encyclicals *Veritatis Splendor*[36] and *Evangelium Vitae*.[37] For Reinders, these are prime examples of how the Catholic tradition has mistakenly sought to account

34. Ibid., 118.
35. Ibid., 93; 96; 112.
36. Ibid., 96; 114. John Paul II, *Veritatis Splendor*, §48.
37. Ibid., 96–97. John Paul II, *Evangelium Vitae*, §§1; 2; 18.

for human life and dignity (the *telos* question) in terms of human nature and condition (the *genesis* question). The text from *Veritatis Splendor* is especially worth attending to as its context is a discussion on the correct relationship between human freedom and human nature. It will be useful to quote the relevant paragraph in its entirety (Reinders quotes only the bolded words; the italicized words are as in the original text):

> [O]ne has to consider carefully the correct relationship existing between freedom and human nature, and in particular *the place of the human body in questions of natural law*. A freedom which claims to be absolute ends up treating the human body as a raw datum, devoid of any meaning and moral values until freedom has shaped it in accordance with its design. Consequently, human nature and the body appear as *presuppositions or preambles*, materially *necessary* for freedom to make its choice, yet extrinsic to the person, the subject and the human act. Their functions would not be able to constitute reference points for moral decisions, because the finalities of these inclinations would be merely "*physical*" goods, called by some "pre-moral." To refer to them, in order to find in them rational indications with regard to the order of morality, would be to expose oneself to the accusation of physicalism or biologism. In this way of thinking, the tension between freedom and a nature conceived of in a reductive way is resolved by a division within man himself. This moral theory does not correspond to the truth about man and his freedom. It contradicts the Church's teachings *on the unity of the human person*, whose rational soul is *per se et essentialiter* the form of his body. **The spiritual and immortal soul is the principle of unity of the human being, whereby it exists as a whole—*corpore et anima unus*—as a person. These definitions not only point out that the body, which has been promised the resurrection, will also share in glory. They also remind us that reason and free will are linked with all the bodily and sense faculties.** *The person, including the body, is completely entrusted to himself, and it is in the unity of body and soul that the person is the subject of his own moral acts.* The person, by the light of reason and the support of virtue, discovers in the body the anticipatory signs, the expression and the promise of the gift of self, in conformity with the wise plan of the Creator. It is in the light of the dignity of the human person—a dignity which must be affirmed for its own sake—that reason grasps the specific moral value of certain goods towards which the person is naturally inclined. And **since the human person cannot be reduced**

> to a freedom which is self-designing, but entails a particular spiritual and **bodily structure, the primordial** moral **requirement of loving and respecting the person as an end and never as a mere means also implies, by its very nature, respect for certain fundamental goods**, without which one would fall into relativism and arbitrariness.[38]

It is clear enough from the bolded sentences, let alone from the context in which they occur, that the Church understands the human being to be a composite creature: a-human-soul-along-with-a-human-body unity. A human being can only be "man" as a soul-body whole.[39] In this way, the faculties of reason and will, along with the faculties of bodily and sense perception—none of which is a discrete function of either the body or the soul—are consequential to "man," and neither the soul nor the body of a human being, nor the individual himself, is reducible to them in any combination. Because every human being is a human soul informing a human body, "man" is first and foremost, always and totally, existential. It is this existential man himself—the uniquely whole and entire individual—that the Encyclical speaks of as being oriented to the resurrection, and not some "essential man" that is the sum of the qualitative faculties with which he may or may not be endowed. Furthermore, this orientation of the whole human individual to the resurrection—his teleological meaning and hoped-for end—is intrinsically grounded; it has been "entrusted to himself," given by God for him to then live.

It is also clear enough from the text that an ontological framework and language is being drawn upon to ground the Church's ethical claims about human beings. A man is substantially a moral being. This framework and language is not employed in any essentialist sense. Human dignity, to take the example from the text, is to be affirmed "for its own

---

38. *Veritatis splendour*, §48. The four words that are not in bold type among the bolded words (i.e., "free," "spiritual and," and "moral") are inexplicably left out by Reinders.

39. Reinders (*Receiving the Gift of Friendship*, 93) correctly notes that the language of hylomorphism has been traditionally employed to explain this reality. However, he incorrectly labels hylomorphism a "doctrine" of the Catholic Church. The actual doctrine remains conspicuously free of such linguistic and conceptual frameworks. Hence, the *Catechism of the Catholic Church* states, "The human person, created in the image of God, is a being at once corporeal and spiritual" (CCC §362), adding that "spirit and matter, in man, are not two natures united, but rather their union forms a single nature" (CCC §365). The Church has never "ordained" hylomorphism or any other particular linguistic expression of the doctrine.

sake," meaning: it is to be affirmed for the sake of the human being who is dignified. Human dignity is not something extrinsic to human beings (even if suited to human beings), in which they participate (as if that participation is contingent). Rather, "human dignity" is another name for "man," so to speak; he is the "human dignity creature." He is not (essentially) dignified, as if "dignity" somehow supervenes on his nature; he is dignity—it is the way he has his humanity. Human beings—who, by purposeful origin, are valued as good—are their dignity; they do not have their dignity. Therefore, human dignity is neither a factor of someone's rational capacity nor of his natural inclinations nor of a self-designating freedom. Certainly, there is an epistemological dimension to this ontological framework, but it plays its role in the process of discovery: a man is human dignity substantially, but he learns of this through his faculties. Hence, the affirmation of human dignity is something learned, something discoverable, but human dignity itself is grounded in what it is to be human as such.

Herein lies the reason why "dignity" and "human dignity" are not to be treated as synonymous (while noting that the text itself does not express the difference in this language). The former is a more general behavioral concept of moral import extrinsic to anything to which it may be applied, and therefore can be won or lost. The latter—"the dignity of the human person"[40]—pertains to a human being as "man," and therefore cannot be gained or lost. Instead, it defines him. "Human dignity" is the dignity proper to human beings, and it says that human beings are always (existentially) good, while not always (essentially) moral.

Recognizing this distinction helps to highlight one further aspect of the anthropology of *Veritatis Splendor*, namely, the notion of "person" as it occurs in the text. "Human person" is treated as synonymous with "human being"; no "division within man himself" is countenanced between being a human being and being a human person. Furthermore, "person" is a value-laden term in that it is the *nomen dignitatis* for "man," pertaining to the substantial existence of all human beings as human beings (it "entails a particular spiritual and bodily structure").[41] Human personhood, understood in this way, identifies the anthropology of the Church as one of continuity, ranging over human nature, purpose and dignity.

40. VS §50 expresses this as "the dignity proper to the person."

41. This is phraseology used by Spaemann in *Persons*, 6, whom Reinders treats as an exemplar of Catholic anthropology. Reinders, *Receiving the Gift of Friendship*, 98–101.

"Person," in the anthropology of *Veritatis Splendor*, is not a certain kind of qualitative description of man, but a certain kind of moral claim to being treated as a man.

While these few ideas drawn from *Veritatis Splendor* are not the only ones to be found there (there is also the matter of the moral significance of bodily life), they do provide us with a sufficient picture of the Church's anthropology by which we may now compare what Reinders draws from the same text. For his part, Reinders has this to say about the first bolded part of the text: "Clearly, this statement entails the conception of the human person as defined by the embodied capacity for reason and will."[42] We may immediately note the essentialist interpretation Reinders is reading into the anthropology of the encyclical. He does not pick up on the unity of human existence that is being stressed, nor on the emphasis given to the way in which someone, whole and entire, is said to have his or her existence personally. Yet, it is precisely these points that are proposed as the true "definitions" (as the text calls them) of man, and the necessary correctives to anthropologies that are reductive, dualistic, and essentialist in character.

Instead of considering how this bedrock of the Church's anthropology comes to influence the particularly "human" of human being, Reinders hones in on the subsequent mention of the capacities of reason and will and raises them to the status of determinants of human personhood, failing to see the restrictive sense given to them in the text itself. He does this by treating them as stand-alone qualitative features of the nature of the human soul, and not in their association with bodily life, as does the text. In a quite confused (and confusing) way, Reinders seems to have missed altogether where John Paul II actually places the anthropological emphasis, namely: away from essentialist categories that would reduce "man" to some set of qualitative requirements and towards an un-qualified understanding, and instead reads into it what he thinks is evidence of essentialist tendencies.

What, then, is Reinders point? It would seem that the phrase "embodied capacity" is being made to carry the interpretive weight for "person," understood in the descriptivist manner we have already seen from him. He interprets the Church's language about capacities as placing emphasis on the things that a human being has via his or her soul and which, once subsequently embodied, goes to make him or her a human

---

42. Ibid., 96.

person. Therefore, he interprets the Church's understanding of the human person as being programmatic of being human, with the human soul being the determinative locus of this programme. Consequently, if the programme is defective, if the capacitated nature is not embodied, then those of human descent who are not so programmed, are rendered defective humans or sub-human, "properly so called."

This, at least, is what Reinders thinks is entailed when the Church employs the language of human personhood. However, this is to equate "person" with the human soul, and to then see it as some kind of embodied personal nature that someone has to have if he or she is to be fully a human being, and not to see it as the way in which an individual is revealed as being a human being. Reinders sees the Church as proposing that a human being is a being who *has* a living human body; however, if the anthropology of *Veritatis Splendor* is saying anything with its emphasis on soul-body unity and the man, whole and entire, it is saying that a human being is a being who *is* the living human body that he is. Furthermore, because Reinders is unable to read "person" in anything other than essentialist terms, the text from the encyclical—with its mention of, though not emphasis on, reason and will—is confusingly misread as an essentialist anthropology. The entailment Reinders "clearly" sees in his interpretation of the first bolded quotation from *Veritatis Splendor* is simply not there to be had. Moreover, the view of personhood he thereby attributes to John Paul is, perversely, the very view that John Paul has devoted the encyclical as a whole to refuting.

There is much that follows from this misreading. Most notably, Reinders concludes that the Church has no means at its disposal to overcome the programmatic understanding of human being he reads into *Veritatis Splendor*:

> Given its venerated principle that anthropology and ethics build on the natural powers of "man," it is doubtful that Roman Catholic moral theology will be allowed any concession in that direction."[43]

Therefore, Catholic doctrine cannot secure the humanity of the profoundly disabled:

> [b]ecause in some human beings there are no intrinsic qualities to build on, [and] any anthropology and ethics that proceeds

---

43. Ibid., 117.

from such qualities cannot be truly universal for that very reason.[44]

If there is no opening onto the true meaning of human life from the substantial nature of human beings, as this understanding entails, then in the face of the profoundly disabled the only option left is to "proceed from the principle that whatever quality there is to build on must be extrinsic."[45] So, Reinders completes the circle, as it were, and goes on to propose friendship as the extrinsic quality the profoundly disabled receive as fulfilling their humanity "properly so called." It is noteworthy that Reinders reveals his own essentialist undercurrents in the very words he uses: it is a "quality" he is looking for, and not a mode or way or manner in which humanity is revealed. This is a crucial presupposition that exposes the true provenance of friendship. He eschews so-called intrinsic qualities like the capacities of reason and will, and all that these have to do with the substantial nature of human beings. Even so, he is not against proposing an extrinsic quality, one that he takes to be entirely relational in nature.

A Return to a Creaturely Form

The rejection of any substantial human quality and the acceptance of the relational quality of friendship turn out to be of paramount importance. For if the substantial human being (Reinders' "human person") is to have no active part in establishing and sustaining the relational human being (Reinders' "human being properly so called"), then we must rely on an epistemological account of the quality of friendship, and not an ontological account of human life, to do the work of securing the humanity of human beings. This is precisely Reinders' thesis: the substantial origins of human beings will not secure the humanity of the profoundly disabled; only their relational ends can do so. (Recall also, in this context, the doubt raised earlier as to whether or not a friendship can actually exist if someone is incapable of knowing they have "drawn apart together" with someone else.)

However, this results in a rather peculiar scenario: the profoundly impaired, who cannot know of God's loving embrace of their humanity (because they do not have the capacity to know), are nonetheless

44. Ibid.
45. Ibid.

established as human beings on the basis of their being in a relationship of friendship with God. It is the only way they can be human because it is the only way that Reinders allows for them to be human. Their bodily life is said to bring nothing to the relationship, their substantial existence is considered devoid of influence. Instead, it is a "relational aptitude" (to borrow a rather apt phrase from the Christian philosopher J. P. Moreland), specifically an openness to befriending, which is made to be the measure of the man.[46] Yet, such an openness presupposes an ability to know what to do when one is befriending. Thus, the one thing that marks out the profoundly impaired as what they are not—that is, beings who have a capacity to know what to do when it comes to befriending—Reinders has placed at the center of his extrinsic quality of friendship.

The upshot of this discussion of the text from *Veritatis Splendor* is that it has not only exposed how Reinders wrongly identifies Catholic anthropology as essentialist in nature by applying a commitment to discontinuity to an anthropology of continuity, but it has also revealed a hidden epistemological essentialism in his own position. A misreading of an anthropology of being is countered with a deeply flawed anthropology of knowing. All of this has come about because of an epistemic commitment to an entirely relational, not substantial, view of humanity, one that results in a complete closure to any existential appreciation of human life. With his sharp conceptual distinction between the *genesis* and *telos* of human being, Reinders sets out to break free of a reliance on human origins and the creaturely principle of human life, but he does not succeed in doing so. Consequently, we have reason to turn to an understanding of "being human" that is centered on our creaturely existence and life—namely, the human condition is determinative of "man," while the condition under which an individual exists is not.

One final comment is called for, before moving on to the more positive account of the crucial role creaturely existence plays in the lives of all human beings. It is this: that despite what has been noted here, there might remain a lingering sense that Reinders is not entirely without justification in confronting the Catholic tradition with an accusation of ontological essentialism. Certainly, it would be uncontroversial to say that seams of essentialist thinking have had a tendency to surface and gain sway in Catholic theology; an inherent risk, it might be said, of espousing a natural law approach to moral discourse. It is this tendency

---

46. Moreland, *Recalcitrant Imago Dei*, 4.

that Reinders has picked up—perhaps reflecting more the neo-Thomistic anthropology of the early part of the twentieth century rather than the renewed anthropology of *Gaudium et Spes*, as outlined earlier—and he has then applied it to the doctrinal statements he considers. It has been our argument, however, that the text of *Veritatis Splendor* does not support an essentialist reading of the Church's anthropology, and Pope John Paul II makes it clear in his references to "biologism" and "physicalism" that this is his intended target. Nonetheless, the question of human essentiality remains a significant factor in the theological outworking of Catholic doctrine.

What is to be made of this? Essentialism is a form—probably the most prominent form—of the elevated anthropology discussed earlier; it is the tendency to take the rational essentiality of human life and to make it foundational to the living of that life. Part of the task ahead, therefore, will be to show how the non-essentialist doctrinal position can be sustained theologically without either denying a moral significance to the rational essentiality of human life (as Reinders does) or allowing it to dominate the significance of human life (as elevated anthropologies do). Key to this task will be not only unpacking what is implied in a creaturely principle to human life but also examining why an anthropology of continuity is the right response to the question of the humanity of all human beings, including those who are profoundly impaired.

6

THE PILGRIM CREATURE
Hope and Human Life

The Creaturely Human

EARLIER WE NOTED HOW in the discussion on friendship, Josef Pieper, in *On Love*, locates the human love of friendship within a creaturely architecture. It is an idea he captures in his oft repeated remark that, at its base, love is an existential declaration: "It's good that you exist; it's good that you are in this world!"[1] As he notes, the "indispensable beginning" of all human love rests on "[the recognition] that the *conditio humana* is that of a created being."[2] However, he does not go on to flesh out in that essay his stance on creaturely life, other than to draw attention to the intrinsic reality implied in human creatureliness: "we are *creatura* and thereby have an existence that is our own."[3]

Where Pieper does elaborate on these claims is in an earlier essay, *On Hope*.[4] He expands his idea further in his book-length essay, *Death and Immortality*.[5] From these he argues for the claim that to be human is to be a *viator*: a pilgrim, a wayfarer.[6] If, as we saw for Arendt, man is always a beginning, then for Pieper, man is always on pilgrimage.

1. Pieper, *On Love*, 164. This is the first time he uses the phrase.
2. Ibid., 223.
3. Ibid., 218.
4. Pieper, *On Hope*, in *Faith, Hope, Love*.
5. Pieper, *Death and Immortality*.
6. The more literal rendering of *viator* into English is "wayfarer." "Wayfarer,"

> It would be difficult to conceive of another statement that penetrates as deeply into the innermost core of creaturely existence as does the statement that man finds himself, even until the moment of his death, in a *status viatoris*, in the state of being on the way.[7]

What Pieper has developed in these three works is a consistent line of thought in which he argues that any cogent understanding of human life requires an understanding of it as fundamentally a creaturely life. His own thinking in this regard was influenced by and in the line of St. Thomas Aquinas, who, as Pieper puts it, had always understood the nature of man to mean: "by virtue of his Creation."[8] Yet Pieper's position is no simplistic replaying of Thomistic themes; he locates his own take on the creaturely life of human beings—the creaturely human—within a deep seam of thought that runs through the entire Western Christian tradition "from Augustine through Thomas Aquinas to Francis de Sales, Leibniz and C. S. Lewis."[9] What we have in Pieper, therefore, is a line of thought that upholds the notion of the creaturely human as being of deep and abiding significance, which has been tried and tested over many centuries and from various traditions, and which presents itself as the one indispensable and foundational insight into a cogent understanding of what it means to be human. For these reasons, his thought on the creaturely human provides a valuable point of departure for the arguments we now want to develop.

The task ahead may be put in the form of a question: What is meant when we speak of human life as being identified by a creaturely principle; what is being referred to by talk of the creaturely human? Of course, the

---

however, has become somewhat romanticized and now carries a sense of someone who is a drifter in search of a purpose to his life. To avoid this connotation, I will translate *viator* as "pilgrim," to bring out the sense of purposefulness inherent in the Latin word.

7. Pieper, *On Hope*, 92.

8. Pieper, *Death and Immortality*, 40. For Aquinas' theological understanding of humanity's *status viatoris*, which he draws from a more ancient tradition, see especially: *ST* II-II.18.4, but also II-II.17.2, II-II.18.2.*ad*1 (concerning Christ's human nature), and II-II.18.3.*resp*. Pieper says elsewhere, "In the philosophy of St. Thomas Aquinas, there is a fundamental idea by which almost all the basic concepts of his vision of the world are determined: the idea of creation, or more precisely, the notion that nothing exists which is not *creatura*, except the Creator Himself; and in addition, that this createdness determines entirely and all-pervasively the inner structure of the creature." Pieper, *Silence of St. Thomas*, 47.

9. Pieper, *On Love*, 218.

wording of this question presupposes that human existence is a creaturely kind of existence, and that it is in holding to this identification that the question about meaning arises. Hidden within the question, however, is the notion of the act of creating. If being a *creatura* is determinative of something significant about being human, then *creatio*—the act of creating—is an integral part of that significance.[10] It will be useful, therefore, to begin looking at the question of human creaturely life by means of the unique position human beings are said to have in the broader scope of God's creative action. By first turning to this question of location, we may then take up the question of the creaturely human on his pilgrim way through life armed with some supporting structural insights.

The Createdness of Human Creation

Karl Rahner's *Sacramentum Mundi* offers the following, theologically-focused definition of creation:

> The term "creation" expresses the way in which the world and everything pertaining to the world have their origin, ground and final goal in God. It can mean, actively, the creative action of God, and passively, the totality of creation.[11]

What makes this a helpful definition to work from is the way in which it locates the meaning of creation in how it is what it is—in emphasizing the createdness of creation, so to speak—rather than focusing simply on what it is. It is a definition that shifts attention away from questions of "What?" and onto questions of "How?" By so emphasizing the createdness of creation, the definition orients us in the direction of making the movement from puzzlement about "human being" to a revealing of something of what is involved in "being human."

The three descriptors by which the parameters of the notion of creation are set—origin, ground, and goal—also make this definition particularly noteworthy.[12] They tell us that the question of creaturely

---

10. As the German theologian Christoph Schwöbel has put it, "[E]very theological description of the world as *creatura* presupposes a view of its constitution, an account of divine creating." Schwöbel, "God, Creation and the Christian Community: The Dogmatic Basis of a Christian Ethic of Createdness," in *Doctrine of Creation*, 161.

11. Smulders, "Creation: I. Theology," in Rahner, *Sacramentum Mundi*, 23. The definition remains unchanged for the concise, single-volume version of the *Sacramentum Mundi* published in 1975.

12. We may note how the three descriptors are theologically equivalent to the

life is properly a question about being in existence, and to understand existence as creaturely is to understand it within God-initiated, God-sustained, and God-directed parameters. These three descriptors establish creaturely life as existence related to, but distinct from, God by demarcating out the kind of relationship that exists between creator and creature, with the emphasis on a relational existence. Such a relationship presupposes distinct subjects who are mutual agents within the relationship. The mention of "distinct subjects" points us in the direction of understanding the relationship in substantial terms, while "mutual agents" delineates the unique position each creature has in relation to the creator. It is this existential condition of being a member of a kind, related to God but also distinct from God, that is being revealed in the definitional emphasis on the createdness of creation. J. P. Moreland provides a philosophical correlation to this theological point when he states,

> [A] thing's functional abilities or relational aptitudes are determined by its kindedness. . . . [A]n entity can stand in certain relations and not others depending on the kind of thing that entity is, and an entity flourishes in certain relations and not others depending on the sort of thing it is.[13]

The French-born Russian Orthodox theologian Oliver-Maurice Clément helps focus our attention on the theological grounding needed for understanding human creaturely life in this dual-aspect (but not dualistic) way when he states, "The human being does not exist by itself but that God is 'its beginning, its middle and its end' . . . So we cannot exist apart from God or outside of God. No one can. By the very life in us we are rooted in the one living God."[14] Clément is adamant that "from the beginning grace is inherent in the very fact of existing" (and in a dramatic flourish) insists that "there is no middle ground. . . . The death of God brings about the death of Man (who cannot actually annihilate [himself])."[15] The point to this flourish is that the (notional) death of God would imply the (notional) death of a man as "man," but as God can-

---

words of St. Paul to the Athenians: "For 'In him we live and move and have our being'; as even some of your own poets have said, 'For we too are his offspring'" (Acts 17:28).

13. Moreland, *Recalcitrant Imago Dei*, 4, 5.

14. Clément, *On Human Being*, 25. Clément attributes the words in inverted commas to the seventh-century Eastern Father, St. Maximus the Confessor, but gives no reference.

15. Ibid., 26, 27. (The bracketed phrase is also Clément's terminology, and is taken from the same at page 10.)

not be abolished in fact, then neither can "man." Human creaturely life exists in a relational mode; we are the kind of creature who is "in God."

This relational mode is itself the only reason given for why human creatures are substantially different from God. That which unites the human creature to the divine creator—namely, the existence of a real relationship—is precisely that which establishes them as fundamentally different from one another. The relationship is not dependent upon some more foundational reality in, or underlying condition of human existence; it is the way in which human creatures and God have their unique existences from each other. Therefore, human beings are in a creaturely relationship to God by way of a real relationship that is intrinsic to them. A man cannot annihilate his being of human kind and remake himself into something else because his relatively autonomous existence in distinction from God is unavoidably in God, nonetheless.

Existing "in God"

What is the theological value for us in noting this mode in which human beings are creatures? The book of Wisdom offers a basis to respond: "For [God] created all things so that they might exist; the creatures of the world are wholesome, and there is no destructive poison in them" (Wis 1:14).[16] Two crucial thoughts are conveyed in this short sentence. First, existing is at the heart of creation. That there be something other than God is itself reason enough for God to create. Secondly, for something to exist means that it has a reason for existing, a purpose, as expressed in the "so that" of God's creativity. From this we may say that "value" and "existence" are coextensive: God saw that his creation was very good because creaturely existence cannot not be good (Gen 1:31).

The implication of these two points, when coupled with the previous point about the relational mode of human existence, is far-reaching. If human beings are beings in existence because they are valuable (good)

---

16. The word "creatures" is a translation of *geneseis*, and simply refers to all things that have been created or generated. See Winston, *Wisdom of Solomon*, 108. The same point is made in *The Theological Dictionary of the New Testament*, 881n46. The Liddell and Scott *Greek-English Lexicon*, however, notes that the word takes on various meanings, most notably: having an origin and being of a kind, drawing attention to Plato's *Phaedrus* (245E). Of course, the book of Wisdom, coming as it does from the Jewish Hellenistic period of second/first century BC, is unique in the Bible for its Greek modes of thought, especially in its correlation to classical Platonism.

in their very existence, then every human being is valuable (good) for no other reason than his or her creaturely existence. If human creatures exist in a relational mode, then their value is not dependent on anything about them other than that they are existing. In other words, simply being of human kind grounds the value of being human, which is, in turn, a function of being "in God." With this insight, we begin to see something of the theological meaning the doctrine of the *imago Dei* may bring to the lives of the profoundly impaired: the relational mode of human existence—our being in God—is what makes human beings in the image of God. Nothing else is required.

This is borne out in the two creation narratives of Genesis 1 and Genesis 2. Genesis 1 is especially marked by a series of separations: light/darkness (1:4); the two waters (1:6); sea/earth (1:10); day/night (1:14). At the center of these separations is the separation of God from creation. It is God as creator who brings about all these separations, and who marks himself out as separate from them all: God looks on his creation, God names his creation, God admires his creation, God even rests from the work of his creation, but God is not present as this creation; he is not a part of it in terms of creaturely existence. The Scottish theologian, David Fergusson, has noted this dynamic of separation, and has pointed to the ontological distinction established in the transcendence of God over creation that is central to understanding the scriptural differentiation.[17] The God/creation demarcation is essential for properly understanding how the positioning of creaturely life is as other than God.

Just as significant to understanding the Genesis narratives is the recognition of a God/creation relationship, or more specifically, of the moments where relationship overcomes the determinability of demarcation. There are only two such moments: when God creates *adam* (Man) as "in our image" (1:26), and when God creates *ishshah* (Woman) from *adam* as "flesh of my flesh" (2:23). Importantly, these two moments have in common the same unique manner in which God creates human beings. In all of God's creative action, only Man and Woman are created within an explicitly relational framework, and it is only in the creation of Man and Woman that God explicitly locates himself in relation to the *creatura* and not just in relation to *creatio*. Only in the vertical God/human relationship and the horizontal man/woman relationship is the gap of separation bridged in creation. In Man and Woman, God no longer separates

---

17. Fergusson, *Cosmos and the Creator*, 8.

himself from his creation. This relationality in creation is further borne out in its negation, when Man and Woman remove themselves from God as a result of their mutual act of sin (3:8–9). In the creation narratives of Genesis, it is the relational characteristic in both God and humanity that marks out a corresponding kindedness of both God and humanity. This does not undermine the relative position of God and human creatures to each other, that is, their opposition as creator and creature, but it does establish the God/human and Man/Woman creation as being fundamentally different in kind from the rest of creation, exactly at the point of relationship, and not just different by a relational degree.

The second insight to be drawn from the book of Wisdom quotation is that the fact of existing, the being in existence, is not ours to make or unmake. This can be derived from the phrase that creatures have "no destructive poison" in them—meaning, creaturely life, by virtue of being created, does not carry in itself the seed of ceasing-to-be. By implication, neither does creaturely life have the power of coming-to-be. We are not talking here of procreation (of participation in the extension of an instance of what already exists) nor of dying (of participation in the ending of an instance of what already exists). Existing as such as a human being—being the being that a human being is—is neither ours to have nor to hold; it is given (as good) as it is. Another way of saying the same thing is to say that the creature is nothing—no thing at all—without the creator, God. Again, the implication of this is far-reaching. The createdness of creation permanently rotates on an axis that has as its two poles everything and nothing, existing and not existing; and we human creatures are always on the verge of nothingness, always longing for immortality, for a permanent existence.

This double-edged sword to creaturely life finds its deepest expression in the most striking aspect of the doctrine of creation *ex nihilo*. It is not so much the claim that some thing came out of nothing that is most remarkable, but the claim that every thing is nothing without God. Creation is only "creation" because of God. This helps to account for why St. Thomas Aquinas, in his famous treatise on the creation of the world, is undisturbed by the lack of an argument to demonstrate definitively that the world was created *ex nihilo* (*ST* I.46.2). It is not whether or not something came out of nothing that matters; rather, it is that there is a proper basis for being in existence at all: and that basis is God, necessarily. Hence:

> God's will is the cause of things. So then the necessity of their being is that of God's willing them ... [T]he world exists just so long as God wills it to, since its existence depends on his will as on its cause. (*ST* I.46.1)

The world could have come about either *ex nihilo* or not, although Christian faith in all its traditions teaches the former as a matter of revealed knowledge. What is crucial for us is the reason for this teaching. The fact itself is unimportant; rather, what matters is that, from the perspective of *creatio*, not only does God initiate created being, but he also sustains and directs it. The same thing is being expressed when we say, from the perspective of the creature, that God is the origin, ground, and goal of created existence. "Human being," from this theologically charged sense in which Aquinas grounds his account of creation, is not so much a description given of a certain class of being existing in creation (though it is that as well), but an expression of the commitment of the creator to be always present for the sake of the existing in creation of a being in a real relationship to him.

Created for Redemption

The point to emerge from this is one in which the ontological significance of human creaturely life in fact turns on the notion, noted earlier, of how human beings are located in relation to God, in the uniquely human way in which they are. On the one hand, our very existence as human creatures is constituted as such "in God": in him we live and move and have our being. On the other hand, it is of the mode of our creaturely living that our being in God is not actually located in God but in our own proper created being. The valued nature of our creaturely being is intrinsic to us, not to God, even though that value is a measure of our relationship to God.

If being human is an acknowledgment that we are always standing before the precipice of nothingness, then this also means acknowledging that we are standing there, nonetheless. It is before the precipice of nothingness, yet "in God," that we discover ourselves to be the human beings that we are, and win for ourselves the value pertaining to that humanity.[18]

18. Clément quotes the nineteenth-century Orthodox Metropolitan Philaret of Moscow (perhaps from his *Catechism*, which was widely used in Russia) as saying, "Creatures are balanced upon the creative will of God as upon a bridge of diamond; above is the abyss of the divine infiniteness and below is the abyss of their own nothingness" (*On Human Being*, 25).

By implication, this bilocality of human existence means that the *genesis* and the *telos* of human life cannot be separated out from each other as if the former pertains to ourselves as ourselves and the latter to ourselves as in God. This is because the ongoing action of God in human life (our grounding) and the future action of God for human life (our goal) cannot be separated out from the creative action of the God of human life (our origin). The creaturely existence of human beings is at the foundation of all of God's work in regard to human life.

A Christian anthropology, therefore, needs a theology of human creation that points us towards our end in God. From the human perspective we may colloquially use the language of beginnings and ends to speak about our ongoing lives, but from God's perspective this rightly becomes speech about our creation and redemption. As the Australian theologian Neil Ormerod has remarked,

> The God who creates is the God who saves and vice versa. Christian faith resists any attempt to separate the two functions. . . . The work of salvation . . . is truly an act of creation *ex nihilo*, a fundamentally creative act.[19]

There are two notions at play in this claim: continuity and directionality. Of the first, the claim is that the structure of God's redemptive action is of the same kind as the structure of God's creative action. When God is redeeming he is not doing something fundamentally different from creating. The implication is that both creating and redeeming are forms of *creatio* and, therefore, the one and same *creatura* is the personal subject of both the creating and redeeming action of God.

Perhaps the words of the book of Revelation—"And the one who was seated on the throne said, 'See, I am making all things new'" (Rev 21:5)—come to mind, tolling a warning not to accept such a claim. But in fact they support it. This is the first time in the text that the first person of the Blessed Trinity speaks, and the Father's words are ones of confirmation of the effects of the redeeming sacrifice already undertaken by the Son. Crucially, the Father speaks in the present tense: what is being newly made—the new creation—is in fact a making of what already is; the end of its newness is to come on the Last Day, but the origin of its newness is located in its making. Creation and redemption are but different forms of the one continuous act of God's will for his creatures.

---

19. Ormerod, *Creation, Grace, and Redemption*, 5. The book offers a useful survey of the current issues in creation theology.

This point tells us something crucial about the relationship between creaturely being and creaturely nature. To hold a position of continuity between creation and redemption is to hold that God created human beings with a nature that is, by its nature, redeemable. To be created a human being is to be created with a nature open to receiving redemption. The suggestion here is this: God had a certain form in mind of human nature when he created us, and we have our existence in this human form because that is how God determines our nature. Therefore, while existence grounds essence from our creaturely perspective, essence grounds existence from God's perspective as creator. To be an instance of a human being is to share in a human nature that has been pre-determined by God. This is because God would have had to have a certain kind of nature in mind—a human kind of nature—when he brought human beings into existence. To suggest anything to the contrary would be to imply that there is no order to God's creative will, and to do that would mean that there is no order to creation; it is utterly arbitrary.

This being the case, acceptance of the notion of continuity with regard to creation and redemption means that any human being, by virtue of existing, possesses all that is necessary for being human and is, therefore, redeemable. We will simply flag at this stage where this will eventually lead: those human beings who never have possessed or who no longer possess certain features that characteristically pertain to human beings, such as agency, are either created with all that is proper and necessary to the nature of being human, including the possibility of being redeemed in (but not from) their individual conditions, or else they are not at all of a human kind, and nothing that pertains to human beings, *qua* being of human kind, pertains to them.

Of the second notion of directionality, which follows directly from the first, the claim is this: that which is redeemed is first that which is created. Creation and redemption are not bi-directional, as if God is not mindful of his former, creative work when operating in terms of his latter, redemptive work. Both a chronological and logical order is revealed in God's actions with regard to his creation. When God redeems, he is redeeming what already is the case—namely, a human kind of creature; but whom God redeems is the individual human being who is the subjective instance of the kind. God is able to undertake the work of redemption for the sake of his human creation by virtue of our existing individually as the kind of creatures that we are. It is the individually created human being, living his or her life precisely as a human kind of creature, who is open to the possibility of glorification.

As with the notion of continuity, so the question of newness arises with the notion of directionality. Does God redeem his human creation as a new creature altogether? Is the created nature of human beings dispensed with at redemption? We may turn to the ancient and constantly held tradition of the Church concerning bodily resurrection ("*Credo in . . . carnis resurrectionem*") to respond to these questions. To express the meaning of the belief negatively: Christianity holds that a dead human being is not reborn into eternal glory as something other than the same human being who once lived; I am reborn as the human being God once created me to be. Seeing the doctrine negatively helps to highlight what bodily resurrection is not: it is not a metamorphosis, whereby one kind of thing ceases to be and an entirely different kind of thing takes its place. The individual who is created as a certain kind is the individual who is redeemed as that same kind. This is not to say that a human being is already all that he or she can be as an instance of a human kind. We who were created redeemable are not yet the new creation redemption promises, but each and every one of us, no matter in what created condition we are living our lives, is already on the way. Thus, we are back with Pieper's *viator*: human beings are pilgrims on the way.

Of course, this does not answer the further question about how the human creature remains the individual he or she is once that individual is in a redeemed, glorified state. This is, in part, a question about the deeply puzzling issue of identity and recognition over time and space, and beyond. How are persons in their glorious state related to their former, fallen state? Which "me" will be the glorified me? Will we recognize each other in our glorified bodies in the same way we recognize each other in our fallen conditions? In what sense are such questions even meaningful? As significant as these questions are, to attempt to answer them here will take us well beyond our task focused on our mortal reality as human beings. Let us simply assert, therefore, that the glorified state of every human being—impaired or unimpaired, embryonic or fully adult—is continuous with the graced condition in which each was created, and to note that Jesus ascended to the Father with wounds in his hands, feet and side, the result of his crucifixion.

We may flag here where this leads in terms of the profoundly impaired: they are, precisely in the condition in which they live their lives, already existing in the manner of the pilgrim common to all those of human kind, and so are already living according to that which is necessary and sufficient for God to bring them to redemption. God does not undo, but perfects that which he has already brought into existence. If it were otherwise the Incarnation becomes redundant, "and we should not be able to make use of the Conqueror's victory, if it had been won outside our nature," as Leo the Great wrote.[20] Therefore, the chief point to keep in mind and to carry forward is this: being human and living a human life are grounded in our thoroughly conditioned creaturely existence; it is "inside our nature." Our human lives are located in terms of our intrinsic human nature, which is created in God. All that pertains to our lives, including the possibility of our salvation and eternal, glorified existence has this reality at its base. God does not create one thing and then save something else; the creature redeemed is first and still the creature created. As an ancient prayer of the Church has put it,

> God our Father,
> Our human nature is the wonderful work of your hands,
> made still more wonderful by your work of redemption.[21]

The Human Pilgrim

We are now in a position to return to the more specific question of the creaturely human, deferred from earlier on. To recall that question: What is meant when we speak of human life as being identified by a creaturely principle; what is being referred to by talk of the creaturely human? The Catholic moral theologian Romanus Cessario, OP, offers a succinct answer: "Being a wayfarer marks human creatureliness."[22] This is a way of saying that it is of the nature of being human to exist provisionally. To hold that being a human creature is structured in terms of a state of wayfaring is to hold that there is an unavoidable incompleteness about human existence. In other words, Cessario's wayfarer is nothing other than Pieper's *viator*:

---

20. Leo I (the Great), "Letter to Pulcheria Augusta," XXXI. 2, 45.

21. This prayer, currently the Collect for the "Mass of Christmas during the Day" of the *Novus Ordo* of the Roman Rite, has its provenance in a collect for Christmas Day found in the *Sacramentarium Veronese (Leonianum)*, dated to the sixth century. This is the oldest extant collection of *libelli missarum* of the Roman Rite.

22. Cessario, "The Theological Virtue of Hope (IIa IIae, qq. 17–22)," 239.

> The state of being on the way is not to be understood in a primary and literal sense as a designation of place. It refers rather to the innermost structure of created nature. It is the inherent "not yet" of the finite being.[23]

Pieper seeks to capture the meaning of this provisionality with expressions like the "becoming-ness" and the "not yet-ness" of human nature, and the "not-yet-existing-being" of human existence.[24] These expressions are indicative of the one notion: that, unlike God, "who is absolute being, in the fullness of whose being essence and existence are one," our human existence reveals how "man is not ipso facto his own essence."[25] Pieper—and Cessario, for that matter—is drawing our attention to the distinctive manner in which the fact of human existence is related to the living out of that existence. He wants to stress that the provisional character of our existence is a defining feature of our nature; to exist as a human being is to take possession, as it were, of a human nature, to live a human life. Our very existence reveals our nature, and our nature determines the manner of our existing.

As we have already seen, human life, *qua* created life, exists on the threshold of nothingness, of not existing. Pieper's intuition is that this provisionality is not self-referencing; human life is not an existence out of nothing into nothing. Rather, while we stand before the objective possibility of our non-existence because of our created nature, nonetheless we do so from the position of our actual existing in virtue of our created nature. This actual existing is both evaluative and directive because it poses an unavoidable question: Is it good that I am, rather than that I am not? If it is good to exist, then there is value in existing and an inbuilt orientation to continue to exist. Pieper calls this the "ontological quality of being on-the-way to somewhere else . . . pointed towards fulfilment, completion and final realization."[26] Human life is not lived out in some arbitrary manner. An orientation towards nothingness comes about because of a rejection of the proper direction towards being, in all its completeness, that existence has by virtue of its inner structure.[27] By this very fact, the

---

23. Pieper, *On Hope*, 93.
24. Ibid., 96; 98.
25. Ibid., 96.
26. Pieper, *Death and Immortality*, 85.
27. Pieper, *On Hope*, 97. Pieper is closely following Aquinas here, seeing existence as a good.

terminus of nothingness faced by human beings is not a *fait accompli*, but a threat. Human beings do not simple cease to be; they proceed towards an end, which comes to an end for them.[28]

The Pieperian commentator Bernard Schumacher has explained this point in the following manner:

> The human being begins at a precise moment in the unfolding of time, in which he has been projected, and advances toward the future by virtue of a "natural" striving toward the actualization of his project for being.... He is not capable of avoiding the dynamic, temporal ontology of *not-yet-being* that directs him toward the future in which he hopes to attain the fullness of possible being.[29]

It is of the nature of human being that we have the project of our lives to pursue precisely as a project for life. Both a determinate and an indeterminate principle, therefore, mark the *status viatoris* of human being. We are ordered towards fulfilling that which we are, yet we are free not to attain this goal. Therefore, it is our human nature that is determined, although it is not historically conditioned, because it is the nature that we have; while it is our existence, which remains undetermined while it is being lived out, that is historically conditioned, because it is the having of the nature that we have. The actual condition under which the project of one's life unfolds is both necessary and sufficient for the actual living out of the project of that life.

To see this relationship in terms of an earlier insight, the *telos* of human being is intrinsic to the *genesis* of human being; being human is necessarily a factor of both origin and end. What the "not yet" of human life adds is a way of saying that the historical condition under which the concrete, individual human being lives his life is bound up with—and is inseparable from—the nature of his life as a human being. Thus, human beings do not so much have a human nature by which they can then live their lives; rather, human beings go about living their lives by having the natures that they have in the condition under which they have it. That is to say, being human is the projecting of the project of human being, and nothing else.

---

28. Pieper, *Death and Immortality*, 88.

29. Schumacher, *A Philosophy of Hope*, from the French, *Une philosophie de l'espérance*, 41.

To think through this insight in terms of the lives of the profoundly impaired, the idea is that the condition under which they exist and live their lives is integral to their own project of human being. This would mean that their claim to being human is contingent upon nothing else other than their being in existence in the condition under which they find themselves. The human essence of the profoundly impaired does not exist hidden behind or underneath or beyond their human condition; it exists as the very condition under which they live. They are, quite uncomplicatedly, ordinary human beings. It is by virtue of the human nature that they have, in the condition that they have it, that they go about winning the project of their lives.

There is nothing more or less, or different, going on here; each and every human being has the nature that he has in the condition under which he has it so as to win the project of his life. There is no change in the relationship between essence and existence for human beings depending on the condition under which each individual lives. Of course, important questions remain about how the profoundly impaired actually go about doing this, especially when they do not have at their disposal the facilities of agency. The ongoing puzzlement thrown up by a life lived at the extremes is not thereby annulled. That being said, the point of the claim that the profoundly impaired win their humanity precisely in the condition under which they live, and not despite it, ought not to be lost: they go about being human in the thoroughly ordinary way in which human beings go about being human. We are each created—impaired and unimpaired alike—to pursue the project of the life uniquely peculiar to each of us in the one human way in which we have been created.

With this insight we have reached a point where we can claim agreement with Reinders' first principal assertion: that human beings with profound intellectual disabilities are people like other people. However, we certainly have not come to this point by employing arguments in support of his other principal assertion: that the best way to understand human beings is not to be found in the human faculties. To the contrary, we have reached this point by affirming the very reality about the profoundly impaired that Reinders sets aside as distinguishing and diminishing them from all other human beings, namely, that their puzzling condition is intrinsic to and essential for the winning of their humanity because it is the only condition under which they can have the human nature that they have. Neither have we reached the end of the argument as such, as the primary question remains: How do the profoundly impaired have their humanity? All that has been resolved is that this question cannot be answered by seeking to overcome or transcend the distinguishing condition under which the profoundly impaired exist *vis-à-vis* all other human beings. (Although, this is not to say that the puzzle of their lack of agency is insignificant.) We are now faced with asking the question in terms of the distinctive way in which the profoundly impaired have the lives that they have. This distinctiveness is to be found in the condition of being human under the condition of being impaired.

The Creature Who Hopes

As we have seen, gain and loss, but especially loss, are the constants of being a *viator*, a pilgrim; it is the lot in life of all who live in a state of becoming and with the threat of oblivion. The distinctive value of being human is recognizable by the way in which human beings are ordered towards fulfilling that which they are by nature, and yet they are free not to attain this end. Therefore, the gain that human beings have by virtue of this teleological ordering is hard-wired, so to speak, into the nature of human being; it is not something that supervenes on our nature or transcends our nature (both of which suggest forms of dualism), but is the mode in which we are our nature. Consequently (and this is both logically and chronologically the case), the possibility of existential loss—the submitting of one's life to the chasm of nothingness—is a threat to our nature, to our essential being.

Significantly, however, gain and loss do not operate as matched opposites in the lives of human beings. "Gain" applies to being human generically; the goodness to which the notion points applies only because of the provisional nature of human beings. Hence, we may say that there is nothing to gain as such in being human, because the gain is already a feature of our nature. "Loss," on the other hand, can only apply to individual human beings; there is nothing generic about it at all. "Man cannot actually annihilate himself," to recall the words of Clément. This is not to say that the sum of humanity cannot experience loss: we may correctly say that the entire human family suffered as a result of the Second World War. Rather, it is to say that the nature of human being is not in question when human loss is in play.

In saying this, we may note an intriguing reversal of fortunes emerging here: it is the unimpaired, those who are most consciously able to take up the project of their lives, who are suddenly in the precarious position *qua* their humanity. This is because it is they, and not the profoundly impaired, who can be more active in the bringing about of loss in their lives. The profoundly impaired, precisely because of the condition under which they have their lives, are vastly less threatened by the possibility of nothingness. "Gain" applies to being human; "loss" applies to one human being at a time.

It ought to be said that such a conclusion stands or falls on the veracity of the presupposition that God does not intend the annihilation of that which he creates as "very good" (cf. Gen 1:31). Consequently, it is not affected by the doctrine of a corrupted, fallen humanity. This doctrine holds that human beings are completely and utterly incapable of attaining the fulfilment or completion of their created nature without the grace of God. As has been already argued, this grace, which is nothing other than the redeeming form of *creatio*, is presumed in the act of creating. In other words, gain is built into created human nature; and its loss is self inflicted. The *status viatoris* of the human condition hangs, in fact, on the reality of fallen humanity; otherwise there could be nothing to aim for in being human, and nothing to lose. Note also that this argument is not dependent on any particular understanding of the nature of fallen humanity; the perennial theological debate over the extent to which fallen humanity is corrupted does not change the argument that God's redeeming grace is a form of his creating grace, and that it is the nature of the created human being that God saves. It does, however, remind us that human nature is in a substantial relation to God, and this is where the relational aspect must come to the fore so that the doctrine of justification may be preserved.

With this distinction in mind, perhaps the term "gain" is not the best antonym for the term "loss," given that only individual human beings can lose the kind of valued life that being human is by virtue of created human nature. We do not make our own lives, but we can lose our own individual lives. This is what makes loss the especially significant constant for human beings on their pilgrimage through life. It is under the possibility of losing one's personal life—the self-generated threat of personal oblivion—that the value of human life is especially revealed.

What is it that will cause this loss? It cannot be the condition under which I am living my life because this is not strictly mine, but that which is given to me. The only thing that I have to lose that is properly mine is my subjective projection of the objective human project. The distinction made earlier between "human dignity" and "dignity" is apposite: the former is something I have regardless of how I live, while the latter is something I can lose because of how I live. All human beings are created to succeed in the project of their humanity, but some fail in the taking up of the task. The true site for the loss of our humanity, therefore, is not something that is "of the kind" but something that is "of the instance."

This, in turn, makes the *status viatoris*, in its positive expression, the existential state of "aiming for" that pertains to being human, but which is played out in the life of each individual human being. In the Christian tradition, "hope" is the word that captures *par excellence* this personal experiencing of that which is being aimed for, while still on the way. Thus, for the kind of creature who is a pilgrim, the proper antonym for "loss" is not "gain," but "hope." Hope is the remedy for the loss of humanity. As Pieper has remarked, "The only answer that corresponds to man's actual existential situation is hope. . . . In the virtue of hope more than in any other, man understands and affirms that he is a creature, that he has been created by God."[30]

To say that hope is the remedy for the loss of humanity is to indicate something distinctive about what it means to hope for the kind of creature who hopes. Hoping not only communicates something about the concept of hope itself, but more importantly it points to the difference that hope makes for being human. Hope, in other words, is not just a concept that is informative about the nature of human beings; more to the point, it is performative for the living of a human life.[31] Hoping makes a difference for the creature created to hope. Recognizing that hope is remedial, therefore, has more to do with responding to the question of how hope is experienced than with answering the question of what hope is in itself, because it is via the former question that our attention is directed towards the meaning that hoping has for living a human life.

A relatively uncontroversial response to the latter question may be quickly sketched in the following terms: a theory of hope will locate hope in terms of desire and virtue, and it will emphasize its more volitional, rather than rational character; theologically, hope will be spoken of in terms of faith and grace, while noting its promissory thrust. (Of course, the whys and wherefores of each of these elements have been, and always

---

30. Pieper, *On Hope*, 98.

31. Pope Benedict XVI has drawn renewed attention to how hope can be understood in both "performative" and "informative" ways. He, too, emphasizes the performative dimension. Benedict XVI, Enclyclical letter on Christian hope, *Spe Salvi*, §2 & §4.

will be fiercely debated. The point, however, is that no well-developed account of hope would deny them a significant schematic place.) Yet such a response does not, by itself, indicate much about hope's distinctiveness for the human being, in the context of the living of his or her creaturely life. For our purposes, then, the more interesting question to ask of hope is a heuristic one: What might be revealed about human beings, those distinctive creatures who have the nature that they have in the condition under which it is had, by asking what hoping means for them as creatures who hope?

Pieper sums up the way in which hoping functions in the life of the one who hopes in the following manner:

> Hope, like love, is one of the very simple, primordial dispositions of the living person. In hope, man reaches "with restless heart," with confidence and patient expectation, toward the *bonum arduum futurum*, toward the arduous "not yet" of fulfilment, whether natural or supernatural.[32]

Pieper is closely following Aquinas here, who is to be credited above all with working out the principal structural elements to the theology of hope that has come down through the Christian tradition to the present day.[33] Aquinas' basic, fourfold structure to hope remains essentially sound: "Hope is concerned with a future and difficult good, but one, nevertheless, that remains possible" (*ST* II.II.17.7.*resp*). The act of hoping involves a movement of "reaching out" towards that which is hoped for (*ST* II.II.17.1.*resp*). What is particularly distinctive about this reaching out is the way in which it grounds hope in the *status viatoris*: the objective possibility towards which the very nature of hope is ordered entails a subject who cannot be other than *en route*.[34] The one who is created to hope,

---

32. Pieper, *On Hope*, 100.

33. Kerstiens, "Hope," in *Sacramentum Mundi*, 3:61–65. Unlike Catholicism, the Protestant tradition seems not to have concerned itself with proposing a distinct, stand-alone theology of hope as such, but sought instead to correct, in the light of biblical faith and eschatology, certain perceived philosophical emphases coming from Catholic Scholasticism. See Stock, "Hope: 2. Theology and Ethics," in Bromiley, *Encyclopedia of Christianity*, 2:595. Besides Pieper, the names who have had a major influence on the contemporary debate include Han Urs von Balthasar and Johann Baptist Metz (Catholic), and Jürgen Moltmann and Wolfhart Pannenberg (Protestant), but none of these has sought to overturn the basic insights of Aquinas. Cf. Lacoste, "Hope," in *Encyclopedia of Christian Theology*, 2:734–39; and Noll, "Hope, Theology of," in Elwell, *Evangelical Dictionary of Theology*, 532–34.

34. In picking up the notion of "being on the way," Aquinas points to the unique

by hoping, is directed towards a future, a "not yet," where the hoped-for outcome presents itself in the form of a looked-for good.

We may fairly invoke St. Paul in support of this last point. He has this to say about the one who hopes in his Letter to the Romans: "For by hope we were saved. Now hope that is seen is not hope. For who hopes for what is seen? But if we hope for what we do not see, we wait for it with patience" (Rom 8:24–25).[35] Clearly, Paul is approaching hope from the perspective of faith. However, this does not preclude recognizing the more anthropological aspect of his insight, as it emerges from the visual metaphor he employs. First, we can readily note in Paul's words the presence of the fourfold structure of hope, either specified (future, difficult) or implied (good, possible). Secondly, hoping is here characterized in terms of a response to that which is unseen, and not as some sort of attaining of knowledge about it, thereby revealing how hope is best located within an ethical, rather than epistemological framework.[36] Most noteworthy for our purposes is the fact that Paul writes these words about hoping in the very same context in which he highlights the way in which redemption is related to creation, as was discussed previously. Then, it was the continuity in the movement from creation to redemption that was especially noteworthy. It would be reasonable, therefore, given the placement of the words we are presently considering, to expect to find the same sense of continuity when it comes to the relationship between hoping and the one who hopes. This is precisely what we do find, for St. Paul goes on to say, "For those whom [God] foreknew he also predestined to be conformed to the image of his Son" (Rom 8:29).

Significantly, this path of continuity evident in the one who hopes is at the level of human nature. The nature that is already given to us (foreknown and predestined) is the nature that is still to come for us (to be conformed), namely: being "in the image of the Son." Hope takes its place in this schema as the apprehension of that which was foreseen yet remains unseen, as that which is looked for. Hope, in this Pauline sense, "sees" that which remains "not yet" as being the "looked-for" good. What

---

way in which Christ is simultaneously both a *comprehensor* and a *viator*, as well as highlighting the sense in which hope is properly a theological virtue when the hoped-for good is God. See, for example, *ST* II.II.18.2.ad1.

35. Aquinas picks up this Pauline insight on hope in *ST* II.II.18.2.*sed contra*.

36. The Dominican, William Hill, notes this insight in his commentary on Aquinas' approach to the Pauline theology of hope. See Hill, "Appendix I: The Revelation of Hope in Sacred Scripture," 126.

this suggests is that hope is an immanent reality for human beings that directs our origin towards our end, in terms of the good that human beings have by existing "in God." Hope is "a sure and steadfast anchor of the soul," as the author of the Letter to the Hebrews puts it, "that enters the inner shrine behind the curtain" (Heb 6:19). In other words, hope posits a real continuity between the present and future nature of human beings, and does so in terms of the human subject.

In this way, hoping is not only indicative of someone's human nature, but it is the signalling to him that he is having it aright. Pieper puts it this way:

> Hope says: It will turn out well; or more accurately and characteristically: It will turn out well for mankind; or even more characteristically: It will turn out well for us, for me myself.[37]

Hoping is the reaching out for that towards which one is *en route* by nature. So, for hoping to be "hope" one must be "on the way," a pilgrim; and to be someone of that kind is to be someone who hopes. Hoping, therefore, is intrinsic to the nature of the *viator*, to that being who is required to go about having the nature that it has in order to be that nature.

This continuity sense of "in order" is precisely the point that the French Dominican, Louis-Bertrand Geiger, was stressing when he wrote: "The human being was created or produced *in order* to be the image of God."[38] Significantly for us, we may note the way Geiger identifies the hoped-for good with the *imago Dei* (picking up Paul's own identification of human nature with the *imago Christi*). The "in order" of Geiger is not to be read as pointing to some entirely future, essentially extrinsic and utterly different state that a human being is yet to receive as his or her (new) nature. Rather, it is the one who is not yet, by nature, who is the one who is reaching out in order to be(come) that nature he is destined to be. As Geiger says,

> If the words "end" or "destiny" are to have any meaning, it is necessary to say that the human being was created, and is thus ultimately wanted and conceived [of] by his Creator, not to be a

---

37. Pieper, *On Hope*, 114.

38. Geiger, "L'homme, image de Dieu," 515. In the original French: "L'être humain a été créé ou produit *pour* être à l'image de Dieu." Geiger was at the center of the twentieth-century Dominican revival in Thomism.

thinking substance, for example, or a reasonable animal, but *in order to be* in his image.[39]

To hope is nothing more (or less) than to be living the life of a wayfarer or pilgrim; and Man is the quintessential pilgrim, the *viator*. Therefore, it is the living human being—the one who is having the nature that he has in the condition under which it is being had in order to be(come) the nature that he is—who hopes.

These brief remarks on hope have the benefit of opening up a new perspective on a lingering question mark about the "not yet" of human life. It has been argued that the "not yet" nature of a human being orients the living of his life towards that which is good for him. We have not learned from this, however, the nature of the good to which he is oriented, other than to have said that it is "in God." So, the question arises: What is the content of this "not yet," and how is it known to human beings, the creatures who have it? Saint Paul solves this question by proposing that there is an "is to be," which qualifies the "not yet," and it is by hoping that this is visualized for human beings. This "is to be" is identified by Paul as the *imago Christi*, the good that the human pilgrim already has, and is to have by conforming to it. The nature of human beings has already been made in *imago Christi*, in order that this nature may be(come) made into the *imago Christi* by the living of one's life. It is the *imago Christi*—or more simply, the *imago Dei*—that hope reaches out towards; it is the unseen, but not unknown, good of being human. We may immediately add, however, that all St. Paul is offering, in identifying the *imago Dei* as the good towards which human beings are to orient their lives in hope, is an affirmation of his experience of hope in terms of the *imago Dei*. He does not thereby provide a theological framework to support this affirmation.

We have, however, completed a significant anthropological circle, moving from the doctrine of the *imago Dei*, to the creaturely human, through the pilgrim creature that hopes, and back to the *imago Dei*. In doing so we have uncovered the presence of two major structural factors in being human. First, being human is necessarily grounded in an immanent human nature: it is about having the nature that one has in the condition under which one has it. This is the stuff of the human project. Secondly, the nature that one has in being human itself exhibits

39. Ibid., 515-16. In the French original: "Si les mots de fin ou de terme ont un sens, il faut dire que l'être humain est, a été créé, et donc voulu et conçu finalement par son Créateur, non pour être une substance pensante, par exemple, ou un animal raisonnable, mais pour être à son image."

continuity and directionality: it is about being the creature who lives out his nature from origin to end. This is the individual projecting of the human project. With these insights in mind, we may now return more fully to the question of the *imago Dei* and whether or not it may inform our understanding of the humanity of the profoundly impaired.

7

IMAGO DEI

"The Nature That We Have"

The Structural Familiarity between the *status viatoris* and the *imago Dei*

IN A FOOTNOTE TO a discussion of the way in which Josef Pieper grounds human hope in the *status viatoris* of human beings, Schumacher briefly proposes the notion that human hope is structurally related to the doctrine that man, in his nature, is made in the image of God. As Schumacher says,

> This orientation of the human being toward full realization can also be inserted into the framework of the theological affirmation that defines the human being as having been created in the image of God, an affirmation that constitutes the heart of Thomistic moral theology.... Although the human being was created in the image of God, one nevertheless must actualize this image over the course of one's life, in order that it may shine forth in all its fullness.... Such an anthropological conception implies an ontology of becoming, of *not-yet-being*, of the *status viatoris*: the human being is not yet perfectly that which he is in the depths of his being, but he has to become it, he has to fulfil the nature he has received.... Every creature that aims to realize itself thereby strives in an intrinsic way to resemble God.[1]

---

1. Schumacher, *Philosophy of Hope*, 60n131.

The footnote is intriguing, both for the claim being made: that being a pilgrim creature is structurally identifiable with being in the image of God, and for what is alluded to in the making of it: the features of being *en route* towards a looked-for good that is possible to attain because it is somehow already present intrinsically. The theologically charged notion of the *imago Dei* both grounds human life, and gives expression to it, in the structural terms of hope. We can note immediately that the second sentence in the quotation is doing most of the work: human beings are created as images of God to be in the image of God; they are already, by virtue of the nature they have, what they are to be, by virtue of their living. This is another way of saying: human beings are the kind of creatures who have the nature that they have. What Schumacher adds is the reason for human beings to go about having this nature, which is simultaneously the looked-for good for which they are *en route* in hope—namely, because their nature is in the image of God.

The use of the word "actualize" in this sentence is especially significant: it functions in an existential mode, and not an essential one. Nothing other than existing—no capacity for human agency, for example, nor a future-expected additional quality or property—is required for this actualization to occur. Being a living human being is all that matters. We may add that this is remarkably close to Geiger's insight, where the only operative factors are: creator, creature, existing. To live—to be a living human being—is all that is needed in order to become the image of God that, of our nature, we are to be.

Schumacher is quite clear about the direction of fit when it comes to the association of a theology of hope with the doctrine of the *imago Dei*: the former inserts itself (to use his language) into the structure of the latter. Presumably, the reverse—*imago Dei* into hope—is not the case. Human beings have their nature in the image of God, then to be had—lived—accordingly. Hope manifests itself structurally as the proper ordering—the actual living—of this way of being human. The rightness of this direction of fit is evident in the lives of the profoundly impaired. Given how deeply puzzling are the lives of those living at the extremes of human life, a dangerous temptation may present itself (say, out of a pastoral concern for their dignity) to ensure their human status by looking for a solution within the theological structure of hope. The temptation is this: to go in search of a fully-blown eschatological grounding to their humanity, which may be expressed in the following manner: *Given the condition of their nature, how can the profoundly impaired be "in the image of God" as things currently stand for them? Let us secure their humanity, therefore, in that state of human life that is to be ours in that yet-to-be promissory future looked for by all human beings. Let us make hope not only the revelation of a well-ordered human life but the very basis for it.*

We should note what this will do to the present circumstances of the profoundly impaired: it will make their humanity entirely promissory and the actual living out of their lives would have no value or purpose. Nothing would be brought about by the living of the natures that they have now because all that it means for them to be human has been postponed into the future. At its base, the temptation is a particularly insidious form of ascription: it renders the living of the lives of the profoundly impaired, in the condition under which they are having their lives, entirely redundant because the condition under which they are having their lives is not the condition under which they are having a human life. That condition is permanently deferred until their nature has been transformed into that which they are not at present.

This kind of thinking is really about metamorphosis, about becoming a different thing altogether from that which is presently the case, and not about hope, about orienting that which is already the case towards its looked-for end. To pursue the temptation of seeing the lives of the profoundly impaired in entirely eschatological terms—*so that they may have hope as the basis of their humanity*—will only have the effect of marking them out as different from human beings. They are no longer *viators*, on-the-way human beings, but *metamorphs*, waiting-to-be-human beings. For the profoundly impaired, under this temptation, ceasing to exist becomes their looked-for good because it is the only way they can become that which they are presently not. By implication, their only claim to humanity, in the circumstances under which they presently live, would be for them to be deemed to be so as something extended to them, say, by an act of charity. The outcome of taking the eschatological path for those living at the extremes of human life is to remove from them that which they have already by virtue of their living.

We have already seen how hope points the way for the human pilgrim in the working out of his own nature towards his looked-for good. As Cessario remarks: "Hope serves the state of the wayfarer."[2] To add to this the claim that the structure of the *status viatoris* inserts itself into the structure of the *imago Dei* implies that the looked-for good of hope

---

2. Cessario, *Theological Virtue of Hope*, 239.

is, in fact, the *imago Dei* itself, and it is by virtue of this relationship that human beings are the creatures that they are. To be the kind of creature who is on the way is to be the kind of creature who is in the image of God. Yet, while we may hold that the *status viatoris* and the *imago Dei* share a structural kinship in hope, they are not synonymous; they are not simply different terms for the same thing in human beings. It is the direction of fit which makes this evident: to be the creature who is a wayfarer is to be, by nature, in the image of God, but being in the image of God does not entail being a creature who is, by nature, *en route* in hope. What, then, is to be made of this relationship between the *status viatoris* and the *imago Dei* in human beings? For as it is now emerging, it is this particular relationship that is pressing hard on the question of how human beings have the nature that they have.

Getting the Question of the *imago Dei* Right

To this end, we may take the direction of fit evident in the relationship itself as suggestive of a way of framing the question at hand. The suggestion is to make being human our point of departure in revealing aspects of the image of the nature that human beings have. The direction of fit from *status viatoris* to *imago Dei* provokes a specific question about the relationship between them: What does being human tell us about being in the image of God? The very posing of this question raises an immediate concern: it looks as if it seeks to turn on its head the expected direction in which the question of the *imago Dei* would be broached. Is there not a taint of incipient anthropocentrism about the question, and a loss of a properly theological focus? Given the scriptural thrust of Gen 1:26–27, surely the question ought to be: What does being in the image of God tell us about the nature of being human? The question being posed here, however, is not meant to be a rejection of either the divine-to-human order, in which human beings are of God, or the divine-to-human priority, in which human beings are in God. This is not, in other words, a question that departs from the orthodoxy of human beings being made in—or "after," as Aquinas stresses—the image of God.[3] On the contrary,

---

3. *ST* I.93.1.*resp*.2. Aquinas expresses the difference as follows: *Homo vero et proper similitudinem dicitur 'imago', et propter imperfectionem similitudinis dicitur 'ad imaginem'*. If "ad" is to be translated as "to," then it is to be read in the sense of measurement, as in the sentence: ". . . made *to* the specifications of . . ." It is the reference to man's imperfect image that is most helpful about Aquinas' point: it may fairly be read as

to say that human beings are after the image of God is precisely to hold that the image of God is in human beings. The whole argument centered on the creaturely life of human beings would be undermined if we were to depart from the presupposition that the human creature follows, in all ways, after the image of his creator.

To suggest that human beings are in and after the image of God is to suggest something about human beings that has "stubbornly resisted reduction or elimination" from any theological account of them, despite Reinders' attempt.[4] It should not be surprising, therefore, that others working in the area of disability theology have taken up the question of the value of the relationship between the *imago Dei* and profound disablement. While Reinders' assessment of the relationship is, by and large, a negative one, two theologians in particular have taken a far more positive stance. Amos Yong (in 2007) and Thomas Reynolds (in 2008) published substantial works in which they take the doctrine of the *imago Dei* to be foundational of their respective theological anthropologies, as seen from the perspective of significant intellectual disablement.[5] For both, the *imago Dei* makes an essential and positive contribution to understanding the humanity of the intellectually disabled. Yong and Reynolds place the creaturely life of human beings at the theological center of their thinking. Their accounts of the relationship between being human and being in the image of God are of interest to us, and on the face of it ought to be of help as well. We must ask whether this is indeed the case. It will be useful to

---

highlighting the way in which human beings have their nature "in hope." The imperfect image rightly belongs to the "not yet" creature who is "on the way" towards his looked-for good.

4. Moreland, *Recalcitrant Imago Dei*, 5. Moreland considers the notion of the *imago Dei* in relation to human beings to be a "recalcitrant fact" about the nature of human beings (ibid., 4).

5. I will be using the phraseology "intellectual disablement/disability" in the context of Yong and Reynolds because both of them are primarily interested in those who are significantly cognitively disabled but not to the extent of the profound and complex cognitive impairment that has been our primary focus. This distinction is of some importance as neither Yong nor Reynolds seems to question the very humanity of the intellectually disabled, only their subsequent moral and pastoral status. Interestingly (and as is a common element amongst most "disability theologians"), both authors are motivated in their theologizing by personal experience: Yong's brother has Down syndrome, while Reynolds' son has a multi-faceted disablement. Both undertake their theologizing from within an overarching pastoral, and not anthropological, concern.

take some time to consider their respective accounts to see what may be learned from them. Let us begin with Yong.

Yong characterizes his theological position as an epistemic posture with regard to the biblical narrative and Christian experience of the Holy Spirit—what he calls a pneumatological imagination—that "opens up space for the possibility of a dialogue with experiences of disability."[6] This methodology is specifically for "the purposes of (re)shaping the Christian imagination and for (re)ordering ecclesial practices" for the benefit of the lives of the intellectually disabled.[7] Key here is the story of Pentecost and the "many tongues" of the Holy Spirit, which, Yong claims, speak to the theological significance of diversity, variety, difference, and otherness for human beings in their commonly shared relationship in God. Consequently, the "many tongues" of the various experiential discourses—personal, professional, pastoral, scientific, medical—may be combined to shape an "emancipatory witness of the Church" to the lives of intellectually disabled.[8] Taking account of such contemporary experiences of disability is crucial to the development of his overall project. (More than half the book—the first two parts of three—is taken up with what these various discourses contribute to the picture, before the theological work is commenced.) Two particular questions will be asked of this theological structure: how are the intellectually disabled to be understood within the doctrines of creation and providence; and how is the doctrine of the *imago Dei* to be understood in the light of the experience of such disability in the modern world. The answering of these questions, says Yong, will provide resources for "understanding the human image of God as embodied, interdependent, and relational."[9]

When Yong takes up the specifically anthropological aspects of his argument (as distinct from ecclesiological, soteriological and eschatological dimensions), he begins with a brief consideration of the doctrines of creation, providence, and the Fall, especially asking how the contemporary experience of disability might inform a response to the question posed by the presence of evil in the world.[10] For our purposes, the key issue to arise from Yong's thoughts in this regard is the way in which

6. Yong, *Theology and Down Syndrome*, 11.
7. Ibid., 13.
8. Ibid., 14.
9. Ibid., 16.
10. Ibid., 157–65.

he seeks to account for disability without resorting to paradigms of impairment, deformation, and suffering. Disability ought not to be placed within the framework of deviation from the substantial norm of human nature but as an integral feature of the variety and difference in human beings as a consequence of the unfolding of creation over time. He points to the genetic variations in the human species over time—his example is the emergence of the chromosomal mutation, Trisomy 21, associated with Down Syndrome—as evidence not of a necessary deviation (because of sin) present in the intellectually disabled, but of a possible catalyst for human variety (because of providence).[11] Yong claims that such a move accomplishes two things:

> it locates sin, death, and judgement in human dispositions, affections, and actions rather than in *ha adam*'s singular headship or in human biology; and it accentuates Christ's redemption of all sinners, nondisabled and disabled alike.[12]

Leaving aside the christological aspect, at first blush this may appear to be a promising way of overcoming the marginalization of the intellectually disabled from the human community. Certainly, this is Yong's intention. It suggests, as we have argued, that the condition of those who are disabled is not determinative of their nature, but that the quality of one's humanity is a feature of what is there to be lost in the living—"dispositions, affections, and actions"—of one's human nature. The implication, it would appear, is that the embodied reality of the intellectually disabled is central to their humanity, and this is certainly something we have also argued for. However, this appearance is misplaced because of the way in which he goes on to argue for the claim by locating the *imago Dei* in human beings within a theology of human emergence. To anticipate the problem, Yong's understanding of the *imago Dei* ends up advocating a capacity-based understanding of human nature, thereby falling foul of the Reindersian critique.

Before seeing how this undermines Yong's apparently helpful suggestion, we may note an initial logical problem with the claim itself. If the condition under which the intellectually disabled exist (e.g., the chromosomal condition of Trisomy 21) is not to be taken as a deviation or

---

11. Ibid., 164. Presumably, the catalytic possibility pertains to some good, which is to come about in the future, that God has always planned for the human species, though Yong does not say this.

12. Ibid., 165.

deformation of the human nature, but as a possible catalyst for a future human nature, then the implication is that any variation in the condition of a human being has the possibility of being the catalyst for a future nature of human beings. What we end up with, therefore, is not a variety of conditions under which human beings live, but a multiplication of possible human natures, resulting in the possibility of a variety of human species existing at any one period of time, yet all presumably claiming the kinship of *homo sapiens*.

Yong approaches the theological account of being human in terms of two questions: What constitutes the image of God? and What defines human nature (what does it "consist[s] of").[13] This approach is very much about the "What is it?" question and not the "How is it?" one. We may also note that Yong favorably acknowledges the contribution made in response to these questions from within a broadly Aristotelian-Thomistic framework, although he does not then develop his own position in light of this tradition.[14] What makes these two *notae* significant may be seen in the following quotation outlining Yong's own stance.

> I prefer to explore the possibility of rethinking what it means to be human in dialogue with more recent views that suggest the soul as an emergent set of distinctive features and capacities constituted by but irreducible to the sum of the body's biological parts.... [E]mergence is a theory of how mental (cognitional) properties—including morality, consciousness and self-consciousness, and aesthetic creativity—are dependent on but not fully explicable by physical (brain) properties.[15]

Yong's stated purpose in adopting this emergentist approach to human nature is to overcome any soul/body dualist tendencies; hence, his affinity with Aquinas. He wants to make sure the human body is integral to his account of the human being. It is not difficult to see where he wants to go in adopting this approach: the human being—man—cannot be reduced to a set of capacities or properties residing in a soul or mind of the

---

13. Ibid., 169-70.

14. Ibid., 170 (in terms of the "human nature" question); 172 (in terms of the "*imago Dei*" question).

15. Ibid., 170. Yong lists his "Christian philosophical" and theological sources for a theory of emergentism in a footnote (322n27), noting along the way his reason for drawing on them: "All these positions hold in common the idea that human minds (or souls) are dependent on the material body in some respect without lapsing into a purely naturalistic or materialistic ontology of human persons."

human nature. To take that path would be to exclude the intellectually disabled from the realm of humanity because of what they lack:

> Severe and even profound intellectual disability cannot be used as the sole measure of determining the personhood and intrinsic value of such individuals. . . . [T]he human person must be understood to be at least embodied, even if one's spiritual capacities are less manifest phenomenologically.[16]

It is the use of the phrase "sole measure" that is particularly noteworthy here, as it lays stress on what the intellectually disabled lack. Yong is looking for some other measure(s) of humanity, other than rationality (or the lack thereof). To this end, "human being" is taken to be something that emerges from various "webs of significance" on human nature.[17] He names in this regard biological, social, political, economic, geographic and transcendental approaches to human nature. In other words, human beings emerge from, though are not reducible to, what may be ascertained about human nature from these various spheres of influence. Yong's approach to being human, therefore, is essentialist in character; it is dependent on a qualitative measuring of human nature as the basis for defining human being. While he does not want to reduce being human to any particular quality or set of qualities that emerge from the so-called webs of significance—and in this sense we may say his approach is more about coherence with than correspondence to—who gets to claim to be a human being is dependent on the emergence of these qualities of human nature, nonetheless. Of course, it may be asked: Is this a problem in itself? The manner in which Yong then broaches the *imago Dei* will help to see why this is, indeed, a problem.

Yong begins by naming, and immediately rejecting, two basic ways of understanding what constitutes the *imago Dei*: a substantial or structural view that understands the image of God as "an inherent human capacity that reflects the character or attributes of God," and a functional view that says it "consists not in what human beings are but in what we do."[18] His reason for rejecting them is the same for both: they propose a capacity-based understanding of human beings, the former in terms of rationality and the latter in terms of agency or "dominion." Over and against these two approaches, Yong proposes instead a relational view,

16. Ibid., 171.
17. Ibid., 172.
18. Ibid., 172, 173.

whereby the *imago Dei* consists in "their [human beings'] relationship with God, their interrelationality with other persons, and their embodied interdependence with the world."[19] This is the approach said to be in line with his emergentist anthropology.

Yong initially adopts Eiesland's disabled God metaphor, and adds to it Christ's *kenosis* on the cross, to suggest the ways in which the *imago Dei* takes on a christological form in relation to a theology of disability.[20] Strikingly, this christological turn is then applied only to the physically disabled. The intellectually disabled specifically are instead brought into the ambit of the *imago Dei* through a different notion, that of embodiment. Yong seems to do this so as to avoid the idea of God, in Christ, as retarded, on the one hand; and, on the other, to suggest that a positive account of bodily difference is better suited to the intellectually disabled. As he notes,

> a disability theology of embodiment is much better able to appreciate, account for, and nurture created particularity, uniqueness, and difference . . . [and] we need a theology of creation and a correlating theological anthropology that accentuates difference.[21]

It is with this turn to a theology of embodiment that Yong's pneumatological imagination and his adoption of emergentism come together as the required theology of creation and correlative theological anthropology. It is the Holy Spirit "[who] creatively enables and empowers our full humanity in relationship to ourselves, others, and God, even in the most ambiguous of situations."[22] This is where "God revels in plurality and difference" and where the Holy Spirit is seen "not as the power to rescue and repair according to some presupposed 'original state' or ideal form, but as the energy for unleashing multiple forms of corporal flourishing."[23] It is in a theological accentuation of difference that the bodily life of the intellectually disabled is seen as providing the qualitative difference for the emergence of the human spirit or soul. Yong's conclusion is that "the *imago Dei* can never be a single attribute, but requires multiple lenses to identify, behold, and appreciate," thereby providing a space in which "a

19. Ibid., 174.
20. Ibid., 174–80.
21. Ibid., 181.
22. Ibid.
23. Ibid.

recognition of the diversity of forms of human embodiment" will lead to an acknowledgment that "the intellectually disabled are no less fully human precisely because of their embodiment."[24]

Two related issues stand out in Yong's approach to the *imago Dei*. First, it is the concept itself that he focuses on. His intention, to be sure, is to draw from it christological, pneumalogical, and trinitarian insights that might then be applied to human beings (presumably analogously). In this regard, the notion of a God who "revels in plurality and difference," yet who is a relational unity is significant. The implication of this focus is that "*imago Dei*" becomes something like a collective term for a set of attributes by which "human being" is defined. As a result, the so-called emergent human spirit, the only term by which Yong distinguishes a creature as a human being as such, is reductively constituted, and in two ways: it is made conditional upon some combination of *imago Dei* attributes emerging from amongst the potential set that are identified with God, and it becomes a hyper attribute itself, separate from but supervening on the lesser attributes.

Secondly, this conceptual approach to the *imago Dei* works only because it depends on a capacity-based account of it. We can see this in the following statement:

> So while the "spiritual antennae" [a term he uses for the experiential capacity to be in a relationship with God] of people who are profoundly disabled will lack a developed cognitive component, since the human soul is not reducible to cognition, other aspects of their embodiment will be activated by the relationships that sustain them.... [E]xperiential faith is not inferior to cognitively engaged forms of faith precisely because we exist in relationship with God as whole beings.[25]

Not only does Yong have here one attribute sufficient to replace another that is lacking, but he is also suggesting that it is an attribute that nonetheless makes the difference. It does not matter, in the end, if it is pre-emergent or emergent, subvenient or supervenient; it is an attribute, a property, a capacity that is determining whether or not a creature is a human being in the image of God. Lose the capacity, lose humanity. This is to say nothing of the deep dualism that is evident in the way Yong speaks of the human soul in relation to human cognition, a dualism that

---

24. Ibid., 182.
25. Ibid., 189.

is precisely the result of operating from within a capacity-based understanding of the *imago Dei*.

Finally, while we have identified various difficulties in Yong's theological anthropology of the *imago Dei* from within the argument itself, something ought to be said about his adoption of emergentism as a theological tool. The rise of phenomenology as a methodological tool has taught the value of coming to understand the meaning of being human as it emerges from the phenomena of human living. This is not, however, the kind of emergence Yong advocates. He employs emergence as an explanatory theory of upward causation, leading to the spiritual soul that is characteristic of human beings. Hence, "human souls are emergent from and constituted by human bodies and brains without being reducible to the sum of these biological parts."[26] To be sure, Yong supplements this epistemological theory with a theologically downward movement, whereby the Spirit of God is determinative of the content of this emergent being. Be that as it may, Yong's emergentism nonetheless commits him to an understanding of human being as a difference of degree, and not of kind. A human being, in this framework, is not an irreducibly complex and unique creature, but an especially well developed animal with certain supervening properties that are distinguishing.[27] The fundamental flaw in adapting any form of emergentist theory as a theological tool is that it seems unable to avoid accepting as a logical conclusion the notion that "human being" is simply the name given to whatever emerges at the end of a causal chain of creation. While Yong is to be applauded for seeking to show how various aspects of the living out of human nature combine to build a picture of the human being as being in the image of God, and where no one attribute is trumps, this is undermined by his advocacy of emergence theory as the tool by which he does this.

As with Yong, Thomas Reynolds' *imago Dei* facade appears, at first glance, to be beneficial. Upon a closer look this facade reveals a structural understanding of the *imago Dei* that also falls foul of a capacity-based critique, and in a much more straightforward way than with Yong. For this reason it will not be necessary to spend much time setting out Reynolds'

---

26. Ibid., 188.

27. There are any number of philosophers who have cogently argued against theories of emergence in terms of accounting for human being. We may note here John Haldane and J. P. Moreland, both of whom work within the Christian tradition. See Haldane, *Mystery of Emergence*, 261–67, and "Rational and Other Animals," in *Reasonable Faith*. See also Moreland, *Recalcitrant Imago Dei*, esp. chapters 1 and 2.

project; we may go straight to the issue at hand instead. In what might be thought of as a decisive marker in all the theological approaches to disability we have considered, the notion of relationship, as being constitutive of human being, looms large. For Reynolds, it is the constituting relationship of creator with creature, manifested in the relationship between creatures, which enables him to propose "vulnerability" as the characteristic feature of both God and human beings. Vulnerability is his defining metaphor for the way in which the disabled may be included, along with all other human beings, under the ambit of human dignity and moral participation. It is used to tell us something about the qualitative kind of relationship between God and his creatures. (We may note that he tells us nothing about how the relationship comes about.)

The relational grounding that is constitutive of being a human creature is what particularly matters here, because: "being in relationship to another attests to the fact that existence is trustworthy and good."[28] In other words, it is the relational existence of human beings which, for Reynolds, establishes the value of being human. The value of human life as such is established entirely by the coming into existence of human beings. We may note in this regard how Reynolds seems to be wanting to avoid any sense of an essentialist anthropology. The motivation for this stance is readily evident in the prevalence of what he calls the "cult of normalcy" in Western society, in which disability is viewed as a mark of "an incomplete humanity—a failure, defect, or sinful nature."[29] To hold that human beings are good simply because they exist-in-relationship, is to counter any notion of a graduating scale to humanity; there is no such thing as a "more or less human" human being. Reynolds then brings to this existentiality the notion of the *imago Dei* as precisely the relationality of human being (seen especially in the vulnerability of one to another): "The creatively relational and available character of human being is what it means to be whole, which is the *imago Dei*."[30] In this way, he is able to conclude,

> Human beings, then, are free persons neither because of a fixed trait embedded in their nature nor because of something they produce, but because of something they are: loved into being by God, created in the image of God as vulnerable beings open to

---

28. Reynolds, *Vulnerable Communion*, 140.

29. Ibid., 186. The notion of a "cult of normalcy" is the chief target of his project. See esp. chapter 2.

30. Ibid.

the possibility of love. All human beings are therefore precious and marked by dignity in relationships with others.[31]

This stance, of course, appears broadly in line with an existential approach to human nature, so it may be wondered what it is that is particularly problematic about it. The answer is to be found in the significance Reynolds places on the adjective "free," which may appear to occupy an innocuous place in the quotation. Consider this further statement by Reynolds:

> There is no trait determinable as the image of God and set against others. In fact, the *imago Dei* appears more as a cluster of loosely defined features than discernable traits like reason and freedom. . . . Perhaps, then, the *imago Dei* can best be seen as a form of creativity, relationality, and availability.[32]

The sense of these words seems to be one in which the various capacities that human beings may or may not have—naming reason and freedom as the key ones—are not to be taken as determinative of the *imago Dei* in human beings. The *imago Dei* is not a set of qualities that are then applied to a creature to make it human, but the way in which human beings exist (i.e., creatively, relationally, accessibly). There is an empowering that comes with being in God's image, but not a corresponding list of capacities.[33] Or so it seems to say. What raises a question mark is the confusion that arises when we juxtapose the "free person" (in the former quotation) with the "trait of freedom" (in the latter). To get a handle on the difference between these different uses of freedom, we may add a third quotation from Reynolds:

> Philosophers and theologians alike have used terms like "reason," "self-transcendence," "freedom," and "openness" to describe this irreducibility [of human experience]. It is what is often called the spiritual dimension to humanity. . . . [T]his quality is not itself a fixed trait or endowment but rather a "potentiality for being." Defined in the context of our discussion, "being" signifies the fullness of possibility for creativity and relationship. . . . Humans

---

31. Ibid.
32. Ibid., 178, 179.
33. The word "empowering," and various cognates of it, feature significantly in Reynolds' thinking about the relationality of human beings, especially as it is taken to relate to our creativity. Thus, for example: "As the creative power of God extends itself in relationship with others, so does the *imago Dei*. Creative power essentially is a relational power." Ibid., 180.

are thus capable of responsibility, which entails the freedom to self-consciously acknowledge and enter into relationships.[34]

Clearly, Reynolds wants to distinguish this "potentiality for being" (which is where he places the first use of freedom), from certain capacities or traits that human beings may or may not have (which is where the second use of "freedom" is placed). Rather than making a distinction of kind, we have rather a distinction of degree between the two freedoms. The first freedom is simply a pre-condition for the presence (or not) of the second. The final sentence in the third quotation is most telling in this regard. The "potentiality for being" is named precisely as a capacity, and that which is exactly of the kind that the profoundly impaired are not capable of having. In fact, what Reynolds does, in confusing the two freedoms, is to associate the first with human willing and the second with human reasoning, and then to suggest that willing is not a capacity, but a way of being. This is not, however, the case. The exercise of human agency is a factor of both reasoning and willing, and both are capacities someone may or may not have. Consequently, rather than an existential understanding of human beings in the image of God, Reynolds ends up unable to escape from an essentialist understanding. In the end, he says as much himself: "Our volitional self-transcendence is a capacity to love constituted fully in relationship to God. . . . As a capacity for love, the *imago Dei* is a capacity for God (*capax Dei*)."[35]

One final remark is in order with respect to Yong's and Reynolds' theological reflections on the *imago Dei*. They are both motivated by a desire to overcome a dominating culture that tends to reduce the intellectually disabled to the status of being a deviation from, or deformation of the human norm, even to the point of doubting their humanity. The point, of course, is to find a way of including the intellectually impaired, by seeking to explain the *imago Dei* in terms of an accommodation of diversity, variety, and difference. Therein lies the problem: a theological affirmation of difference will not answer the question of what it means to be human because the differences among human beings are not what need to be established. There may be good pastoral reasons for acknowledging and even celebrating the variety of differences that mark human beings out from one another, as Yong and Reyonlds do. A pastoral concern to include the profoundly disabled in the community of persons

---

34. Ibid., 182.
35. Ibid., 184.

more effectively, by shifting abled people's attitudes towards them from a negative paradigm of deviation to a positive one of difference, is a different concern from the anthropological questions pertaining to deviation and difference.

More will be said in the next chapter about the deviation/difference approaches to the profoundly impaired. At this point, however, we may say that difference among human beings cannot be the basis upon which the humanity of human beings is secured. The question that concerns us is about whether or not someone is a human being and how this is recognized, and not about the condition in which she has her humanity. Either we are all human beings, impaired and unimpaired alike, or we are not. Therefore, it is at the juncture of humanity itself, at the juncture of being a human creature and not something else, and not at the juncture of how we come to live out that humanity, that we need to show that the *imago Dei* can do the work being required of it. Having now cleared away some of the issues that have accrued to or been misread into the doctrine, we may turn to the question of whether or not it can be a sure way of securing the humanity of the profoundly impaired.

Reinders, Aquinas and the *imago Dei*

When we began our discussion on the doctrine of the *imago Dei*, we noted how much of the renewed interest in it has been focused on how it plays out in the lives of human beings, on how it is "received" by the individual who has it, and on how it may be lost. The focus has been predominantly on the kind of good that the *imago Dei* is for the creature who is in the image of God by nature, and not on how it is had by that creature. What this suggests is that the underlying question concerns how being in the image of God reveals something of what it means to be a human being. The issue that primarily concerns us, however, is the reverse: How does being the human beings that we are reveal something of what it means for us to be in the image of God? The same emphasis was being made in asking the question: What is the significance of being made in the image of God for the creature who is a *viator*? This is the right way to ask the question because knowing how a human being lives with the *imago Dei* does not help to answer the question as to whether or not someone is that special and distinct creature who is made in the image of God.

To take up this question, it will be helpful to return to Reinders' project a final time, for this question of the humanity of the creature who is made in the image of God is also his concern. Reinders' position towards the *imago Dei* has already been spelt out in some detail: according to him, it is empty of any properly theological insight into human beings and is a hindrance to securing the humanity of the profoundly disabled. Saint Thomas Aquinas comes under sustained scrutiny in this regard, because he supposedly removes the doctrine of the *imago Dei* from its proper theological moorings, and sees it only in philosophical and, consequentially, anthropocentric terms.[36] For Reinders, Aquinas is the exemplar of "[t]he tradition [which] is to a large extent dominated by the explanation of the divine image in terms of the human faculties, most of all . . . the faculties of human reason and will."[37] Accordingly, reason has been elevated to the point of being the "mark of the divine image," with the result that those who have no or only an underdeveloped capacity for agency are excluded from this "higher class" of human beings, with the implication that "beings without the capacity of reason cannot reflect the [divine] image."[38] Now compare this claim by Reinders, whereby Aquinas is said to have located the doctrine of the *imago Dei* in a philosophical framework, with Schumacher's claim, located in the quotation noted at the beginning of this chapter, that a properly theological affirmation of the *imago Dei* is at the heart of the moral theology of Aquinas.

It is obvious enough that these are two very different interpretations of Aquinas on the doctrine of the *imago Dei*. Which "Thomas" is the real Thomas, then? We have only a hint from Schumacher as to his reading of Aquinas, but Reinders draws substantially on Question 93 from the *prima pars* of the *Summa Theologiæ* to make his case. So, we may fairly turn to *ST* I.93 to judge if Aquinas is indeed guilty of an incipient anthropocentrism (or elevated anthropology) driven by an understanding of the doctrine in terms of human capacity, or to see if there are reasons to support Schumacher's affirmation instead. To anticipate the outcome, it is Reinders who gets Aquinas wrong; but in noting the way that he does so we will be able to pick up on the question of the relationship between

---

36. John Swinton also retrieves aspects of Thomas' theologically grounded account in the context of a welcoming ecclesiology in his article, "Building a Church for Strangers," 48

37. Reinders, *Receiving the Gift of Friendship*, 228.

38. Ibid.

the *status viatoris* and the *imago Dei*, in the form in which it has been posed.³⁹

To begin, it will be helpful to situate Q93—which is concerned with "the purpose or term of man's production, in so far as he is said to have been made after God's image and likeness" (I.93.prologue)—within Aquinas' broader *Treatise on Man* (I.75-102). Aquinas divides it into two parts: what man is (I.75-89) and how he came to be (I.90-102). The question of human origins, therefore, follows on from the question of human nature. Q93, and discussion about the *imago Dei*, falls into the second part. Significantly, from the outset Aquinas treats the question of the origin of human beings theologically, and grounds his thinking in the creation narratives of Genesis 1 and 2. His concern is to show how God has brought about the creation of his image in human beings. This emphasis on a theological grounding to the purposeful origins of human beings is consolidated when the treatise itself is viewed in the light of the systematically theological layout of the entire *prima pars*. All along Aquinas is concerned with one key question: how to "make God known, not only as he is in himself, but as the beginning and end of all things and of reasoning creatures especially" (I.2.prologue). As Aquinas says elsewhere, what shows that the question of human beings and the *imago Dei* is properly answered theologically is that it is a question which considers human beings "as they are related to God—the fact, for instance, that they are created by God, are subject to Him, and so on."⁴⁰ We may say, therefore, as the English Dominican Edmund Hill does,

> Thus the principal part of the treatise on man in the *Summa* is this second half, which is directly investigating for the most part what Scripture has to say about man's origins and his divinely given status and stature. The first half was introductory.⁴¹

Contrary to Reinders' view, therefore, it would appear on the face of it that a theological, and not philosophical, approach to being human drives Aquinas' thinking, with the implication that the question of human nature, while addressed first, is nonetheless to be read in the light of the

---

39. A third interpretation of Aquinas *ST* I.93 has been offered by Molly C. Haslam in her *Constructive Theology of Intellectual Disability*, 95-99. However, the analysis of Q93 we are now undertaking should suffice to show how she, too, "gets Aquinas wrong."

40. Thomas Aquinas, "That the philosopher and the theologian consider creatures in different ways," in *Summa Contra Gentiles - Book Two: Creation*, SCG II.4.§2; 35.

41. Hill, "Introduction," xxii.

question of human origins.[42] This evidently theological grounding suggests this is the best way in which to approach Q93. The question is clearly focused on the end or purpose of the human being, but Aquinas makes it equally clear that this question can only be examined from within the question of human creation; origins and ends—*genesis* and *telos*—are not to be separated out in the theology of being human. Furthermore, origin and nature are likewise not to be treated independently of each other and as if they are separate questions requiring separate lines of inquiry. (The philosophical question of human nature may be asked, of course, but it is always to be asked with the more fundamental theological grounding of man in mind.) This is emphasized by Aquinas in that he approaches the theme of Q93—*de homine facto ad imaginem Dei*—precisely from the perspective of the distinctiveness of man *qua* man, of being the creature that he is, and not man *qua* nature. The way in which human beings are after the image of God is revealed, in large part, by the showing that human beings (93.1) are different from non-rational creatures (93.2) and angels (93.3). With these brief contextualizing thoughts in mind, we can turn to the argument itself.

It is the question Aquinas asks in 93.4—*utrum imago Dei inveniatur in quolibet homine*—that will be of most interest to us. Reinders' claim is that, although Aquinas asserts that all human beings are made in the image of God, the profoundly disabled are marginalized from this inclusion by the very argument he employs. Here are the steps of Reinders' argument: first, he points to a particular sentence in Aquinas' argument that he sees as the crucial one.

> Since man is said to be after God's image in virtue of his intelligent nature, it follows that he is most completely after God's image in that point in which such a nature can most completely imitate God. (93.4.*resp*)

As we know now, it is the question of capacity that drives Reinders' thinking, so it ought to be expected that he will understand Aquinas' point accordingly. This is precisely what he does, arguing that Aquinas holds that it is our capacity for rationality that make us capable of imitating God.[43]

---

42. Reinders, *Receiving the Gift of Friendship*, 230.

43. Ibid., 228. As Reinders puts it, "This claim, according to Aquinas, holds true for every human being. He does not consider the question of what that means for people whose capacity of reason remains underdeveloped."

Nonetheless, Reinders does see in another quotation from Aquinas a qualitative limitation being placed on certain human creatures, at the point of rational capaciousness:

> While all creatures bear some resemblance to God, only in a rational creature do you find a resemblance to God in the manner of an image.... Now what puts the rational creature in a higher class than others is precisely intellect or mind. (93.6.*resp*)

From this Reinders concludes (in terms of the profoundly disabled): "beings without the capacity of reason cannot reflect the image."[44]

What is to be made of this line of argument? The key issue is clearly centered on whether or not Aquinas is making an argument based on human capacity when it comes to the question of how the image of God is supposedly in all human beings. The question is really one of whether or not Aquinas' "intelligent nature" is to be equated with "rational capacity," as Reinders would have it. At first blush, this identity seems plausible as Aquinas does suggest that nature is a matter of degree, at least to the extent that it may be considered as more or less like God's image. Reinders takes the "imitation of the nature" to refer to a likeness that pertains to the level of capacity for intelligence. This initial appearance of equality does not stand up to further scrutiny, however, for Aquinas goes on to say:

> Thus God's image can be considered in man at three stages [*tripliciter*]: the first stage [*modo*] is man's natural aptitude for understanding and loving God, an aptitude which consists in the very nature of the mind, which is common to all men. The next stage is where a man is actually or dispositively knowing and loving God, but still imperfectly; and here we have the image by conformity of grace. The third stage is where a man is actually knowing and loving God; and this is the image by likeness of glory. Thus . . . a threefold image [may be distinguished], namely the image of creation, of re-creation, and of likeness. The first stage of image [*prima ero imago*] then is found in all men, the second only in the just, and the third only in the blessed. (93.4.*resp*)

The word "stage," as it occurs in the Blackfriars translation, may suggest a certain qualitative take on human nature, in the sense of a threefold progressive development of the nature of human beings into greater

44. Ibid.

degrees of being in the image of God. However, it fails to recognize that Aquinas makes a distinction of image, not nature. It is the mode in which the image is present to human beings that differs, and not the nature of human beings. Aquinas' point is that there are three ways or modes in which the one image may be experienced or had in the lives of human beings: "by nature," "by grace" and "by glory." There is nothing here, in other words, that would indicate Aquinas is concerned with the level of capaciousness of our intellectual nature, with whether or not we are capable of moving ourselves upward along some graduating scale towards the perfecting of our natures, *qua* our humanity. Need it be said that, just as human beings cannot make themselves or annihilate themselves, neither can they save themselves, no matter how hard they try?

Even more significant than this linguistic support to understanding of the *imago Dei* as applying to all human beings non-qualitatively, is Aquinas' ontological argument in Q93.3. In this article, comparing angels and humans (the only two creatures taken to have the requisite rational natures needed to be in God's image), the third objection and reply deals with the question of being "more or less" in the image of God (93.3.obj3 & ad3). Aquinas' position, which the argument of the article looks to defend, is that "God's image is found more perfectly in angels than in men, because their natures are more perfectly intelligent." Again, we have the appearance of a capacity-based reading of the *imago Dei*: angels are more perfectly in the image of God because they are more intelligent; they have a more capable rational nature. The implication is that it is the level of one's rational capacity that will make all the difference to the level at which a creature can have the image of God in it. The difference, so it seems, comes down to the degree of intelligence the individual creature has, and quite clearly some human creatures lack the capacity for rationality. So it is that Reinders' concern with Aquinas would seem to be justified.

Unfortunately, this is not a correct reading of how Aquinas understands "intelligent nature." Aquinas sets out the third objection of 93.3 like this:

> Again, a creature is said to be after God's image in virtue of its having an intelligent nature. But there can be no "more" or "less" about such a nature, since it is a question of essential substance, not of some concomitant quality. So you cannot say that angels are more after God's image than man. (93.3.obj3)

And he offers this reply to the objection:

> When it is said that there is no "more" or "less" in substance, it does not mean that one kind of substance cannot be more perfect than another, but that one and the same individual does not belong to its kind sometimes more and sometimes less. Nor do various individuals belong to their kind, some more, some less. (93.3.*ad*3)

It is important to grasp the difference Aquinas makes between the essential substance (*in genere substantiae*) of a nature and its concomitant quality (*de genere accidentis*). The presupposition he is working from is that a human being is a bodily person, and a person is (following Boethius) "an individual substance of a rational nature" (*ST* I.29.1.obj1). In the same context Aquinas goes on to say, "the essence of anything, signified by the definition, is commonly called nature. And here nature is taken in that sense" (29.1.*ad*4). "Nature," therefore, is a sortal term for Aquinas in this context. A thing's nature is that which distinguishes it—sorts it out—from every other thing; it defines the kind of thing that it is, essentially. Consequently, this understanding of nature does not admit of degree: either a thing is the kind of thing that it is or it is another thing altogether. The meaning Aquinas gives to "nature" in terms of this definition is the same as he gives to "essential nature" in Q93. As it turns out, both angels and human beings are creatures of a rational nature; they are both essentially that kind of thing; hence, the point to the objection that there can be no "more or less" concerning the nature of angels and humans in terms of the *imago Dei*. (They are distinguishable, of course, by their respective spiritual and bodily having of this nature.)

The sense that Aquinas gives to "concomitant quality," consequently, can be picked up in the distinction he goes on to make between "kind" and "individual" in the reply. If "kind" goes with "nature" and does not admit of degrees, then "individual" goes with "quality" and does so admit of more or less. The use of "concomitant" tells us that Aquinas is associating the quality to the kind, so we may deduce that it is the rational or intellectual quality that is more or less present in individual human beings. Here we have a rather important revelation: human beings, *qua* the kind of creatures that we are, are always rational creatures, but individual human beings, *qua* the qualities we each have, will differ from each other to the extent to which they are capable of exercising their rationality. Most importantly, there is no distinction to be made between individual human beings in terms of the kind of creature human beings are: if an individual is of a human kind he or she is a human being, absolutely. Nonetheless, there are legitimate grounds to recognize the (obvious) differences between individual human beings in terms of the relative ability to engage their nature. This is the same as saying: human beings have the nature that they have in the condition under which they have it.

For Aquinas, all human beings are rational creatures by definition, but each individual human being is free from being determined by the extent to which that rationality is exercised. His anthropology is not capacity-based, as Reinders would claim. Incidentally, this allows for the recognition that other creatures (i.e., non-human animals) do exercise rational or intellectual qualities, even at a relatively high degree, without them being of a rational kind, while at the same time recognizing how it is possible for human beings who lack the said qualities to be, nonetheless, absolutely of a rational kind. Human beings are in a "higher class" not because of the individual quality of their faculties but because of the common kind of nature they share in, namely, the nature of the image of God. While there is certainly a hierarchy of quality evident in Aquinas' argument, therefore, he cannot be accused of falling into the trap of proposing a hierarchy of being.[45]

Does this solve the problem of the marginalizing of the profoundly impaired on moral grounds? Certainly not. All that it shows so far is how the notion of the *imago Dei* in Aquinas, contrary to what Reinders says, is not capacity-based but grounded in the natural kind of human being. It is an existentially based understanding, not an essentially based one. What this position does suggest, however, is that the problem of a doubtful humanity in the profoundly impaired is not in them, as such, but in those who would judge the extent of their humanity according to the quality of their lives. In this regard, Reinders is quite right: capacity, or the lack of it, can make all the difference in the world.

The ongoing issue, of course, is whether or not it ought to make a difference. So, the question of the relationship between human capacity and the *imago Dei*—the question of what role, if any, the quality of one's life comes to play in the securing of one's humanity in that image—remains an open one. While Aquinas does not deal directly with this particular issue in Q93, there are hints there nonetheless, which may assist in

---

45. Whereas Reinders concludes the opposite: "Aquinas's notion of a 'higher class' confirms that the Christian tradition is not alien to a hierarchy of being that marginalizes people in whom the faculties of reason and will remain underdeveloped." Ibid.

constructing an argument that will shift the burden of proof of humanity from the profoundly impaired to those who would rely on a judgment of quality in the first place. In these hints we will find a way back to the pilgrim creature who is in the image of God in hope.

In amongst the replies to the objections of 93.4, Aquinas provides further information about the three modes of the *imago Dei*. We already know from the *responsio* that the image is imperfectly had "in nature" and "in grace," but perfectly "in glory"; and he associates these three modes with creation (*creationis*), recreation (*recreationis*) and likeness (*similitudinis*). It is the use of "likeness" here that is most interesting. With this information Aquinas hints at how the relationship between image and likeness is to be understood. To hold, as Gen 1:26 says: "Let us make man in our image, according to our likeness," does not mean that image and likeness are to be treated as synonymous. Aquinas confirms this when, in a later article, he draws a distinction between two notions of likeness (93.9.*resp* & *ad*1). First, there is the more general, commonsense way in which "likeness" is simply included in the meaning of "image." This is the sense in which it occurs in Gen 1:26—namely, as a reference to the original. In the second sense, "likeness" can be thought of as signifying the exactness and perfection of "image," to the extent to which it is a true reflection of the original.[46] It is in terms of this second sense of likeness that Aquinas makes his distinctions within the threefold mode of image.

This points to the notion that, while it is in God's image that human beings are created, it is in their likeness to that image that the lives of human beings tend (or not). The image is given, but the likeness is lived. The former is of God and therefore does not admit of change; it is received absolutely in the nature of human beings. The latter is of human beings and is relative to the life being lived, thereby admitting of a better/worse quality. This is what Aquinas is hinting at in 93.4.*ad*1 when he says of the equality that men and women have "after the image": "the idea of 'image' is principally realized [in the] intelligent nature." By emphasizing that the principal manner in which the image is had is in terms of imperfect kindedness, Aquinas highlights how likeness is being used in the second sense when it comes to questions of the *imago Dei*. It is in the mode of

---

46. Aquinas makes a similar point about the distinction in 93.1.*ad*2. We can see here why it is better to translate the Latin "*ad*" as "after" instead of "in" in relation the *imago Dei*: the first sense of "likeness" points out how human beings are the image of God by nature, whereas the second sense refers to how they are, in the having of the nature they have, "after the image."

nature, where the likeness is most imperfect, that all human beings are most evidently after the image of God.

At this point, perhaps the chief temptation to avoid is the one whereby the question of likeness is pressed onto the condition under which human beings have the nature that they have. The issue has to do with how likeness (in the second sense) is here being understood in the sense of approach: as human perfection is approached, so too is likeness after the image. As Aquinas says,

> Since man is said to be after God's image in virtue of his intelligent nature, it follows that he is most completely after God's image in that point in which such a nature can most completely imitate God. (93.4.*resp*)

The issue is this: What, precisely, is doing the imitating in the approaching of perfection? It would appear to be something associated with the nature already possessed, which could lead, in turn, to asking about the relative quality of the nature being had by the individual concerned, or more simply, the particular condition under which that nature is being had. There are two reasons, however, for rejecting such a placement of imitation. First, just as the nature of human beings is a given, so too is the condition. There is a difference between the two in that the nature points us towards the essentiality of the human being concerned, while the condition points us towards his or her existentiality. Even in this difference the absoluteness of the nature is carried over, as it were, and preserved in the condition. So, there can be no sense of better/worse, no notion of relativity in the human condition, and consequently no need for a rapprochement between the human condition and the movement towards perfection. Secondly, Aquinas points out where the rapprochement of nature is to be had, namely: "in grace" and "in glory," and both of these have to do with the living of one's life, and not with the condition under which that life is lived.

Importantly, both grace and glory are about what God does in human beings outwith his initial creative impetus, and with how human beings consequently live in conformity with these gifts. In other words, conformity in living, not quality of condition, is the way of imitation. A human being imitates the image of God to the extent that he or she lives a life in conformity with it. If this is the case, then the issue of imitation is not so much a concern about the movement towards likeness, as it is a concern about ways in which human beings may choose to move away from it (for example, through sinning, as Aquinas notes in 93.4.*obj3* & *ad3*). The presupposition is that the image is there to be lost.

We have seen this direction of movement before: a human being is precisely a human creature in his existing, and it is the prospect of nothingness that most readily shows up the intrinsic value of human existing. The operational structure of the *imago Dei* follows this same pattern. Just as it is the movement away from existing (and towards nothingness) that is the sign of a human life being undermined, so it is with the movement away from likeness after the image of God: being human is "being on the way towards," and not "being away from that which already is the case." To see how this brings us into the ambit of hope: the good that is the image of God is already there to be lived, and failure to live according to this good—understood as a choosing not to pursue life accordingly—is to abandon being *en route* in hope towards the perfection of that good.

As it turns out, recognition of this structural familiarity proves to be highly significant for those living under the condition of profound impairment precisely because of their unchosen, given condition. If, indeed, the operative feature of imitation is best measured in terms of loss, and not gain, then the profoundly impaired find themselves in a rather advantageous position. By virtue of their inability to choose against grace and glory (because of their lack of agency) the profoundly impaired are less able to move away from imitating the nature that they already have after the image of God. It is those who are capable of choosing who are most at risk of losing the good of their humanity, of becoming less perfectly after the image of God. With this, the judgment of quality is reversed because it is in the having of the nature that one has, and not in the condition under which it is had, that the qualitative aspects of being human come to the fore. It is now the rationally capacious who are challenged to judge the quality of their own living in conformity to the image of God in which they are created.

The extent to which the profoundly impaired do not lose the dignity of being after the image of God because they cannot lose it by choice, is the extent to which they may be taken to be exemplars of, not exceptions to, being human. This is not to claim—as in, for example, a well-meaning, though theologically misconstrued pastoral desire to "raise up the lowly" (Luke 1:52)—that the profoundly impaired are somehow better than or more fully human because of their impairment. The deep puzzlement of their lives has not suddenly dissolved away. Nor does it mean that the profoundly impaired are somehow exempt from living the natures that they have; their having of their nature remains as bound up with qualitative considerations as does every human life, otherwise they would not be human.

Rather, to say that the profoundly impaired emerge as real examples of being human is to recognize that the condition under which they live means they are less prone to moving away from the image of God after which they are made. Being less prone, they stand out as being a better measure for what it means to be that creature who is, according to the kind of creature that he is, after the image of God. In this sense, we may venture to say: the rationally capacious would do well to judge the quality of their own humanity according to the measure of the profoundly impaired, and not the other way around. The problem of a doubtful humanity is not to be located in the profoundly impaired, as it were, but in those who would judge the extent of their humanity according to the quality of their own lives.

At the center of the forgoing reflections into the *imago Dei* has been a concern to come to grips with how God has brought about the creation of his image in human beings. In the early part of our discussions on the pilgrim creature who hopes, we saw how it is only the individual human being who can lose the kind of valued life that being human is, because it is the only thing that a human being has that is properly his own. In this sense, all human beings are created to succeed in the project of their humanity by virtue of the good in which they have been created, but some fail in the taking up of the task. What Aquinas' understanding of the *imago Dei* (unlike Reinders' capacity-based one) adds to this picture is the realization that the good to be lost—which is also the looked-for good in hope—is identical with the *imago Dei*, which is the ultimate good of human being, and subsequently to be had according to the "not yet" mode so thoroughly characteristic of the pilgrim creature.

Far from being some static either/or arbitrating property of inclusion, the modal *imago Dei* makes it clear that the natural kind that human beings are is the basis for all human living, and therefore of human spontaneity and flourishing. Human beings are, by nature, on the way towards that by which they are created; human beings are created in order to be the image of God (to recall the phraseology of Geiger). This destiny of the image is the destiny of the creature who is of that image. The emphasis, once again, focuses in on human existence, neither anything more nor anything less. To be living the life one has—to be living for one's life—is to be in the image of God.

We may conclude that there is, in a modal understanding of the *imago Dei*, good reason to say that the profoundly impaired ought to be recognized as being human because they have the nature that they have precisely in the condition under which they have it. This entire project is premised on the reality that what ought to be the case is not always actually taken to be the case; the profoundly impaired are excluded by some (and in practice) from the community of persons precisely because of the condition under which they have their human nature. Are we left, therefore, with an impasse in which a normative position takes the condition of the profoundly impaired to be integral to their being human ("precisely in") and a descriptive position that takes that same condition to be integral to their not being human ("precisely because of")? We must ask whether there is a way of overcoming such an impasse. At the heart of this apparent divide lies the real difference between human nature and the condition of that nature (between "the existential human condition" and "the essential condition of humans"), the way in which each is measured, and how they then relate to each other. Thus, a new question arises: How are we—if we are—to account for the measure of a life such that it is taken to be a human life? It is a question that says that taking the measure of our lives is important, and it leads to questions about what it is that we are measuring when we measure our lives, and how we are to go about taking that measure. These questions about measuring the human condition, the last major set of questions to be dealt with, will open up onto the implication of the doctrine of the *imago Dei* for a Christian anthropology.

8

DRAWING NEAR TO CHRIST
Measuring the Human Condition

Measuring Our Human Nearness to the Man Jesus Christ

THE FIRST QUESTION TO ask when enquiring into taking the measure of the human condition is: What is meant by "measure"? Are we after a biological or genetic measure of the human species; a psychological or social measure? Is it a measure of what a human being is or a measure of how it is what it is? An absolute measure of human beings or a relative measure between human beings? To get some handle on how this question will be broached here, consider the following remark, made from the perspective of the Christian faith, by Cardinal Josef Ratzinger (Pope Emeritus Benedict XVI) concerning the lives of those who suffer from mental illness:

> [T]he light of divine love lies specifically upon suffering people, in whom the splendour of the creation had been externally dimmed. Because these people are in a special way similar to the crucified Christ, to the icon of love, they have drawn near to a special shared nature with him who, alone, is *the* image of God.[1]

---

1. Ratzinger, "The Likeness of God in the Human Being," *Dolentium hominum*, 18, opening address given at an international conference sponsored by the Pontifical Council for Pastoral Assistance to Health Care Workers on the problem of mental illness, entitled "In the Image and Likeness of God: Always? Disturbances of the Human Mind."

It is the language of "similarity" and "nearness" that is especially interesting here. In the eyes of faith, the humanity of those whose lives are conditioned by the impairment of mental illness is said to be similar to that of the crucified Jesus, and therefore exhibiting a certain shared nearness. In the context of the quotation, "similarity" takes on a sense of resemblance to the object that the subject of measurement is being measured against; and "nearness" suggests a closeness of relationship with or between the subject and the object. It is these two senses of measurement—"resemblance to" and "relationship with"—that we will take to be the kind of measurements of the human condition we are pursuing. We might ask: But why these two? And we might respond: because, as we will see, they speak to the question of the difference between "the existential human condition" and "the essential condition of humans." This requires an initial justification.

Clearly, the object by which the humanity of the mentally ill is being measured against by Ratzinger is the man, Jesus Christ. The great Christian insight into the mystery of the pilgrimage of all human life is that we human beings both are, and are meant to be, like Christ. He is the answer to the question concerning the true measure of man, in virtue of him being human. As Ratzinger notes, human beings, who are after the image of God, are made after the one whose existence is the true image of God. A very simple intuition lies at the heart of this belief: to approach Christ is to approach the true measure of ourselves as human beings. As the author of the Letter to the Hebrews says: "for the one who sanctifies and those who are sanctified all have one Father" (Heb 2:11). This journey towards Christ is a journey for all human beings to make by virtue of, and for no other reason than our shared participation in, one and the same human nature. Furthermore, in approaching the man Jesus Christ—in drawing near to him—human beings are actually approaching the fullness of themselves in all their God-given glory. We may "approach the throne of grace with such boldness" precisely because in the man Jesus Christ we do not have someone "who is unable to sympathize with our [human] weaknesses, but we have one who in every respect has been tested as we are, yet without sin" (Heb 4:15–16). Christ's humanity, therefore, is enough for us to approach the full meaning of our own humanity because he represents to all of humanity what it is to be human. To draw near to the humanity of Christ is to draw near to our own humanity.

To say that we are, and are meant to be, like Christ is to make a twofold claim about our own humanity, namely: there are two senses of "nearness to Christ" in operation whenever we approach the question of the measure of man *qua* man. First (and logically prior), there is the nearness of human beings to Christ in virtue of sharing in a common nature. This sense of nearness is captured in the first quotation from Hebrews and in the language of "resemblance to." Secondly, there is the nearness of human beings to Christ in virtue of sharing in a common life, captured in the second Hebrews quotation and the language of "relationship with." If the nature that we have and the life that we live are not synonymous, which is evidently the case, two quite different things about human beings are being signified when we say human beings both are, and are meant to be, like Christ. Something of the picture of this difference is captured in the both/and of "are" and "are meant to be." We must remember, however, that this is only a picture, a way of perceiving the difference; it is not to be relied upon to carry the theological argument.

In this regard, however, we may reintroduce C. S. Lewis to our discussions as he makes a helpful distinction between kinds of nearness, which we may profitably employ to help understand the picture. He distinguishes between "nearness-by-likeness" and "nearness-of-approach."[2] We may immediately note the correspondence of these terms with our own "resemblance to" and "relationship with." The context for Lewis' distinction is the way in which human beings love, and especially how they come closest to God—confirmed by God himself (cf. Ps 81:10; Matt 11:28)—in their loving need for him. This need-love (as he calls it), which is integral to human living, reveals, however, a strange paradox:

> Man approaches God most nearly when he is in one sense least like God. For what can be more unlike than fullness and need, sovereignty and humility, righteousness and penitence, limitless power and a cry for help?[3]

It is this paradox that leads Lewis to draw the distinction between nearness-by-likeness and nearness-of-approach. The former pertains to the nearness human beings have that comes from the image of God impressed upon their nature. It is nearness by way of a status conferred because of the nature received. When it comes to something like rationality, for example, human beings are nearer to God than other non-human animals, while angels are nearer to God than human beings. It is a gift

---

2. Lewis, *Four Loves*, 4–11.
3. Ibid., 4.

conferred, not a merit gained. This sense of nearness is fixed; there is nothing one can do to draw nearer to God in terms of resemblance. We may say: nearness-by-likeness speaks of a certain natural likeness, a likeness in kind.

Not so with nearness-of-approach, which does admit of degree. Here, it is the state of human living, and not the status of human life, that matters. Such a state speaks to us of a contingent likeness, a likeness that is accidental (not necessary). To come nearer to God in this latter sense is to do something: it involves, as Lewis says, "our willed imitation"; but an imitation of whom?[4] Here Lewis makes the point that while nearness-of-approach is distinct from nearness-by-likeness, they are not unconnected in as much as the approach is only possible because of the pre-existing resemblance, so that the imitation is of like unto like. Thus:

> Our imitation of God in this life ... must be an imitation of God incarnate: our model is the Jesus, not only of Calvary, but of the workshop, the roads, the crowds, the clamorous demands, the interruptions. For this, so strangely unlike anything we can attribute to the Divine life in itself, is apparently not only like, but is, the Divine life operating under human conditions.[5]

What makes Lewis' distinction between the two senses of nearness particularly interesting for our purposes is the way in which it provides a nuanced and fine-grained way of taking the measure of being human. Likeness and unlikeness are typically set up as opposites, but this dichotomy can be overcome for human beings, as Lewis' distinction indicates: at one and the same time, a human being may be very much like God in one sense but quite unlike God in another. This is possible because the object in view is different in each sense of nearness. In terms of nearness-by-likeness, the measure of a human being is made in relation to a comparison between kinds of natures: specifically human nature to God's nature. A human being is near to God not in terms of fellow human beings, but in terms of other, non-human beings. The object in view, therefore, in measuring humanity in this sense, is the nature of human being in comparison with the nature of other beings, with the nature of God being the common rule of measure. There is no comparison being made here of the individual lives of human beings nor a comparison of the relative condition under which they individually have their common nature.

4. Ibid., 7.
5. Ibid.

In nearness-by-approach, on the other hand, human lives do come into play. The relative nearness of the life of one human being to the life of God may be set alongside the relative nearness of another. Again, this is not a bare comparison of one human being over and against another, with no rule of measure independent of them. Rather, the measuring is of each individual human being in relation to a commonly held rule of measure—namely, the man, Jesus of Nazareth (noting Lewis' emphasis on the quotidian Jesus). The object in view, therefore, is the living human being, Jesus Christ, who is how God is as a human being. The object remains God, but in his humanity.

The upshot of this way of distinguishing between senses of nearness is this: to speak of how human beings are near to God is to speak in one way of their nature ("the nature that they have") and in another way of their lives ("the having of the nature that they have"), but never in a way that involves having to measure off one human being over and against another, *qua* their humanity. There is a measurability to being human that is being brought into play here that does not depend on an either/or comparison unto likeness between human beings. Neither nearness-by-likeness nor nearness-of-approach is about human beings as they are in comparison with each other; instead, they are two ways in which human beings relate to God as the one true rule of measure of the human condition.

"Human Being" in Psalm 8 and Psalm 144

In previous chapters, we have been tracking the way in which certain recent theological thinking that centers on the profoundly disabled has sought to respond positively to the reality of the condition under which they live. The intention has been to overcome the like/unlike dichotomy that so often marginalizes, even negates, the humanity of the profoundly disabled in comparison with the lives of others. The question that has concerned them all has been this: What is the status of disability in relation to humanity? As we have seen (especially in Yong and Reynolds), one way of answering this has been to prefer difference over deviation, whereby the lived condition of the profoundly disabled is viewed as a sign of variety in human nature rather than as a deformity of that nature. This proposal seeks to reconfigure the way in which the humanity of human beings is measured, such that the lives of the profoundly disabled may be included under a like-to-like comparison with the lives of others. (Reinders, of course, adopts a position of not measuring the human condition at all because of his radical rejection of any value role for immanent creaturely life.)

Besides the commonsense problem of justifying the move from the suffering of deviation to the celebration of difference—Would someone want to continue living with a profound impairment if, *ceteris paribus*, she could live without it?—we may also note, in the light of Lewis' distinction, the confusion that is generated by making this move. The measure of humanity in this approach is dependent upon the lived condition of someone's life, because the presence or absence of a characteristically human feature about someone's life only becomes relevant because of its presence or absence in the living of that life. This suggests that the kind of measure needed is one that takes into account the lives of human beings, their lived reality. The one that does this is the one that measures in terms of nearness-of-approach.

However, by giving preference to difference-in-nature over deviation-within-nature, the disabling condition is made to be a feature of human nature itself and not a feature of the living of that nature. Importantly, this preferencing of difference over deviation is a commitment to an ontological position about human nature; it is not a way of sympathetically accommodating the condition of impairment. Therefore, the measure actually being looked for is the one that will operate at the level of nature, not lived experience, and that measurement pertains to nearness-by-likeness. Consequently, by making the move that some theologians of disability have made, rather than clarifying what is measurable about disability, as it pertains to being human, they have muddied the waters to the extent that it is quite unclear as to what they really want to measure.

The question therefore remains: Where does someone's profound disability—or, more broadly, impairment—sit in relation to his or her very humanity? To bring out the sharpness of this question for the Christian thinker: How is someone, in the context of his or her impairment, like Christ in his humanity? To answer these questions we need to begin by getting a handle on how—that is to say, in what way or ways—being human is, in fact, measurable. For the claim is that the question of being human is a question of likeness, and this, in turn, is a question of measurement (*contra* Reinders), although of the right kind (*contra* Yong and Reynolds).

It is a significant feature of biblical faith that the question—Human being?—has been posed as a question pertaining to the measure of humanity before God. Nowhere is this more strikingly expressed than in the book of the Psalms: "[W]hat are human beings that you are mindful of them, mortals that you care for them?" (Ps 8:4). There is an obvious sense of measurement being conveyed by this question. The kind of measure implied, however, is specific: it is not about what a human being is by definition, but about how human beings are who they are as human beings vis-à-vis God: *How admirable is God! What is man in comparison?* As the scripture scholar Konrad Schaefer has noted,

> This awe and questioning is the distinction of Psalm 8 and the key to its interpretation. The worshipper gazes on eternity then targets the self. How small the human is when compared with divine greatness, yet how great by God's favor![6]

The actual value that comes to be placed on the measure—the concluding judgment of the measurement made—is neither here nor there in terms of the present argument. What is significant about Ps 8:4 is that the question: Human being?, which is asked vis-à-vis God, entails making a measurement of being human. Furthermore, the kind of measure entailed, in asking the question in the way it is asked, can tell us something about being human which pertains to being of human kind. Finally, this kind of measure is value laden: being a human being means something; there is a value (whatever it may be) to being human in kind.

It is the second of these three points, however, that is most significant for the present argument. We may ask, in the light of Lewis' distinction, what kind of nearness is implied in the question of Ps 8:4. The cosmological context into which human beings are positioned in the psalm places the emphasis on a measurement between kinds of things in creation. It is before the awesomeness of the heavenly cosmos (v. 3) that the question of man is first asked, but it is before God himself that the question of man is subsequently answered (vv. 5–8). In both the question and the answer there is no mention of the life that man lives. Instead, the measuring of humanity in the sense posed by v. 4 is about the status conferred on human beings by virtue of the nature they have received from and in God. The whole emphasis of these verses from Psalm 8 is of how the personal God is the measure of the generic man. God is the subject ("You") and man is the object ("Him") of vv. 4–8, thereby situating humanity—the

---

6. Schaefer, *Psalms*, 23

kind of being that human creatures are—within its proper placement in relation to all else. Again, what that position is is not relevant for the moment; what counts is that being human has been measured and so placed. This kind of measurement is an exact fit with Lewis' nearness-by-likeness: a certain status is conferred because of the nature received. The merit gained from a life lived does not enter into the vision of Psalm 8. It is the place of human beings—their position in God's creation—that is being marked out when the psalmist declares in answer to his question, "Yet you have made them a little lower than God, and crowned them with glory and honor" (Ps 8:5).

Verse 4 specifically, and Psalm 8 more generally, has been referred to in much theological anthropology (including theologies carrying a concern for the profoundly impaired), as a kind of summary of the biblical indication of the special status human beings have by virtue of being human (and not some other kind of created being). As Edmund Hill has noted,

> Psalm 8 makes a very suitable introduction to what God's revelation has to say about man, since it both refers back explicitly to the creation of man, to Adam, and is also interpreted by the New Testament as referring forward to the new man, Jesus Christ.[7]

What does not seem to have been considered by these authors is the parallel quotation of Ps 8:4—virtually word for word, and certainly with the same meaning—in Psalm 144: "O Lord, what are human beings that you regard them, or mortals that you think of them?" (Ps 144:3).[8] Perhaps this lacuna has occurred because Ps 144:3 has been taken to be nothing more than a simple repetition of Ps 8:4, adding nothing new of concern to theologians. In the light of Lewis' twofold nearness, however, there is good reason to ask if this non-treatment of Ps 144:3 is justified.

There does not seem to be any need to make a fuss of the very slight variation in the wording of the question as it occurs in the two psalms. So, let it be taken that one and the exact same question is being asked in both occurrences; that Ps 144:3 is a direct and unchanged quotation of Ps 8:4. That being said, this does not mean that the response given to the question asked on each occasion is the same. In Ps 8.4 we have seen how

---

7. Hill, *Being Human*, 9. Hill placed the question asked in Psalm 8 at the beginning and heart of his major study on being human.

8. Hill fails even to note Psalm 144 in his extensive index of biblical references. Ibid., 303–8.

the question fits with seeking a measure of humanity that corresponds with nearness-by-likeness. Is this the same measure being looked for in Ps 144:3? Certainly, Psalm 144 does not convey anything of the sense of the glory of God already given, which Psalm 8 bestows on the status of being human. Man is not made "a little lower than the heavenly beings" but is "like a breath"; he has not been "crowned . . . with glory and honor"; rather, "his days are like a passing shadow." Also unlike Psalm 8, which is focused on what is already the case about human beings, Psalm 144 is future-oriented, focused on what is desired by the warrior poet to be received from God: "deliver me and rescue me" (144:7, and repeated at v. 11). As the biblical scholar Samuel Terrien notes: "The hero of this psalm became a happy warrior, for he looked beyond military triumph towards an era of universal peace."[9]

These two features combine to emphasize how Psalm 144, in contrast to Psalm 8, does not respond to the question asked by considering the status of human beings in virtue of their being human but by reflecting on the divine influence that may be brought to bear on the lives of human beings who turn to God. Thus, vv. 12–14 set out the good effects of God's deliverance in a series of "Then will . . ." statements for those human beings "whose God is the Lord" (v. 15). This psalm, therefore, is not saying something about the status already conferred on human beings, but about the grace of God, who responds to those who have called on him.

There is another significant difference to be noted about the way in which each psalm responds to the question: Human being? Psalm 8, as noted, focuses the answer on human beings as a whole, about the nature of being human. Psalm 144, however, makes a point of separating out certain human beings from human being generally. This specification of the few over the many is conveyed in two ways. First, nearly all of Psalm 144 is written from the first person perspective, unlike in Psalm 8. Throughout it, the language is of the "I" and the "me" of the first person singular and the "we" and "our" of the first person plural. Secondly, the psalm seeks to compare human beings, one with the other, whereas Psalm 8 compares human beings with other beings/things. The hope of the psalmist is that some—"them"—will be "scattered" and "routed" by God (v. 5), while others—"us"—will be "saved" and "rescued" (v. 7). Coupled with the fact that it is the lives of these few over the many that

---

9. Terrien, *Psalms*, 901.

is being emphasized in Psalm 144, and not the nature that they have by virtue of being human (as in Psalm 8), the point that may be drawn from this is that its response to the question: Human being? is in terms of the living out of individual human lives.

With this in mind, we may now ask with Lewis: What kind of measure is in play when the question: Human being? is being asked in Psalm 144? How is man coming near to God? Evidently the answer is: man is being measured in terms of nearness-of-approach, because at stake is not the status conferred by virtue of the nature received in resemblance to God, but the closeness gained from the life lived in a relationship with God. This measure is of an individual human life; this is not a measure of humanity as a whole. By implication, the question—Human being?—of Ps 8:4 and Ps 144:3 is open to two quite distinct answers: the former proposing an answer pertaining to the humanity of human beings as a whole and the latter proposing an answer pertaining to the lives of individual human beings. In both psalms the question of measurement pertains to being human *vis-à-vis* God (and, therefore, is a question of nearness to God), but the kind of measurement being made is different in each case: the former as nearness-by-likeness, and the latter as nearness-of-approach. This is a significant difference between the two psalms, and one that deserves attention when it comes to the theological questions of anthropology.

The Letter to the Hebrews: The Measure of Man in the Measure of Jesus

Our own interest in Psalm 8, to recall, flows out of a question about the measure of being human and the implication this has for consideration of the humanity of the profoundly impaired. Specifically: How is someone, in the context of his or her impairment, like Christ in his or her humanity? We have reached a point where, in responses to the anthropological question of Ps 8:4 and Ps 144:3, we have found biblical support for a distinction in how human beings are measurable *vis-à-vis* God, by making use of C. S. Lewis' notions of nearness-by-likeness and nearness-of-approach. We began this chapter, however, by noting in very simple terms the doctrine in which the true measure of a man, in virtue of him being human, is grounded—namely, that human beings both are, and are meant to be, like Christ. In approaching the man Jesus Christ—in drawing near to him—human beings are actually approaching the fullness of themselves in all their God-given glory. To approach Christ is to approach one particular man out of all human beings, and to approach that man is to draw near to God. It is now time to bring these three insights—the doctrine, the biblical support, and the philosophical distinction—together, to see what they may reveal for a theological anthropology attentive to the profoundly impaired.

To this end, the question posed by Psalm 8, and repeated in Psalm 144, proves a very helpful point of departure because it has found a christological setting in the Letter to the Hebrews.[10] Of course, the play between the anthropological and the christological in Hebrews is well attested, and we have already hinted at this in the earlier quotations made from the letter.[11] Nonetheless, the question of what it means to be human, and the measure of that humanity, as it is expressed in Ps 8:4–6, is specifically taken up in Heb 2:5–9 in the context of the one man, Jesus Christ. It is worth quoting the relevant passage in full:

> Now God did not subject the coming world, about which we are speaking, to angels. But someone has testified somewhere: "What is man that you are mindful of him, or the son of man that you care for him? You have made them for a little while lower than the angels; you have crowned them with glory and honor, subjecting all things under their feet." Now in subjecting all things to them, God left nothing outside of his control. As it is, we do not yet see everything in subjection to them, but we do see Jesus, who for a little while was made lower than the angels, now crowned with glory and honor because of the suffering of death, so that by the grace of God he might taste death for everyone. (Heb 2:5–9)

It is clear enough from the text that the author takes Ps 8:4–6 to be applicable to Christ, drawing from it the implication that Jesus "as

---

10. Just how crucial Psalm 8 is to the questions of Christian anthropology from a christological perspective is attested to by the fact that it is also quoted by St. Paul in 1 Cor 15:27 and alluded to in Eph 1:22.

11. Craig Bloomberg has noted, "In the first half of the twentieth century, the anthropological view [of Heb 2.6, quoting Ps 8.4] seemed to reflect the consensus of [biblical] scholars but today the Christological approach appears to have captured the majority vote." I will not take a particular position myself as to which emphasis is to be favored. I simply note that, theologically speaking, we may legitimately remain open to both the anthropological and the christological elements that are in play. See Bloomberg, "'But we See Jesus,'" 88.

the incarnate Son of God is both the representative man and the one in whom man's appointed destiny will be fully realized."[12] In Hebrews it is this man who is made the representative of all humanity in the question: "What is man . . . ?" As Richard Bauckham has noted (alluding to Heb 2:14–18, which is the conclusion drawn from the argument made in Heb 2:5–9),

> Hebrews portrays Jesus as the high priest who can fulfil his ministry only by sharing fully the human condition, becoming like his brothers and sisters in every respect, tested in every respect through suffering and death, so that he understands human weakness and now, from his heavenly throne, exercises mercy and grace to sinners.[13]

In the context of our own concerns, the question to be asked is this: With its explicit reference to the question—Human being?—of Ps 8:4, does the Letter to the Hebrews show signs of the two modes in which the measure of humanity can be expressed? If this is the case, what does this tell us about Christ himself, about his humanity, and our being and becoming like unto him?

The eschatological dimension to Heb 2:5–9 is evident enough from the opening sentence. The glorious future being offered to listeners is nonetheless presented to them as having already been inaugurated in Jesus. The eschatological, in other words, is grounded in the incarnational, giving us the reason needed to ask the anthropological question, rather than the narrower christological question. What is particularly interesting for our purposes is the way in which this move is made, for a subtle but real distinction in measurement is detectable in how the author interprets the humanity of Jesus in the light of Psalm 8. Initially, Jesus as the one who is a man like us by nature ("made lower than the angels"), but then Jesus as the one who is transformed ("crowned with glory and honor") by the experience of suffering death. Of this difference, Alan Mitchell notes,

> The humanity proclaimed in the psalm is none other than that of the Son, who in the incarnation participated in the lowered state of humanity . . . [Yet], Christ's exaltation results not merely

---

12. International Bible Society, *NIV Commentary*, 776.

13. Bauckham, "The Divinity of Jesus Christ in the Epistle to the Hebrews," in *Epistle to the Hebrews and Christian Theology*, 26.

from the incarnation but from the acceptance of humanity to its limits, suffering, and death.[14]

It is the "not merely" which is worth highlighting, for it indicates where the shift occurs. The movement from Jesus, the incarnate human being, to Jesus, the exalted human being, is dependent upon the experience he has in living out that humanity. At this stage, it is not the specificity of that lived experience—the suffering that he took upon himself—that is of interest, though its significance will emerge a little further on in our discussion. Rather, it is simply that the shift that occurs is one from the nature in which Jesus appears and the subsequent manner in which he shows that appearance. It is evidently a shift in the way in which the humanity of Jesus is being measured: initially, his humanity is measured according to his conformity to human nature, but then his humanity is measured according to his conformity to a manner of human living. Furthermore, this same shift is marked by a reversal in the direction in which the relationship between Jesus and other human beings is registered: initially Jesus is described as fitting according to the image of human beings—he is made like us (through his incarnation); but then it is human beings who are described as fitting according to the image of Jesus—we are made like him (through our experience of Christlike suffering and death). The first was necessary so that the second may occur.

The correspondence is striking between the structure of the argument centered on the humanity of Jesus in Heb 2:5–9 and the distinct modes of human measurement identified by Lewis. The humanity of Christ, as a question directed towards his nature, is measured in terms of nearness-by-likeness; and as a question directed towards his life lived, it is measured in terms of nearness-of-approach. Moreover, the passage from Hebrews presents an order in which the measure of Jesus' humanity is made: first in terms of human nature, and only consequentially in terms of human life. As the author of the letter explains it, "Therefore he had to become like his brothers and sisters in every respect, so that he might . . . make a sacrifice of atonement for the sins of the people" (Heb 2:17). In that "so that" we have a definite progression in which the measurement of Jesus' humanity is to be undertaken, and as there is the anthropological aspect operating in this text, with Christ as the representative of human being, we may accept that the same order applies to all human beings.

---

14. Mitchell, *Hebrews*, 66–67.

The conclusion we may fairly draw, therefore, from the foregoing discussion of asking the question—Human being?—in the light of Lewis' distinction between nearness-by-likeness and nearness-of-approach is this: these two modes of human measurement, and their ordering, have universal application. What emerges from the anthropological setting of Psalms 8 and 144 is confirmed in the christological setting of Hebrews 2: any and all human beings are measurable according to this structure. Whether it is someone who is profoundly impaired or someone who is not, or whether it is Jesus of Nazareth who is being considered, the mode of measurement is the same for all human beings, without exception.

One final point is worth noting about the measurement of human beings before considering how the conclusion we have arrived at plays out in the lives of the profoundly impaired. The Christian faith has always exhorted men and women to take the measure of themselves from the subjective perspective, that is: the personal measurement of oneself as a human being. Only, it has done so with an eye to employing the right rule of measure. Jesus said, "Do not judge, so that you may not be judged. For with the judgment you make you will be judged, and the measure you give will be the measure you get" (Matt 7:1–2). Thus, the wrong rule of measure would be one that measures oneself over and against others (the word "others" being presumed in the exhortation: "Do not judge"). Saint Paul took the same line of argument when he told the community at Corinth, "But when they measure themselves by one another, and compare themselves with one another, they do not show good sense" (2 Cor 10:12). The positive teaching that both Jesus and Paul go on to make about the measured judgment of oneself, may be stated as follows: that which is measurable about oneself is that which is relatable to God by virtue of God's humanity in Christ. Thus, Paul speaks of "[coming] to the measure of the full stature of Christ," adding, "we must grow up in every way into him who is the head, into Christ" (Eph 4:13; 15). Jesus presents himself as the true rule of measure by which we are to measure ourselves: "I am the way, and the truth, and the life. No one comes to the Father except through me" (John 14:6). It is the one man, Jesus Christ, who is the sure measure of man for all men and women; and to make the point once again, this is the case without exception.

The biblical measure of oneself, therefore, is presented as a measure made in relation to the nature and life of Jesus. This measuring of oneself in relation to Christ as a rule does mark out the one difference between him and the rest of humanity. As a rule, Jesus becomes the instrument, so to speak, by which the measurement is made, and not just the subject of the measurement, although he must be that as well for him to be assured of his humanity. But, how can this be? Again, we may turn to Lewis' modes of measurement.

In nearness-by-likeness (to recall), the measure is of the nature of being human, and in this Jesus must be subject to measurement: key to the christological status of Jesus is establishing that he is truly a human being (as the great christological debates of the Church testify), and this requires the measuring of Jesus' human nature. In terms of nearness-of-approach, Jesus stands apart from other human beings as the one who is being approached, and not the one who is approaching. Thus, in terms of nearness-of-approach, Christ is no longer a subject of measurement, but the instrument, the rule, by which the measurement is made. Importantly, therefore, when Christ stands apart from other human beings as representative of humanity, he does not do so because he is the "perfect specimen" of that kind of being who is human in nature, but because of the state of the life that he lived. This is confirmed when we consider that the measure of oneself is not a measure of one's nature, but a measure of the living of one's life, which corresponds with nearness-by-approach. Jesus Christ is a subject by nature: needing to prove himself along with everyone else; he is a rule by life: being the representative towards whom everyone else may draw near.

Associating the Condition of Impairment with the Sufferings of Christ

It is time to consider how the insights from the foregoing discussion may be brought to bear on those whose lives are marked by profound impairment. To this end, perhaps the most contentious implication to arise from this discussion, and the one that most demands attention, is this: the humanity of the profoundly impaired can be assured if and only if, by their nature and by their lives, they are measured as human beings in exactly the same way as every other human being. That is to say, they are recognizably human, by status conferred and by state lived, precisely to the extent to which they are measurable, as human beings are measurable, in terms of the modes of nearness-by-likeness and nearness-of-approach *vis-à-vis* the one man Jesus Christ. If this is the way that human beings are assured of their humanity, then this is the only way that the profoundly impaired are assured of theirs; there is no exception-clause for the subjects of this way of answering the question: Human being?

What makes this position contentious is that those who have recently written theologically about the profoundly disabled would have it that the human status conferred on them is differently measured, by virtue of the condition under which they live their lives, or it is not open to measurement at all. The profoundly disabled, so this position maintains, are indeed human beings, but differently so, with the condition under which they live their lives being the only cause of that differentiation. (*"The disabled are not deviant; just different."*) Consequently, the measure of their humanity must be taken differently to accord with the differentiated humanity. We have, therefore, two markedly different positions being advocated, with the condition under which the profoundly impaired live their lives emerging as the touchstone upon which judgment is to be made between the two. It is this touchstone, therefore, we need to contend with as the question—Human being?—is broached specifically in terms of the profoundly impaired. We may do this by taking up the question of human suffering, which was mentioned without elaboration in the discussion on Hebrews 2, in the light of Lewis' twofold distinction.

To state the issue: If our concern is to show how, for example, the humanity of a woman who is profoundly impaired both is, and is meant to be, like Christ's in exactly the same manner as anyone who is a human being, then the question of the measurement of her humanity needs to be asked and answered. According to the Lewisian way of measuring human beings, this means showing how she is near both in likeness and in approach to Christ, who, as the representative human being, is the rule of measure for being human, both by nature and by living. Intervening into the smooth rendering of this measurement is the impaired condition under which she is living her life. Let it be taken to be the one distinguishing feature about her which presents itself as raising a doubt as to her claim on humanity. So, the question becomes: how does the condition, under which this profoundly impaired woman lives, get measured in virtue of her humanity? Is it a feature influencing the measure of her nature (nearness-by-likeness) or the measure of her living (nearness-of-approach)? Is it both or neither? This then raises the question: Does one aspect of this measurement take precedence over the other? Which is the one that really matters for the question at hand? This is, in other words, a question about the status of, and the part played by, the condition under which the profoundly impaired find themselves living. The association of this condition with the notion of human suffering in the light of the Gospel offers a way of addressing this issue theologically.

It has become almost commonplace in Christian theology and ethics to associate the abiding care and concern of God with certain groups of human beings. Sometimes this is done at the level of the identity of God, as with some queer, feminist, and black theologies. Affinity with God in his Incarnation is also significant: the poor, sick and suffering, the widow and the orphan, the stranger and the possessed—the *anawim*—are all biblical examples of this phenomenon of association. The contemporary associations are attempts to extend more or less the gospel picture into new scenarios of perceived forms of human suffering, especially as they might relate to poverty, oppression, and marginalization. While the relative merit of some of these associations is a matter of ongoing debate and controversy, it is without doubt that the associating of God with the disabled—as exemplars of the biblical form of unmerited human suffering—has played a crucial and valuable role in highlighting human disability as a topic of theological concern in its own right. Nancy Eiesland's groundbreaking work, *The Disabled God*, has become the *locus classicus* in this regard, and no text in the disability genre is written without some reference to it.

The assertion common to these theological associations is that an identifiable group of human beings, by virtue of some unlooked-for condition under which they live, is especially close to Christ, "who is the image of God" (2 Cor 4:4). It is by establishing the association that the status, and therefore the dignity, of the group so conditioned is assured. Importantly, then, it is the presence of the condition itself that brings about the possibility of making the association, for it is through the experience of living under a certain condition that a particular group of human beings may then be thought of as being especially like the suffering Jesus in virtue of their condition. Take the condition away (and its concomitant marginalization) and there is no reason left to consider looking for the association.

Given this factor, we may add two aspects of general Christian concern towards the *anawim* that might lead theologians to see value in the associating move. First, there is a desire to uphold certain human beings as especially representative of the suffering, crucified Jesus by virtue of living under a particular human condition. Pope John Paul II, for example, called the intellectually disabled "living icons of the crucified

Son."[15] Secondly, there is a desire to present those who are living under that condition as exemplars of how God's salvific plan is meant to unfold for all human beings. To quote John Paul II again: "disabled people are humanity's privileged witnesses."[16] These twin desires express something of the general Christian disposition towards, or intuition about, those who so suffer innocently because of the condition under which they have come to live their lives. Josef Ratzinger gives expression to this intuition in the quotation that opened this chapter in the context of a conference on mental illness. (It must be stressed, however, that this general intuition differs markedly from those aspects of the associating move that would place the suffering of God in Jesus Christ—and the conditions of those who suffer with him—into the very identity of his divine being.)

Having so identified the rudiments of this general Christian intuition, the question that arises is one of how it is then handled by the associating move. What seems to happen is that the move seeks to give a certain theological trajectory to the intuition whereby the specialness of the condition—and the association of it with the sufferings of Jesus—marks the difference in someone being like Christ, or not, in terms of his or her humanity. It is the humanity of Jesus, therefore, and not simply that he suffered, that is the end towards which the associating move is aimed; his suffering is but the means by which his humanity is manifest. The end is not to establish, say, that the profoundly impaired suffer like Christ suffered, but to assure them that they are indeed like the human being, Jesus Christ, precisely because of their suffering. This being the end in view, the means to it is one of identifying an appropriately significant form of unmerited suffering or marginalization—be it determined biologically, psychologically, economically, culturally, or so on—which, in the experience of it, reflects something of the human suffering experienced by Jesus of Nazareth.

While a condition suffered is required for the associating move to work, once an appropriate connection is made to the sufferings of Jesus, then all that is subsequently required is a mere act of affirmation that the humanity of the group identified is—must be, surely!—like unto the humanity of Christ. Because they suffer like Christ, so the associating move

---

15. John Paul II, *Message on the Occasion of the International Symposium on the Dignity and Rights of the Mentally Disabled Person*, §6. As was noted in *Part I*, this is the speech where Jean Vanier thinks the Pope finally got his own thinking right concerning the disabled.

16. Ibid., §6.

suggests, then they must be like Christ, the man, and not simply sharers with him in the experience of suffering. The condition lived confirms the nature conferred. The only determinative question, therefore, that the associating move seeks to ask is this: Is the condition being suffered sufficiently serious to warrant identification with the sufferings of Christ?

Besides the obvious logical leap of faith that is being called for, we may note for our purposes how the whole structure of the associating move uses something that would be measured by nearness-of-approach (namely, the condition lived) to say something about that which would be measured by nearness-by-likeness (namely, the nature conferred). Is this a problem? Yes, it is, and it can be readily shown by way of a thought experiment. What would happen to someone who, having come to identify herself in her humanity with Christ in his, because of a common experience of unmerited suffering they share, no longer had the condition under which that suffering is experienced? In terms of the general Christian intuition of concern for the *anawim*, we may legitimately ask in this (fortuitous) scenario: Does she thereby cease to be a "living icon" of Christ or a "privileged witness" to him? The answer to the question could be either yes or no, for it would evidently depend on how she continues to live her life, now that she is free of the suffering experienced as a result of the condition lived. We may say this because "Icon?" and "Witness?" are not questions we ask of the nature of something, so their measurement is not dependent upon the presence or absence of the condition itself. Consequently, someone's nearness to being an icon or witness would be appropriately measured in terms of nearness-of-approach, the kind of measure that pertains to the life being lived.

According to the structure of the associating move, however, where the lived condition confirms the nature conferred, the condition itself becomes the overriding, determinative factor in the woman's nearness to Christ's humanity. This measure of her humanity is made in terms of nearness-by-likeness, the form of measure pertaining to her nature and not to her living. The associating move, therefore, requires a further (rather unfortunate) question to be asked of this woman because of her fortuitous turn of events: Does she cease being a human being at all? And, bizarrely, the logic of the associating move suggests that it could—would have to—countenance an answer in the affirmative. Remove the condition as it has come to be lived, and a doubt is raised about the very humanity of the woman. This flawed outcome is a result of the way in which the associating move takes the focus proper to one form of nearness as reason to use that form to measure something that is properly the focus of the other. As the thought experiment shows, such confusion should be avoided.

Measuring the Humanity of the Profoundly Impaired

The basic thrust of the associating move is a deeply appealing one to theologians concerned with securing the humanity of the profoundly impaired. Consider, for example, the following remarks by Reynolds (who is, on this point, relying on the support of Eiesland):

> At the cross [the fully human person] Jesus subjects himself to disability . . . as a sign of God's solidarity with humanity. . . . It suggests that disability indicates not a flawed humanity but a full humanity. Our bodies participate in the *imago Dei* in and through vulnerability and its consequent impairments, not despite them.[17]

What seems to be driving the appeal of the associating move is the way in which it approaches the question of the humanity of the profoundly impaired from the perspective of belonging. How can certain people, who, for whatever reason, are perceived to be marginalized through no (moral) fault of their own doing, be assured of their full human status and dignity in the human community? To quote Reynolds again:

> Disability is redemptive . . . because God affirms [it] by embodying it in Christ, contesting exclusion and ratifying vulnerability and relational interdependence as normative.[18]

This desire to belong leads to essentially the same thing we encountered earlier in terms of friendship, namely: "the need for an act of inclusion."[19] As was noted in the case of friendship, when the drive for inclusion dominates, confusion in the argument seems to follow. In the present case, what has emerged as problematic is the confusion generated by treating the condition suffered as the sign and locus of being fully human, as measured in terms of the human nature of Christ. The task this presents, therefore, is one of finding a path out of this confusion, without abandoning the basic Christian intuition affirming the humanity of those

---

17. Reynolds, *Vulnerable Communion*, 207.
18. Ibid., 210.
19. Wannenwetsch, "Angels with Clipped Wings," 183.

who suffer innocently because of the condition under which they have come to live their lives. To this end, it will be helpful to consider the question of how the associating move goes from the conditioned suffered to the nature conferred (and not just what the move is and why it is made).

From the perspective of a Christian anthropology, the question of our humanity cannot be separated out from the question of the humanity of Christ. This is the evangelical given that, as we have seen, finds an explicit voice in the Letter to the Hebrews, but which is also amply present in the Pauline corpus and in the New Testament, generally. The doctrinal expression for this anthropological tradition, however, comes with the christological formulae of the Council of Chalcedon.[20] It was there that the Church settled on a language and concept—"person"—to use for talking about the man Jesus Christ, and in so doing for talking about humanity in general. As Spaemann has noted about the Chalcedonian contribution,

> It was the concept "person," the equivalent of the Greek *hypostasis*, that made it possible to understand the application of the personal pronoun . . . without making Jesus appear as a theophany clothed in human form.[21]

With this "application of the personal pronoun," what proved significant for the one human being, Jesus Christ, thereby proved significant for all human beings; Chalcedon was not only a christological doctrine, but also an anthropological one.

---

20. Here is a translation of the pertinent paragraph (§34) from the fifth session (22 October 451) of the Council: "Following, therefore, the holy fathers, we all in harmony teach confession of one and the same Son our Lord Jesus Christ, the same perfect Godhead and the same perfect in manhood, truly God and the same truly man, of a rational soul and body, consubstantial with the Father in respect of the Godhead, and the same consubstantial with us in respect of the manhood, like us in all things apart from sin, begotten from the Father before the ages in respect of the Godhead, and the same in the last days for us and for our salvation from the Virgin Mary the Theotokos in respect of the manhood, one and the same Christ, Son, Lord, Only-begotten, acknowledged in two natures without confusion, change, division, or separation (the difference of the natures being in no way destroyed by the union, but rather the distinctive character of each nature being preserved and coming together into one person and one hypostasis), not parted or divided into two persons, but one and the same Son, Only-begotten, God, Word, Lord, Jesus Christ, even the prophets from of old and Jesus Christ himself taught us about him and the symbol of the fathers has handed down to us." Price and Gaddis (trans.), *Acts of the Council of Chalcedon*, 2:203.

21. Spaemann, *Persons*, 27–28.

What makes the anthropology of Chalcedon especially worth noting at this point, however, is the specific trajectory it takes: it seeks to establish Jesus Christ as truly a human being—as like unto human nature—and not the other way around. This is important because the associating move, for its part, reverses this trajectory in making its argument. Instead of working from the Chalcedonian position: "He is like us in all things . . .," the associating move strikes out for the position: "They are like him in key things . . ." This is not to suggest that making such a reversal is problematic in and of itself. We have already seen how it is important to consider the extent to which our own lives approach that of the life of Jesus Christ, the rule of measure for living a human life.

Yet, here is the rub: the reversal of trajectory would appear to come into its own only when the question—Human being?—is being asked about a human life lived, measurable, as this is, in term of nearness-of-approach. In this case, the very humanity of someone—Is she a human being, or not?—is neither the point of focus nor the measure being sought; the life she is living, and the measure of it, is subsequent to the question of her humanity. Yet it is her very humanity—measurable as it is in terms of nearness-by-likeness—that the associating move is aiming to assure with its reversal of the Chalcedonian trajectory. At the very least, this suggests that the difference in trajectory is substantially significant, and not just a matter of grammatical preference. So, the question to pursue now is this: What difference does the direction of the trajectory make to understanding the humanity of the profoundly impaired?

By way of an initial point, consider how the two trajectories are concerned with markedly different kinds of questions about human beings. In its anthropological form, the Chalcedonian trajectory concerns itself with how one human being relates to human beings generally. As such, the point of focus is the nature conferred, and not the life lived. This is because there is no such thing as a generic "human life lived" against which the measure of one individual life may then be taken. There is, however, a way of considering human beings generally, and that is in terms of their being of human kind. This seems to be the key question the Chalcedonian trajectory seeks to answer. This is confirmed in the formulae of Chalcedon itself: the Council Fathers were not interested in establishing the kind of human life Jesus lived, but with whether or not he was truly a human being, "consubstantial with us in respect of the manhood." Consequently, we may say that the measure proper to the

Chalcedonian trajectory is that which is concerned with the question of the nature conferred, namely, nearness-by-likeness.

The trajectory adopted by the associating move, on the other hand, is concerned with the relationship of some human beings to one other human being. Unlike with the Chalcedonian trajectory, however, there is no general anthropological form to this trajectory; it is always specific. This is because the "one other" must be specified or there is nothing by which a measurement can be made. Because the form of the trajectory demands that a specific other is chosen, then it is something about the life of the other—something revealed through the lived experience—which becomes important. In the associating move, we know this something to be the human suffering experienced by Jesus Christ, so we immediately enter into a question of the way in which his human life has been lived. The corresponding measure to the question of a human life lived is that which measures in the form of nearness-of-approach. It is only in the universalizing of the life of Jesus, by designating him the representative human being, that the associating move can claim the experience itself to be determinative for being fully human.

To sum up the point being made, the relational difference—on the one hand, one human being related to human beings generally; and on the other, some human beings related to one other human being specifically—neatly highlights how each trajectory is, in fact, focused on a different way of measuring being human. The former lends itself to questions asked about the "kindedness" of human beings, while the latter lends itself to questions about the life lived by human beings, with each drawing on its corresponding form of measure.

What is to be made of this difference in trajectories, when seen from the perspective of measuring Christ's humanity, for those who live lives of profound impairment? In seeking to answer this question, let us take it that either trajectory may be adopted for the same sound reason: to ensure that certain conditioned human beings—the profoundly impaired—are "one of us," that is, they are full members of the human community and indeed exemplars of humanity ("icons" and "witnesses"). Furthermore, let us assume that both trajectories also aim to show how such individuals are, in a special way, near to Christ, who became "one of us" in the fullest sense. Now to the question itself.

Achieving Humanity under the Condition of Being Impaired?

An effective way of seeing what difference the two trajectories make is to consider the way in which each takes the measure of the "fullest sense" of the humanity of Jesus. We may recall that the trajectory adopted by the associating move seeks to relate the condition suffered by "the some" (that is, the profoundly impaired) to the experience of suffering of "the other" (that is, Jesus Christ). Accordingly, the specific manner in which the humanity of Jesus is measured, and the measure by which the humanity of the profoundly impaired is subsequently assured, focuses in on the details of how he came to live his human life. In this regard, it is not that Jesus suffered a human's death that matters, but that he experienced human suffering in his death. What counts for the full sense of Jesus' humanity, therefore, is the measure of his humanity by-virtue-of-his-living, and not his humanity in-virtue-of-which-he-lived. It is this measure of Jesus' humanity that the associating move then takes up in presenting its argument: given that Jesus suffered like a human being (thereby "proving" that he was a human being in the fullest sense), and if the profoundly impaired can be shown to suffer like Jesus suffered, then the profoundly impaired are "proved" to be human beings in the same manner as Jesus was.

We should note carefully what has just occurred: simply being a human being is no longer enough to be human "in the fullest sense." Humanity becomes an achievement when this trajectory is adopted. Jesus is said to be fully human because of the suffering he experienced (humanity by-virtue-of-his-living). We must ask what caused the suffering. What made the experience so measurably significant? We seem to have no option but to posit some condition Jesus had as a human being, something that was more than him simply being human, to do the work. The one unmentioned, but implicit "condition" of Jesus that is readily at hand is his divinity: through experiencing the "condition" of his divinity, the suffering of Jesus takes on the fullness of humanity.[22] As one theologian, who advocates a form of the associating move with regard to those suffering from dementia, has put it: "the God who validates our existence must in some sense participate in it."[23] What is made to happen in Jesus is

---

22. I have placed "condition" in inverted commas to highlight the obvious unorthodoxy that is entailed here by mixing the natures of Jesus.

23. Kevern, "What Sort of a God," 180. In keeping with the pattern, Kevern also draws on Eiesland to support his claim.

subsequently mirrored in the profoundly impaired: they, too, need their condition so as to achieve the fullness of their humanity. They are shown to have, like Jesus, that "something extra" that makes all the difference. The measure of the humanity of Jesus and of the profoundly impaired is reduced to the condition itself; it is made to carry the weight of their being human in the fullest sense. Remove the condition, whatever it is, and the individual's hold on humanity is undermined.

The opposite is the case in terms of the Chalcedonian trajectory, in which one human being is related to human beings generally. Here, the claim is that the fullest sense of the humanity of Jesus is measured as the humanity in-virtue-of-which-he-lived. The veracity of this claim may be confirmed by returning briefly to the Letter to the Hebrews, and to the passage where the author makes the link between Jesus, the man, and his suffering:

> Therefore he had to become like his brothers in every respect, so that he might be a merciful and faithful high priest in the service of God, to make a sacrifice of atonement for the sins of the people. Because he himself was tested by what he suffered, he is able to help those who are being tested. (Heb 2:17–18)

The "so that" in the first sentence is the key; it says that Jesus' life of suffering is the achievement of his humanity, and not the precondition for his humanity. To read this passage otherwise would be to render the "so that" pointless. According to Hebrews, then, it is because Jesus is a man, a human being, that his suffering is in any way meaningful for us, who are (also) human beings. This is not to say that the life that Jesus lived, as a man, was not of crucial value for us; clearly from the text, his suffering was seen to be efficacious. Only because Jesus' life was a human life did it take on the specific value that it did. It is essential to the Christian revelation that Jesus did not save the world because of the fine words he spoke or the wonderful deeds he performed; nor that he saved it because of certain (or the sum of) personal experiences he had. He saved the world by his becoming a human being and dying a human death.

Herbert McCabe provides a wonderfully droll way of driving home the point: "Of course he was crucified: he was human wasn't he?"[24] The sense of his comment is that the death Jesus suffered was efficacious because of his humanity, his being a man, and not because of the suffering condition in which he died. The suffering is an achievement of the

---

24. McCabe, *God Still Matters*, 96.

humanity, not the humanity an achievement of the suffering. "Jesus died of being human," as McCabe goes on to say.[25] The suffering he bore, the death he endured, is meaningful for us because, and only because, he was a human being; it was his being a man that made all the difference. (Conversely, Jesus' humanity—his being a man—is of no saving value to any other creature, other than fellow human beings.) Importantly, "likeness" in this context ("like his brothers") is not that of approach, but that of identity. Jesus was not deemed a human being—he did not approach the achievement of humanity—because of the way he suffered and died; he was a human being who suffered and died. The Chalcedonian trajectory, in other words, does not posit a condition of humanity to do the work of measurement; instead, it presents the human being whose condition it is simply to live as the human being he is. McCabe sums this up well when he says,

> The gospel we preach is not about memories or ideas or profound thoughts [or, we may add, experiences had]. It contains all these things, but what it is about is the human person, Jesus, alive and present to us and loving us from his human heart.[26]

This final remark confirms that there is a real difference between the two trajectories we have been considering, with the expectation that it will make a corresponding real difference to how the question—Human being?—is answered, including when asked of the profoundly impaired. All along, the task of responding to the question of their humanity has been one of showing how they are the human beings that they are. When it has come to taking the measure of that humanity, the issue of the condition under which they live their lives has risen to the surface. What we now have seen is that the associating trajectory takes this issue of condition to be referring to something about the individual in question, which then determines the question of his or her humanity; whereas the Chalcedonian trajectory understands it to be concerned with the task of living, which the individual does in virtue of his or her humanity. In the former, "condition" is a state of living under which a life achieves humanity (humanity by-virtue-of-one's-living), while in the latter "condition" is simply the concrete state of being human (humanity in-virtue-of-which-one-lives).

---

25. Ibid.
26. Ibid., 227.

Why should we expect this to make a difference to how we may secure the humanity of the profoundly impaired? Recall the Christian intuition, as expressed in the remarks of Pope John Paul II and Benedict XVI, whereby the condition suffered by the profoundly impaired is a sign of assurance to them (and to us) that they are like Christ in the suffering he experienced. What is particularly characteristic of this intuition is that the measure of it has to do with the lives being lived, not the natures conferred. In other words, the condition under which someone is living like Christ is relative to the life he is living, not to the nature he has. In the associating move, the condition that a profoundly impaired individual brings to the measuring table is related to his nature, something that has been conferred on him. So we are left with a situation where either the wrong kind of thing is being measured or the wrong measure is being applied. Either way, the manner in which the associating trajectory understands "condition" leaves the humanity of the profoundly impaired confused and undermined.

The Human Condition Lived

It is in taking the measure of the human condition itself—humanity in-virtue-of-which-one-lives—that the humanity, and thereby the dignity, of the profoundly impaired may best be secured. It is the anthropological trajectory evident in the formulae of Chalcedon that offers a theologically sound way for how this is to be done. This is the conclusion we may draw from the preceding discussion. For in the end, if the profoundly impaired both are, and are meant to be, like Christ in the same way as all other human beings, then this must be reflected in how their humanity is measured. Because the Chalcedonian trajectory answers the question—Are they human?—in terms of nearness-by-likeness, and the question—Are they meant to be human?—in terms of nearness-of-approach, it gets right the combination of measurement and thing measured.

It has always been the case for the profoundly impaired that the condition under which they live their lives is the issue that matters. What our discussion has helped to clarify is that the measure of their impairment is properly placed in the context of the lives that they are living, and not in the context of the natures that they have (as it is with the associating move). In a way, we have come to the point where we may say that the condition of their impairment is both sufficient and necessary for answering the question—Human being? It is sufficient because, *qua* the human nature conferred, the condition of their impairment is simply the concrete particular expression of their humanity; and it is necessary because, *qua* the human life lived, it is the only location, as it were, in which they may live the lives that they have. By implication, the profoundly impaired are both secure in their humanity and still in need of continually winning through to their closeness to Christ. It is how they have come to live their lives, under the condition in which they have their lives, that matters; not the condition itself. In this way, the suffering of the profoundly impaired is like Christ to the extent that they draw close to him in the lives they live, and this is measured by nearness-in-approach, in exactly the same way as it is for all other human beings. We might say that, for the profoundly impaired, as with all other human beings, it is not a matter of being "one of us" that counts, but living well "all of me." To take on as our own the words of Rowan Williams: "God accepts [human] bodiliness in its actual condition."[27]

---

27. Williams, "On Being a Human Body," 409.

CONCLUSION

"BEYOND INCLUSION!"
Humanity Lived under the Condition of Impairment

Moving Beyond the Paradigm of Inclusion

THE HOMEPAGE OF L'ARCHE International's website begins with the bold declaration "Beyond inclusion!" complete with exclamation mark to drive home the point.[1] Born out of the lived experience of Jean Vanier, who made his home with the profoundly disabled more than fifty years ago, L'Arche describes itself as an organization centered on "people, with and without an intellectual disability, who share their lives in homes, workshops and day programmes which are grouped into . . . communities." In this light, we might say that the slogan "Beyond inclusion!" is something akin to the mission statement of L'Arche; its corporate brand. As the website goes on to say, "L'Arche works closely with people with an intellectual disability so that each person can play their full role in society. . . . More than just inclusion, it is about making the most of life!"

We have in L'Arche's opening declaration both an encouraging acclamation in support of the lives of those who are intellectually disabled and something of a bold challenge to anyone who would envisage their lives in less supportive ways. As we come to the conclusion of this book, it is the challenging dimension to go beyond inclusion that is particularly pertinent. The point of the slogan seems to be about shifting attitudes of negativity, closure, and denial towards the profoundly disabled to

---

1. http://www.larche.org/home.en-gb.1.0.index.htm.

something more positive, open, and accepting. Furthermore, the use of the exclamation mark suggests that this is not to be taken as a tentative proposal proffered for consideration; rather, it is a bold declaration to those who would make inclusion the sole criterion upon which the personal status of the profoundly disabled is to be measured.

It has been our contention in this book that recognizing the moral status of the those who live their lives at the extremes of human life—recognizing them to be the persons that they are—cannot work from within an anthropological framework that would place notions aimed at achieving inclusion, such as friendship, at the heart of the question—Human being? The slogan adopted by L'Arche suggests, at the very least, that the notion of inclusion is something problematic for the intellectually disabled that needs to be overcome and moved beyond if their moral status within human society is to be supported. What the L'Arche headline declares in relation to the lives of the profoundly disabled, therefore, we may adopt as a kind of slogan for the position developed throughout this book in relation to the profoundly impaired, more generally. Thus (and to make the point in the more familiar phraseology of the book): the notion of inclusion of the profoundly impaired amongst the community of persons is such a negative thing for them that we need to move beyond the notion itself if we are to adequately acknowledge and respect—that is, recognize—their claim to humanity; we need to go beyond inclusion.

The drive to place a paradigm of inclusion at the heart of a re-imagined Christian anthropology attentive to the lives of the profoundly impaired was both the point of departure for and the undercurrent of the book. This group of persons, we noticed, is identifiable by the fact that their cognitive faculties of reason, will and self awareness—those characteristics of a human being commonly associated with the moral status of being a person—are, or have come to be, grossly undermined or entirely absent. The nature of such conditions of impairment are often perplexing in the extreme, and the lives of those so conditioned are often considered a tragic mystery. Yet, it is the usual practice in contemporary human culture—both domestically and institutionally—to foster their dignity and to attend to their wellbeing. It is by means of such commonplace practices that the profoundly impaired are generally recognized as peers within the human community.

However, we also identified that there are those who would deny that the profoundly impaired are persons precisely because of the impaired condition in which they live their lives. And there are others who would uphold the personhood of the profoundly impaired precisely by side-lining their impairment. In both positions, it is the condition of the impairment that makes the difference. So, if we are to accept the intuition that the profoundly impaired are recognizably persons precisely in the condition in which they are living their lives, as is evidenced in our practices of care towards them, then we need to ask how is it that they are recognizably the persons that they are. This is to suggest that there is something at stake precisely in their being the particularly conditioned human beings that they are, yet we would not want it to be the case that their claim to personhood is dependent upon the condition of their impairment.

This is where the notion of inclusion has taken up a significant explanatory role in the lives of the profoundly impaired, especially in the emerging field in Christian theology that proposes a distinct theology of disability that seeks to re-imagine Christian anthropology for the profoundly impaired such that their humanity is secured without the condition of their humanity becoming an obstacle to their personal recognition. Key to this re-imagining is the adoption of a framework or paradigm of inclusion around which the condition of human impairment is separated out from the question of our human nature. The profoundly impaired, so the argument goes, can be seen to be included in the community of persons when human nature is not defined in terms of the human capacity for reason and will. The condition of their impairment is not made to be determinative of their claim to being human.

Most noteworthy in this regard, and the chief protagonist with which we have engaged, is the Dutch theologian Hans Reinders and his work, *Receiving the Gift of Friendship*. As we have seen, Reinders is concerned with two related claims: that the profoundly intellectually disabled are "people just like other people" and that, therefore, whatever it is that makes human beings distinctive "it cannot be the human faculties," those features of personhood that the profoundly disabled do not have. His basic thesis is this: because the profoundly disabled lack in their natures the requisite characteristics of personhood—especially rationality, volition, and self-awareness—then any theology centered on the notion of personhood cannot secure for them their moral status within the human community. Therefore, how might we view human life without reference to reason and will? Reinders' answer is that it is only in the concept of friendship—in being chosen as a friend—that the life of someone who is profoundly disabled can come to transcend the impaired condition of their lives, and so be seen as a full member of the human community. Friendship, in other words, and not personhood, is the only sure way of securing the humanity of the profoundly impaired.

The Ambivalence of "Inclusion"

There is no reason for rehearsing the fatal flaws in Reinders' project. There are two points, nonetheless, worth recalling as we ourselves move beyond inclusion. First, his entire position stands or falls on finding a way in which the profoundly disabled can be fully included in the human community: they cannot be included as persons, but they can be included as friends. In other words, a paradigm of inclusion drives his project to secure the humanity of the profoundly impaired. Secondly, his project depends on separating out the condition in which the profoundly impaired find themselves—in particular their lack of certain capacities—from their status as human beings. Reinders does not want their condition to complicate or get in the way of their claim to inclusion in the human community.

To begin with, the first claim. The very idea that "inclusion" is itself the one sought-after good necessary for securing the humanity of the profoundly impaired falls at the first hurdle because it fails to ever ask what it is that the profoundly impaired are being included into; and in failing to ask this question, it fails to recognize that what precisely they are included into may not be at all good for them. The British journalist Ian Birrell, when he was deputy editor of *The Independent* newspaper, makes this point well in two written opinion pieces about the experience of being the parent of his severely disabled teenage daughter, called Iona.[2] Iona has suffered from a complex epileptic condition that has left her blind, unable to walk or talk, and in need of twenty-four-hour care. Her life is one of pain and struggle, and the Birrell family has lived with the constant proximity of her death: "Each fit damages her brain, slowly stripping away her ability to smile, to eat, to hold our hands. The only certainty is that each one could be her last."

In these articles, Birrell writes of a particular kind of inclusion that comes from being a parent of a profoundly disabled child: "We have been thrust into the hidden world of disability, a land shockingly ignored by

---

2. Birrell, "How a disabled child changed my politics, and those of David Cameron," and "Iona and Ivan—a tale of two children and two families."

the rest of society." He notes how inclusion into this world, to which he did not choose to belong, has not only come to impact on all facets of their lives, but also has come to be the overriding directive of their lives and loves. The inclusion being spoken of here is of an intimate and personal kind; it is about how the circumstances of one member of a family have influenced the lives of the rest. Iona's life has meant that the whole family has had to journey together into an "unwanted, unique" world, setting them apart from most other people. Yet, it is also a world they have come to cherish.

Birrell also writes of another kind of inclusion, one that equally has been thrust upon his family as a consequence of Iona's condition. It is not, however, an inclusion in which they find much value, either for the family or for Iona personally. It is an institutional inclusion, for want of a better word, born of a certain political and social ideology that is concerned with the integration of the disabled into the normal structures of society. Of this kind of inclusion he concludes: "Inclusion is a fine aim, but it has become an over-riding dogma at a time when there is a rise in the number of kids born with multiple disabilities."

The language Birrell uses of a "hidden," "unique" world in which the profoundly impaired are to be found, "shockingly ignored" by society, points to the experience of having become immersed into a way of living significantly removed from the usual world of human interaction and activity. This experience of immersion into one world and removal from another has exposed the entire Birrell family to an existence both unknown and shunned by most other people. Yet it is precisely the life they have immersed themselves into that is described as bringing joy and meaning. In doing so, Birrell does not present himself as two men: he is not one man who lives in the world of the impaired and then another, different man who lives in the world of the un-impaired. He is, instead, the man who stands before the un-hidden world as the man who has been begotten, so to speak, of the hidden one. In being this man that he is, the true value of his daughter's humanity, which becomes present to the world of the unimpaired through his humanity, is revealed in his incorporation into her impaired life. Crucially, his humanity has been revealed only because of his incorporation into her impaired life, and not because of her incorporation in his un-impaired life. As a result, he has come to recognize the human being that he is by immersing his life into the life of the human being that Iona is. Birrell has "won his own humanity" in recognizing the humanity of his daughter precisely in her impaired condition.[3]

This is Birrell's personal experience, of course, and it is written with a journalist's eye to making a political point. Nonetheless, his article highlights how the notion of inclusion can be experienced both as a good and as an evil, as something creative and as something destructive. It certainly raises questions about the value of expressing the humanity of the profoundly impaired within the context of a paradigm of inclusion. It also suggests that we do indeed have good reasons for seeking to go beyond the notion of inclusion in securing their personal presence amongst the human community.

Wannenwetsch offers a helpful theological insight into what lies behind Birrell's ambivalent experience of inclusion, when he says,

> We are tempted to understand the predication of a disabled human being as "person" as a kind of benevolent stretching of the concept from the usual case toward the unusual. In other words, we are led to think of this "including" of the disabled within the protected zone which we inhabit—"even the disabled!"—as a required moral act. . . . I rather wish to call attention to the mistaken assumption on which [this notion] is based: the need for an act of inclusion that, in turn, rests on an abstract and preconceived concept of personhood that is to be merely applied to disabled human life, instead of being won from a perceptive understanding of the phenomenon [of personal life] itself.[4]

This dense commentary actually offers a simple point: the mistaken assumption of a paradigm of inclusion is that it calls for the impaired to be incorporated into the notion of personhood as it is applied to someone who is unimpaired. In other words, it views personhood as an achievement of humanity, as something to be gained by the profoundly impaired. Whereas, the Christian perspective is that personhood is something that is waiting to be discovered—recognized—in the midst of someone's impairment. The profoundly impaired do not have to measure up to humanity, as a paradigm of inclusion would have it; instead, they are already the measure of humanity.

---

3. Wannenwetsch, "Angels with Clipped Wings," 183.
4. Ibid.

"Descending the Ladder"

Where, then, are we to go instead, if we are to leave behind the notion of inclusion? Helpfully for those who look for a gospel-centered understanding of the lives of the profoundly impaired, Jean Vanier offers a way forward. As noted early in the book, Vanier has often written about the need for the strong and powerful, those who stand at the top of the social ladder, to descend that ladder to the place where the weak and broken find themselves. He argues that it is only by descending this ladder that human beings will come to discover their humanity. Vanier has described his own life in communion with the profoundly disabled as a sign "touching the roots" of our humanity, and he speaks often of how he himself has been transformed by "descending the ladder." Consider his words:

> The vision of God is to go down the social ladder to take the lowest place in order to *be with* the weak and the broken. Then God rises up *with* them to build a new community which does not forget or exclude anyone. Many people want to climb up the social ladder of individual success and promotion . . . [It is] a cycle in which each one tries to push and hold down the other motivated by the fear of being dominated by someone stronger. Jesus tells us: "Stop being so frightened and forever trying to protect yourself! Stop trying to defend and justify yourself! Stop associating only with people like yourself! . . . Go down the ladder. Become a friend of the weak and the broken, and a friend of God.[5]

As is evident from this quotation, Vanier wants to distance our understanding of God—and the understanding of ourselves who are made in God's image—from "our society's obsession with images of mastery and autonomy."[6] While notions of inclusion and friendship are present in Vanier's picture, their true, God-given nature will not be found within human activity that is centered on self-justification. Instead, Vanier uses the ladder metaphor to indicate that befriending and including do not make the human being, but are themselves dependent on a certain vision of human life which is not dominated by notions of capacity, autonomy, and the like.

Our humanity comes through an act of self-emptying, of giving up what we cling to, and thereby of opening up to a similarly self-emptied

---

5. Vanier, *Befriending the Stranger*, 41, 43.
6. Wannenwetsch, "Angels with Clipped Wings," 192.

life. By descending the ladder, just as Jesus did, by being with similarly self-emptied people, we are open to accepting them into our lives, and thereby discovering their personal presence. The view of friendship and inclusion from the bottom of the ladder, therefore, is one where I am free to be with others, which is a reversal of the image from the top of the ladder where I consent that others may be with me.[7]

Humanity Lived under the Condition of Impairment

The insight to be drawn from Vanier's use of the ladder metaphor is that the true measure of our humanity is not to be found in ascribing personhood to others but in accepting that we are persons in virtue of the life we are called to live, in the condition under which we are living it (be it impaired or unimpaired). The personal presence of the creature who hopes is already there to be lived—and possibly lost; it is not something always waiting to be gained. In the end, if the profoundly impaired are truly personally present in the human community, in the same way as every other human being, then this must be evident precisely in the lives that they are living under the condition of their impairment.

This question of the relationship between one's existence as a human being and the condition in which one lives out that existence brings us back to the second of the issues raised by Reinders' reliance on a paradigm of inclusion. Should the condition of impairment itself have an influence on how we might come to recognize the humanity of someone who is profoundly impaired? Is one's impairment crucial to one's very humanity? The answer developed in this book is to say: yes, it does make a difference, but not in any undermining way, as a paradigm of inclusion might view it. To say that the profoundly impaired are truly personally present in the human community through the lives that they are already living under the condition of their impairment is another way of saying that the profoundly impaired can only be the human beings that they are in the condition in which they are living. There is no way of being human outside of the condition in which that humanity is lived. This issue of one's condition, therefore, has to do with the task of living, which an individual does in virtue of his or her humanity. We do not have to

---

7. A more detailed examination of the anthropological implications in Vanier's ladder metaphor is offered by the author in "Descending the Ladder: The Theological Anthropology of Jean Vanier's Key Metaphor."

have a certain condition—for instance, a certain level of rationality or self-awareness—so as to achieve humanity. Rather, the condition of our humanity is simply the concrete state in which we are being human.

Why should we expect this to make a difference to how we may secure the humanity of the profoundly impaired? We need only recall the intuition with which we began—namely, the practices of care that society generally shows towards the profoundly impaired is a sign that they are recognizably persons. What is particularly characteristic of this intuition is that the measure of it has to do with the lives being lived, and not some status extended to them as an act of inclusion. It is not the condition of their humanity that determines this recognition of personhood; rather, it is the recognition of their personal presence that prompts us to attend to their condition.

The measure of our humanity, therefore, is not determined by the condition of it; personhood is not something to be achieved, either by the capacities we already have or by an act of moral inclusion when we lack those capacities. Someone's humanity is not determined via an invitation into the club of being "one of us." Yet the condition of our humanity is the only means we have by which we live out our humanity. Personhood is always a lived reality, and not merely a category to be applied. In this sense, the moral claim that the profoundly impaired make upon us is made via the condition of their humanity—their "all of me," so to speak. It is not about finding ways in which they might be included as "one of us." The human condition is determinative of being human, while the condition under which a human being exists is the location of their humanity.

When all is said and done, it has always been the case for the profoundly impaired that the condition under which they live their lives is the issue that matters. What this book has sought to do is to shed light on the ways in which the measure of their humanity is properly secured in the context of the lives that they are actually and already living, and not in some idealized life that we, the unimpaired, might hope for them. By implication, the profoundly impaired are both secure in their humanity, and still need to continually win through to it, just like every other human being. It is how they have come to live their lives, under the condition in which they have their lives, that matters; not the condition itself. It is not a matter of the profoundly impaired being included amongst "one of us" that counts, but that we and they together may discover the extent to which we are each living well "all of me" in the condition in which we each are living our lives.

The inclusion of the profoundly impaired amongst the community of human persons has been a central theme running through this book, prompted by the emergence of the theological trend to re-imagine Christian anthropology from within a paradigm of inclusion attentive to the lives of the profoundly impaired. Questions have been raised, from the perspective of a Catholic anthropological imagination, about the soundness of these attempts to configure the lives of the profoundly impaired in terms of such a paradigm. The notions of human friendship and the creaturely life of human beings have been the principal prisms through which this task has been undertaken.

It is not to be doubted that the condition of impairment of the profoundly impaired needs to be front and center in any question that seeks to ask about the recognition of their personhood. If they are recognizably persons, as has been our guiding presupposition, then they are the persons that they are in the condition under which they live. What this book has drawn attention to is that this cannot be shown to be the case by re-imagining the anthropology of the profoundly impaired in terms of friendship. This is not to deny the crucial and integral role that ought to be given to friendship in the living of any human life; befriending and being befriended are truly humanizing activities. It is to say, however, that the notion of friendship cannot ground what it means to be the human being that one is because it does not deal with the question of who it is that that human being is.

Friendship, in the end, demands to know something about what it is to be human, because it wants to know who it is who is being befriended. Only a robust theology of created human nature can provide an adequate response to this demand. This is the conclusion towards which the arguments of this book have been moving. The God who befriends human beings is the God who created human nature so as to be befriendable, and is faithful to his creation to the point of entering it. Friendship does not precede human nature, therefore; it gives expression to that which is made in the image of God.

It is within this reality that the lives of the profoundly impaired are to be located. They are not extended the hand of human personhood because they are befriended by God; they are, instead, befriended by God because they are being the human beings that God created them to be. They are human creatures made in the image of God. For the profoundly impaired, that means the condition of their impairment is indeed a crucial feature of their humanity because it is the condition under which they are living out their humanity. Consequently, they cannot be the human beings that they are without the recognition of this reality. That is to say: the condition of their humanity is determinative of them being the persons that they are, but not determinative of them being persons as such. Even though the lived experience of the profoundly impaired often leaves them exposed to exclusion from enjoying a personal presence amongst the human community, they do not need firstly to be extended the hand of friendship for them actually to be included because they are there already. A robust Christian anthropology is called to attend to this, but it will not do so unless it moves beyond inclusion.

BIBLIOGRAPHY

Agius, Emmanuel. "Disability, Bioethics and Human Rights." Conference paper: received electronically from the author, 2007.
Anscombe, Gertrude Elizabeth. "Under a Description." 1979. Reprinted in *Metaphysics and the Philosophy of Mind*, 208–19. Collected Philosophical Papers 2. Oxford: Blackwell, 1981.
Aquinas, Thomas. *Commentary on Aristotle's Nicomachean Ethics*. Translated by C. I. Litzinger. Notre Dame: Dumb Ox, 1993.
———. *Summa Contra Gentiles*. Translated by J. F. Anderson. Notre Dame: University of Notre Dame Press, 1975.
———. *Summa Theologiæ*. Edited by T. Gilby and T. C. O'Brien. Blackfriars edition. 61 vols. London: Blackfriars, 1964–81.
Arendt, Hannah. *The Human Condition*. 2nd ed. Chicago: University of Chicago Press, 1998.
Ashley, Benedict. "What Is the End of the Human Person? The Vision of God and Integral Human Fulfilment." In *Moral Truth and Moral Tradition: Essays in Honour of Peter Geach and Elizabeth Anscombe*, edited by Luke Gormally, 69–86. Dublin: Four Courts, 1994.
Ashley, Benedict, and Kevin O'Rourke. *Health Care Ethics: A Catholic Theological Analysis*. 5th ed. Washington, DC: Georgetown University Press, 2006.
Augustine. *Concerning the City of God Against the Pagans: A New Translation*. Translated by H. Bettenson. Harmondsworth: Penguin, 1972.
———. *Letter to Jerome (CLXVI)*. Translated by W. Parsons. In vol. 4 of *Letters*. Fathers of the Church 30. New York: Fathers of the Church, 1955.
———. *The Nature and Origin of the Human Soul*. In *Answer to the Pelagians I*, translated by R. J. Teske, edited by J. E. Rotelle. The Works of St. Augustine I/23. New York: New City, 1997.
Balthasar, Hans Urs von. *The Glory of the Lord: A Theological Aesthetics*. Vol. 6, *Theology: The Old Covenant*. Edinburgh: T. & T. Clark, 1991.
———. "On the Concept of Person." Translated by Peter Verhale. *Communio: International Catholic Review* 13 (1986) 18–26.
Barrow, Robert H., trans. *Introduction to St. Augustine: The City of God, Being Selections from the De Civitate Dei, Including Most of the XIXth Book, with Text*. London: Faber and Faber, 1950.
Barth, Karl. *Church Dogmatics*. III, 1: *The Doctrine of Creation*. Edited by G. W. Bromiley and T. F. Torrance. Edinburgh: T. & T. Clark, 1958.

Bauckham, Richard. "The Divinity of Jesus Christ in the Epistle to the Hebrews." In *The Epistle to the Hebrews and Christian Theology*, edited by R. Bauckham et al., 15–36. Grand Rapids: Eerdmans, 2009.

Benedict XVI. Encyclical letter on Christian hope, *Spe salvi*. November 30, 2007. *Acta Apostolicae Sedis* 99 (2007) 985ff.

———. *Midday Angelus*. St. Peter's Square, July 12, 2009. http://www.vatican.va/holy_father/benedict_xvi/angelus/2009/documents/hf_benxvi_ang_20090712_en.html.

Birrell, Ian. "How a Disabled Child Changed My Politics—and Those of David Cameron." *The Independent*, October 20, 2005. http://www.independent.co.uk/voices/commentators/ian-birrell-how-a-disabled-child-changed-my-politics-and-those-of-david-cameron-320772.html.

———. "Iona and Ivan—a Tale of Two Children and Two Families." *The Independent*, February 26, 2009. http://www.independent.co.uk/opinion/commentators/ian-birrell-iona-and-ivan-ndash-a-tale-of-two-children-and-two-families-1632390.html.

Block, Jennie W. *Copious Hosting: A Theology of Access for People with Disability*. New York: Continuum, 2002.

Bloomberg, Craig L. "'But we See Jesus': The Relationship between the Son of Man in Hebrews 2.6 and 2.9 and the Implications for English Translations." In *A Cloud of Witness: The Theology of Hebrews in Its Ancient Contexts*, edited by R. Bauckham et al., 88–99. London: T. & T. Clark, 2008.

Bromiley, Geoffrey W., trans. and ed. *The Encyclopedia of Christianity*. 5 vols. Grand Rapids: Eerdmans, 1999–2008.

Brunner, Emil. *Man in Revolt: A Christian Anthropology*. Translated by O. Wyon. Cambridge: Lutterworth, 1957.

Carlson, Licia. *The Faces of Intellectual Disability: Philosophical Reflections*. Bloomington: Indiana University Press, 2010.

Carmichael, Liz. *Friendship: Interpreting Christian Love*. New York: Continuum, 2004.

Catholic Church. *Catechism of the Catholic Church*. New York: Doubleday, 1995.

Cessario, Romanus. *Introduction to Moral Theology*. Washington, DC: Catholic University of America Press, 2001.

———. "The Theological Virtue of Hope (IIa IIae, qq. 17–22)." In *The Ethics of Aquinas*, edited by S. J. Pope, 232–43. Washington, DC: Georgetown University Press, 2002.

Clément, Olivier. *On Human Being: A Spiritual Anthropology*. Translated by Jeremy Hummerstone. London: New City, 2000.

Coleman, Gerald D. "The Irreversible Disabling of a Child: The Ashley Treatment." *National Catholic Bioethics Quarterly* 7 (2007) 711–28.

Colloquium of the International Association of Catholic Bioethicists. "Consensus Statement on Dignity in Illness, Disability, and Dying: And a Response to the UNESCO Universal Draft Declaration on Bioethics and Human Rights." *National Catholic Bioethics Quarterly* 5/4 (2005) 767–81.

Congregation of the Doctrine of the Faith. "Instruction on Respect for Human Life at Its Origins and for the Dignity of Procreation, *Donum Vitae*." February 22, 1987. *Acta Apostolicae Sedis* 80 (1988) 70–102.

———. "Instruction on Certain Bioethical Questions, *Dignitas personae*." September 8, 2008. *Acta Apostolicae Sedis* 100 (2008) 858–87.

Corbon, Jean. *The Wellspring of Worship*. Translated by M. J. O'Connell. San Francisco: Ignatius, 2005.
D'Arcy, Martin C. *The Mind and Heart of Love: Lion and Unicorn; A Study in Eros and Agape*. 2nd ed. London: Faber and Faber, 1945.
Eberl, Jason T. *Thomistic Principles and Bioethics*. London: Routledge, 2006.
Eiesland, Nancy L. *The Disabled God: Toward a Liberatory Theology of Disability*. Nashville: Abingdon, 1994.
Elwell, Walter A., ed. *Evangelical Dictionary of Theology*. Grand Rapids: Baker, 1984.
Engelhardt, H. Tristam, Jr. *The Foundations of Bioethics*. 2nd ed. New York: Oxford University Press, 1996.
Faggioni, M. "Life and Forms of Life: The Relationship between Biology and Anthropology." In *The Culture of Life: Foundations and Dimensions*, edited by J. V. Correa and E. Sgreccia, 40–63. Vatican City: Libreria Editrice Vaticana, 2002.
Fergusson, David A. S. *The Cosmos and the Creator: A Introduction to the Theology of Creation*. London: SPCK, 1998.
Fitzgerald, Allan D., ed. *Augustine Through the Ages: An Encyclopedia*. Grand Rapids: Eerdmans, 1999.
Flannery, Kevin L. "Marriage, Mental Handicap, and Sexuality." *Studies in Christian Ethics* 17 (2004) 11–26.
Foyer, Dominique, Dominique Greiner, and Dominique Jacquemin, eds. *Oser parler du handicap: Approches éthiques et théologiques*. Paris: Cerf, 2009.
Francis, Pope. *Evangelii Gaudium: The Joy of the Gospel*. November 24, 2013. Acta Apostolicae Sedis 100 (2013) 1019–1137.
Gaita, Raimond. *A Common Humanity: Thinking about Love and Truth and Justice*. Melbourne: Text Publishing, 1999.
Garcia, Laura L. "Natural Kinds, Persons, and Abortion." *National Catholic Bioethics Quarterly* 8 (2008) 265–73.
Geiger, L. B. "L'homme, image de Dieu: A propos de Summa Theologiae I.93.4." *Rivista di Filosofia Neo-scolastica* 66 (1974) 511–32.
Gilges, Kent. *A Grace Given*. Canandaigua, NY: Cider, 2008.
Gillibrand, John. *Disabled Church—Disabled Society: The Implications of Autism for Philosophy, Theology and Politics*. London: J. Kingsley, 2010.
Grant, Colin. "For the Love of God: Agape." *Journal of Religious Ethics* 24 (1996) 3–21.
Grisez, Germain. *The Way of the Lord Jesus*. Vol. 1, *Christian Moral Principles*. Chicago: Franciscan Herald, 1983.
Haldane, John J. "The Mystery of Emergence." *Proceedings of the Aristotelian Society*, n.s., 96 (1996) 261–67.
———. *Practical Philosophy: Ethics, Society and Culture*. Exeter: Imprint-Academic, 2009.
———. "Rational and Other Animals." In *Reasonable Faith*, 120–28. London: Routledge, 2010.
———. "Recognising Humanity." *Journal of Applied Philosophy* 25 (2008) 301–13.
Haslam, Molly Claire. *A Constructive Theology of Intellectual Disability*. New York: Fordham University Press, 2012.
Hauerwas, Stanley. *Suffering Presence: Theological Reflection on Medicine, the Mentally Handicapped, and the Church*. Notre Dame: University of Notre Dame Press, 1986.

Hauerwas, Stanley, and Charles Pinches. *Christians among the Virtues: Theological Conversations with Ancient and Modern Ethics*. Notre Dame: University of Notre Dame Press, 1997.

Hauerwas, Stanley, and Jean Vanier. *Living Gently in a Violent World: The Prophetic Witness of Weakness*. Downers Grove, IL: IVP, 2008.

Hill, Edmund. *Being Human: A Biblical Perspective*. London: G. Chapman, 1984.

———. "Introduction." In vol. 13 of Thomas Aquinas, *Summa theologiæ*, xxi–xxxi. English Dominicans edition. London: Blackfriars, 1964.

Hill, W. J. "Appendix I: The Revelation of Hope in Sacred Scripture." In vol. 33 of Thomas Aquinas, *Summa theologiæ*, 123–28. English Dominicans edition. London: Blackfriars, 1966.

Innocent III, Pope. *On the Misery of the Human Condition: De miseria humane conditionis*. Edited by D. R. Howard. Translated by M. M. Dietz. Indianapolis: Bobbs-Merrill, 1969.

International Theological Commission. *Communion and Stewardship: Human Persons Created in the Image of God*. July 23, 2004. http://www.vatican.va/roman_curia/congregations/cfaith/cti_documents/rc_con_cfaith_doc_20040723_communion-stewardship_en.html.

Iozzio, Mary Jo. "Genetic Anomaly or Genetic Diversity: Thinking in the Key of Disability on the Human Genome." *Theological Studies* 66 (2005) 862–81.

———. "The Writing on the Wall . . . Alzheimer's Disease: A Daughter's Look at Mom's Faithful Care of Dad." *Journal of Religion, Disability & Health* 9 (2005) 49–74.

Isaacs, Marie E. *Reading Hebrews and James: A Literary and Theological Commentary*. Macon, GA: Smyth & Helwys, 2002.

Jeanrond, Werner G. *A Theology of Love*. London: Continuum, 2010.

John Paul II. Address: "The Mentally Ill Are also Made in God's Image." *Dolentium Hominum* 34/12 (1997) 474.

———. "Encyclical letter on the value and inviolability of human life." *Evangelium vitae*. March 25, 1995. *Acta Apostolicae Sedis* 87 (1995) 486–522.

———."Encyclical letter regarding certain fundamental questions of the Church's moral teaching." *Veritatis splendor*. August 6, 1993. *Acta Apostolicae Sedis* 85 (1993) 1133–1228.

———. "The Gospel of Life." *Evangelium vitae*. March 25, 1995. *Acta Apostolicae Sedis* 87 (1995).

———. *Man and Woman He Created Them: A Theology of the Body*. Translated by M. Waldstein. Boston: Pauline, 2006.

———. *Message on the Occasion of the International Symposium on the Dignity and Rights of the Mentally Disabled Person*. January 5, 2004. *Acta Apostolicae Sedis* 96 (2004).

Johnstone, Brian V. "The Self as Receiver and Giver: A Critique of the Modern and Post-modern Self." *Australian E-Journal of Theology* 7 (June 2006). http://aejt.com.au/__data/assets/pdf_file/0010/395128/AEJT_7.2_Johnstone_Self.pdf.

Kasper, Walter. "The Theological Anthropology of *Gaudium et Spes*." *Communio: International Catholic Review* 23 (1996) 129–40.

Kavanaugh, John. *Who Counts as Persons? Human Identity and the Ethics of Killing*. Washington, DC: Georgetown University Press, 2001.

Keenan, James F. "The Moral Argumentation of *Evangelium Vitae*." In *Choosing Life: A Dialogue on Evangelium Vitae*, edited by K. W. Wildes and A. C. Mitchell, 46–62. Washington, DC: Georgetown University Press, 1997.

Keener, Craig S. *The Gospel of John: A Commentary*. Peabody, MA: Hendrickson, 2003.

Kelly, Thomas F., and Philipp W. Rosemann, eds. *Amor amicitiae: On the Love That Is Friendship; Essays in Medieval Thought and Beyond in Honor of the Rev. Professor James McEvoy*. Leuven: Peeters, 2004.

Kelsey, David H. *Eccentric Existence: A Theological Anthropology*. Louisville: Westminster John Knox, 2009.

Kerr, Fergus *Theology After Aquinas: Versions of Thomism*. Oxford: Blackwell, 2002.

———. *Theology After Wittgenstein*. 2nd ed. Oxford: Blackwell, 1997.

———. *Twentieth-Century Catholic Theologians: From Neoscholasticism to Nuptial Mysticism*. Oxford: Blackwell, 2007.

Kevern, Peter. "What Sort of a God Is to Be Found in Dementia?" *Theology* 113 (2010) 174–82.

Kittay, Eva, and Licia Carlson, eds. *Cognitive Disability and Its Challenge to Moral Philosophy*. Malden, MA: Wiley-Blackwell, 2010.

Kittel, Gerhard, ed. *The Theological Dictionary of the New Testament*. Translated by Geoffrey W. Bromiley. 10 vols. Grand Rapids: Eerdmans, 1964–76.

Kotva, Joseph J. *The Christian Case for Virtue Ethics*. Washington, DC: Georgetown University Press, 1996.

Kuhse, Helga, and Peter Singer. *Why Should the Baby Live? The Problem of Handicapped Infants*. Oxford: Oxford University Press, 1985.

Lacoste, Jean-Yves, ed. *Encyclopedia of Christian Theology*. 3 vols. New York: Routledge, 2005.

Lebech, Mette. *On the Problem of Human Dignity: A Hermeneutical and Phenomenological Investigation*. Würzburg: Königshausen & Neumann, 2009.

Lee, Patrick, and Robert P. George. *Body-Self Dualism in Contemporary Ethics and Politics*. Cambridge: Cambridge University Press, 2008.

Leo I. "Letter to Pulcheria Augusta." Translated by C. L. Feltoe. In vol. 12 of *A Select Library of Nicene and Post-Nicene Fathers of the Christian Church*, Second Series. Edited by P. Schaff and H. Wace. Grand Rapids: Eerdmans, 1956.

Lewis, C. S. *The Four Loves*. New York: HarperCollins, 2002.

Liddell, H. G., and R. Scott. *A Greek-English Lexicon, With a Revised Supplement*. 9th ed. Revised and augmented by H. S. Jones and R. McKenzie. Oxford: Clarendon, 1996.

Luther, Martin. *Luther's Works*. Vol. 54, *Table Talk*. Edited by H. T. Lehmann. Philadelphia: Fortress, 1967.

MacIntyre, Alasdair. *Dependent Rational Animals: Why Human Beings Need the Virtues*. Chicago: Open Court, 1999.

Maguiness, Gerard H. *Assisted Suicide, Self-Love and a Life Worth Living: A Re-examination of St Thomas Aquinas' Arguments against Suicide in the Summa Theologiae II.II.64.5, with Reference to Assisted Suicide and Euthanasia in the Magisterium, and the Writings of Peter Singer*. Rome: Pontifical Lateran University, 2002.

Mantel, Hilary. *Wolf Hall*. London: Fourth Estate, 2009.

Matthews, Pia. *God's Wild Flowers: Saints with Disabilities*. Herfordshire, UK: Gracewing, 2016.

———. *John Paul II and the Apparently "Non-acting" Person*. Herfordshire, UK: Gracewing, 2013.
McCabe, Herbert. *God, Christ and Us*. Edited by B. Davies. London: Continuum, 2003.
———. *God Matters*. London: G. Chapman, 1987.
———. *God Still Matters*. Edited by B. Davies. London: Continuum, 2002.
———. *Law, Love, Language*. London: Sheed & Ward, 1968.
———. *On Aquinas*. Edited by B. Davies. London: Continuum, 2008.
McEvoy, James. "Friendship and Love: For Theodore Crowley." *Irish Theological Quarterly* 50 (1983–84) 35–47.
Meilaender, G. *Friendship: A Study in Theological Ethics*. Notre Dame: University of Notre Dame Press, 1981.
———. *The Taste for the Other: The Social and Ethical Thought of C. S. Lewis*. Grand Rapids: Eerdmans, 1978.
Mitchell, Alan C. *Hebrews*. Sacra Pagina 13. Collegeville, MN: Liturgical Press, 2007.
Moltmann, Jürgen. *The Power of the Powerless*. San Francisco: Harper & Row, 1982.
Moreland, J. P. *The Recalcitrant Imago Dei: Human Persons and the Failure of Naturalism*. London: SMC, 2009.
Niebuhr, Reinhold. *The Nature and Destiny of Man: A Christian Interpretation*. Vol. 1, *Human Nature*. London: Nisbet, 1941.
Nouwen, Henri J. *Adam: God's Beloved*. Maryknoll, NY: Orbis, 1997.
Nussbaum, Martha. *Hiding from Humanity: Disgust, Shame, and the Law*. Princeton: Princeton University Press, 2004.
———. "Hiding from Humanity: Replies to Charlton, Haldane, Archard, and Brooks." *Journal of Applied Philosophy* 25 (2008) 335–49.
Nygren, Anders. *Agape and Eros*. Translated by P. S. Watson. London: SPCK, 1953.
O'Daly, Gerard. *Augustine's City of God: A Reader's Guide*. Oxford: Clarendon, 1999.
O'Donovan, Oliver. "Again: Who Is a Person?" In *Abortion and the Sanctity of Life*, edited by J. H. Channer, 125–37. Exeter: Paternoster, 1985.
———. "Augustine's *City of God* XIX and Western Political Thought." In *The City of God: A Collection of Critical Essays*, edited by D. Donnelly, 135–49. New York: P. Lang, 1995.
———. *Begotten or Made?* Oxford: Clarendon, 1984.
———. *The Christian and the Unborn Child*. 2nd ed. Bramcote, UK: Grove, 1975.
———. *The Desire of Nations: Rediscovering the Roots of Political Theology*. Cambridge: Cambridge University Press, 1996.
———. "The Object of Theological Ethics." *Studies in Christian Ethics* 20 (2007) 203–14.
———. *Resurrection and Moral Order: An Outline for Evangelical Ethics*. 2nd ed. Grand Rapids: Eerdmans, 1994.
O'Donovan, Oliver, and Joan L. O'Donovan. *Bonds of Imperfection: Christian Politics, Past and Present*. Grand Rapids: Eerdmans, 2004.
Oord, Thomas J. *Defining Love: A Philosophical, Scientific, and Theological Engagement*. Grand Rapids: Brazos, 2010.
Ormerod, Neil. *Creation, Grace and Redemption*. Maryknoll, NY: Orbis, 2007.
O'Rourke, Kevin D. "The Embryo as Person." *National Catholic Bioethics Quarterly* 16 (2006) 241–51.
Ouellet, Marc. *Divine Likeness: Toward a Trinitarian Anthropology of the Family*. Grand Rapids: Eerdmans, 2006.

Pailin, David. *A Gentle Touch: From a Theology of Handicap to a Theology of Human Being*. London: SPCK, 1992.
Pannenberg, Wolfhart. *Anthropology in Theological Perspective*. Edinburgh: T. & T. Clark, 1985.
Parfit, Derek. *Reasons and Persons*. Oxford: Oxford University Press, 1984.
Pasnau, Robert. *Thomas Aquinas on Human Nature: A Philosophical Study of Summa Theologiae Ia.75-89*. Cambridge: Cambridge University Press, 2002.
Paul VI, Pope. "Encyclical letter on the development of peoples." *Populorum progressio*. March 26, 1967. *Acta Apostolicae Sedis* 59 (1967) 257-99.
Pieper, Josef. *Death and Immortality*. Translated by R. Winston and C. Winston. London: Burns & Oates, 1969.
———. *On Hope*. Translated by M. F. McCarthy. In *Faith, Hope, Love*, 87-138. San Francisco: Ignatius, 1997.
———. *On Love*. Translated by R. Winston and C. Winston. In *Faith, Hope, Love*, 139-282. San Francisco: Ignatius, 1997.
———. *The Silence of St. Thomas: Three Essays*. Translated by J. Murray and D. O'Connor. South Bend, IN: St. Augustine's Pres, 1999.
Pinckaers, Servais. *The Pinckaers Reader: Renewing Thomistic Moral Theology*. Edited by J. Berkman and C. S. Titus. Washington, DC: Catholic University of America Press, 2005.
———. *The Sources of Christian Ethics*. Translated by M. T. Noble. Washington, DC: Catholic University of America Press, 1995.
Pontifical Council for Justice and Peace. *Compendium of the Social Doctrine of the Church*. Vatican City: Libreria Editrice Vaticana, 2004. [Authorized English edition: Strathfield: St. Paul's Publications, 2005]
Price, Richard. and Michael Gaddis, trans. *The Acts of the Council of Chalcedon*. Vol. 2. Translated Texts for Historians 45. Liverpool: Liverpool University Press, 2005.
Rahner, Karl., et al., eds. *Sacramentum Mundi: An Encyclopedia of Theology*. 6 vols. London: Burns & Oates, 1968-70.
Ramsey, Paul. *The Patient as Person: Explorations in Medical Ethics*. New Haven: Yale University Press, 1970.
Ratzinger, Joseph. "The Likeness of God in the Human Being." *Dolentium Hominum* 34 (1997) 16-19.
———. "Retrieving the Tradition: Concerning the Notion of Person in Theology." Translated by M. Waldstein. *Communio: International Catholic Review* 17 (1990) 439-54.
Redrado, J. L. "The Role and Importance of Pastoral Care for Disabled People in the Ministry of the Church." *Dolentium Hominum* 68 (2008).
Reinders, Hans S. *The Future of the Disabled in Liberal Society: An Ethical Analysis*. Notre Dame: Notre dame University Press, 2000.
———, ed. *The Paradox of Disability: Responses to Jean Vanier and L'Arche Communities from Theology and the Sciences*. Grand Rapids: Eerdmans, 2010.
———. *Receiving the Gift of Friendship: Profound Disability, Theological Anthropology, and Ethics*. Grand Rapids: Eerdmans, 2008.
Reynolds, Thomas E. *Vulnerable Communion: A Theology of Disability and Hospitality*. Grand Rapids: Brazos, 2008.
Roger of Taizé (Shütz, R.). *A Path of Hope: Last Writings of Brother Roger*. London: Continuum, 2006.

Rousselot, Pierre. *The Problem of Love in the Middle Ages: A Historical Contribution*. Translated by A. Vincelette; reviewed and corrected by P. Vandevelde. Milwaukee: Marquette University Press, 2001.

Rowland, Tracey. *Ratzinger's Faith: The Theology of Pope Benedict XVI*. Oxford: Oxford University Press, 2008.

Schaefer, Konrad. *Psalms*. Berit Olam: Studies in Hebrew Narrative and Poetry. Collegeville, MN: Liturgical Press, 2001.

Scheffczyk, L. "Image et ressemblance." In vol. 7, pt. 2 of *Dictionnaire de spiritualité*. Edited by M. Viller, F. Cavallera, and J. de Guibert. Paris: Beauchesne, 1971.

Schindler, David L. "Christology and the Imago Dei: Interpreting *Gaudium et Spes*." *Communio: International Catholic Review* 23 (1996).

Schmude, Karl. *G. K. Chesterton*. London: Catholic Truth Society, 2008.

Schumacher, Bernard. *A Philosophy of Hope: Josef Pieper and the Contemporary Debate on Hope*. Translated by D. C. Schindler. New York: Fordham University Press, 2003.

Schwöbel, Christoph. "God, Creation and the Christian Community: The Dogmatic Basis of a Christian Ethic of Createdness." In *The Doctrine of Creation: Essays in Dogmatics, History and Philosophy*, edited by C. E. Gunton, 149–76. Edinburgh: T. & T. Clark, 1997.

Scola, Angelo. *The Nuptial Mystery*. Grand Rapids: Eerdmans, 2005.

Singer, Peter. *Practical Ethics*. 2nd ed. Cambridge: Cambridge University Press, 1993.

———. *Rethinking Life and Death: The Collapse of Our Traditional Ethics*. Oxford: Oxford University Press, 1995.

Sokolowski, Robert. *Eucharistic Presence: A Study in the Theology of Disclosure*. Washington, DC: Catholic University of America Press, 1994.

———. *Phenomenology of the Human Person*. Cambridge: Cambridge University Press, 2008.

Spaemann, Robert. *Persons: The Difference between "Someone" and "Something"*. Translated by O. O'Donovan. Oxford: Oxford University Press, 2006.

———. "Death – Suicide – Euthanasia." In *The Dignity of the Dying Person: Proceedings of the Fifth Assembly of the Pontifical Academy for Life (Vatican City, 24–27 February 1999)*, edited by J. de D. V. Correa and E. Sgreccia, 123–31. Vatican City: Libreria Editrice Vaticana, 2000.

———. "On the anthropology of the Encyclical Evangelium Vitae", in J V Correa & E Sgreccia (Eds), *Evangelium Vitae: Five Years of Confrontation with Society*. Vatican City: Libreria Editrice Vaticana, 2001.

———. "Ars longa, vita brevis", in J V Correa & E Sgreccia (Eds), *Ethics of Biomedical Research in a Christian Vision*. Vatican City: Libreria Editrice Vaticano, 2004.

———. "When does the human being [begin] to be a person?, in E Sgreccia & J Laffitte (Eds), *The Human Embryo before Implantation: Scientific Aspects and Bioethical Considerations*. Vatican City: Libreria Editrice Vaticana, 2006.

———. translated by G de Graaff & J Mumford, *Essays in Anthropology: Variations on a Theme*. Eugene, Or: Cascade Books, 2010.

Stony Brook University. *Cognitive Disability: A Challenge to Moral Philosophy*. Stony Brook University, September 18–20, 2008. www.stonybrook.edu/sb/cdconference/index.shtml.

Summers, Steve. *Friendship: Exploring Its Implications for the Church in Postmodernity*. London: T. & T. Clark, 2009.

Swinton, John. "Building a Church for Strangers." *Journal of Religion, Disability & Health* 4 (2001) 25–63.

———, ed. *Critical Reflections on Stanley Hauerwas' Theology of Disability: Disabling Society, Enabling Theology*. Binghamton, NY: Haworth Pastoral Press, 2004.

———. *Dementia: Living in the Memories of God*. London: SCM, 2012.

———. "Introduction: Re-imagining Genetics and Disability." In *Theology, Disability and the New Genetics: Why Science Needs the Church*, edited by J. Swinton and B. Brock, 1–26. London: T. & T. Clark, 2007.

———. *Resurrecting the Person: Friendship and the Care of People with Mental Health Problems*. Nashville: Abingdon, 2000.

Swinton, John, and Esther McIntosh. "Persons in Relation: The Care of Persons with Learning Disabilities." *Theology Today* 57 (2000) 175–84.

Terrien, Samuel L. *The Psalms: Strophic Structure and Theological Commentary*. Grand Rapids: Eerdmans, 2003.

Teske, Roland J. "Saint Augustine on the Incorporeality of the Soul in Letter 166." *The Modern Schoolman* 60 (1983) 170–88.

Torrance, A. J. *Persons in Communion: An Essay on Trinitarian Description and Human Participation, with special reference to Volume One of Karl Barth's Church Dogmatics*. Edinburgh: T. & T. Clark, 1996.

Torrance, T. F. *The Soul and Person of the Unborn Child*. Edinburgh: Handsel Press for the Scottish Order of Christian Unity, 1999.

Vacant, Alfred, and Eugene Mangenot, eds. *Dictionnaire de Théologie Catholique*. Vol.7, pt. 1. Paris: Letouzey et Ané, 1922.

Vacek, Edward C. *Love, Human and Divine: The Heart of Christian Ethics*. Washington, DC: Georgetown University Press, 1994.

Vanier, Jean. *Becoming Human*. New York: Paulist Press, 1998.

———. *Befriending the Stranger*. London: Darton, Longman & Todd, 2005.

———. *Drawn into the Mystery of Jesus through the Gospel of John*. London: Darton, Longman & Todd, 2004.

———. *Encountering the Other*. New York: Paulist, 2006.

———. *From Brokenness to Community*. New York: Paulist, 1992.

———. *Jesus the Gift of Love*. London: Hodder & Stoughton, 1994.

———. *Man and Woman God Made Them*. Rev. ed. London: Darton, Longman & Todd, 2007.

———. *Our Life Together: A Memoir in Letters*. London: Darton, Longman & Todd, 2008.

Vatican II. Pastoral Constitution on the Church in the Modern World, *Gaudium et spes*. December 7, 1965. *Acta Apostolicae Sedis* 75 (1966) 1025–1115.

Volpe, Medi A. "Irresponsible Love: Rethinking Intellectual Disability, Humanity and the Church." *Modern Theology* 25 (2009) 490–501.

Von Hildebrand, Dietrich. *The Heart: An Analysis of Human and Divine Affectivity*. Edited by J. H. Crosby. New ed. South Bend, IN: St. Augustine's Press, 2007.

Wadell, Paul. *The Primacy of Love: An Introduction to the Ethics of Thomas Aquinas*. New York: Paulist, 1992.

Wannenwetsch, Berndt. "Angels with Clipped Wings: The Disabled as Key to the Recognition of Personhood." In *Theology, Disability and the New Genetics: Why Science Needs the Church*, edited by J. Swinton and B. Brock, 182–200. London: T. & T. Clark, 2007.

Waters, Brent, and Ronald Cole-Turner, eds. *God and the Embryo: Religious Voices on Stem Cells and Cloning.* Washington, DC: Georgetown University Press, 2003.

Williams, Rowan D. "Interiority and Epiphany: A Reading in New Testament Ethics." *Modern Theology* 13 (1997) 29–51.

———. "On Being a Human Body" *Sewanee Theological Review* 42 (1999) 403–13.

———. *Resurrection: Interpreting the Easter Gospel.* London: Darton, Longman & Todd, 1982.

Wilson, R. McLellan. *Hebrews.* New Century Bible Commentary. Grand Rapids: Eerdmans, 1987.

Winston, David. *The Wisdom of Solomon: A New Translation with Introduction and Commentary.* Anchor Bible 43. Garden City, NY: Doubleday, 1979.

Wright, N. T. *Hebrews for Everyone.* London: SPCK, 2003.

Yong, Amos. *The Bible, Disability, and the Church: A New Vision of the People of God.* Grand Rapids: Eerdmans, 2011.

———. *Theology and Down Syndrome: Reimagining Disability in Late Modernity.* Waco: Baylor University Press, 2007.

Zaborowski, Holger. *Robert Spaemann's Philosophy of the Human Person.* Oxford: Oxford University Press, 2010.

Zimmermann, Nigel. *Facing the Other: John Paul II, Levinas, and the Body.* Eugene, OR: Cascade, 2015.

Zizioulas, John D. *Being as Communion: Studies in Personhood and the Church.* London: Darton, Longman & Todd, 1985.

———. *Communion and Otherness: Further Studies in Personhood and the Church.* London: T. & T. Clark, 2006.

INDEX

abortion, 7, 7n8, 23, 23n14
Acts of the Apostles, 135–36n12
agapao love, 86n47
agape love, 53–54, 58, 77
agape love of God, 70
agape/caritas, 63
Agius, Emmanuel, 16n4
angels, 176, 177, 194
Anscombe, Elizabeth, 5n5, 73
anthropology
    anti-anthropological notion of speciesism, 4–5n3
    of childlikeness, 26–27
    of discontinuity, 122–24
    elevated view of, 30
    epistemological, 124
    existential configuration of *imago Dei*, 20–22
    one for all, 28–31
    theologically re-imagined, 6–10
anti-anthropological notion of speciesism, 4–5n3
Aquinas, Thomas (saint)
    on creation, 115, 139–40
    on friendship, 63–64
    friendship with God, 39
    on hope, 151, 151–52n34
    human person qualities, 30
    on *imago Dei*, 159, 159–60n3
    nature of man, 134, 134n8
    Reinders on Aquinas and, 171–83
Arendt, Hannah, 118–19
"Aren't We All Eugenicists Anyway?" (Mahowald), 7n8
Aristotle, 69, 76, 101–2
Ashley, Benedict, 16n4

Augustine of Hippo
    doctrine of the *reliquiae*, 52
    on goodness, 44–52
    on human soul, 50–51
    on *imago Dei*, 115
    on learning, 51n47
    Letter to Jerome, 50–51, 50–51n44

Balthasar, Hans Urs von, 15n1, 113, 115
Barth, Karl, 115
being human, 3, 4, 11
being of human descent and living a human life, distinction between, 121
belonging, 43
Benedict XVI, pope, 17–18n6, 150n31, 184, 210
    See also Ratzinger, Josef
Birrell, Ian, 216–18
blindness, scriptural meaning of, 55–58
Bloomberg, Craig, 194n11
bodily resurrection, 143
Boethius, 29, 30, 177
Bonds of Imperfection (O'Donovan & O'Donovan), 50–51n44
Brock, Brian, 8n11
Brunner, Emil, 113, 115

Carmichael, Liz, 88n1, 91n9
Cartesian turn to psychological self, 73, 73n34
Catechism of the Catholic Church, 13, 126n39

Catholic Church. *See* Roman Catholic Church
Centre for Spirituality, Health and Disability, 8n11
Cessario, Romanus, 144, 145, 158
Chalcedon Council, 6, 123, 204–6, 204n20
charity, friendship as, 63
Chesterton, G. K., 19
childlikeness, anthropology of, 26–27
choosing paradigm, 36
Christian anthropology
    Catholic perspective, 12–14
    theological re-imagined, 6–10
Clément, Oliver-Maurice, 136, 140n18
concomitant quality, 177
Congregation for the Doctrine of the Faith (CDF), 113, 115
A Constructive Theology of Intellectual Disability (Haslam), 7–8n10, 113n6, 173n39
Corinthians I, Letter to, 117, 194n10
Corinthians II, Letter to, 117, 197, 200
Creamer, Deborah Beth, 7, 7n10
creation
    creaturely existence and humanity, 118–22
    creaturely form, a return to, 130–32
    creaturely human, 109, 133–35
    theological definitions of, 135–36n12, 135–37
creatures
    hope for, 148–55
    term usage, 137n16
"Critical Reflections on Stanley Hauerwas' Theology of Disability" (Swinton), 7n10
Cromwell, Thomas, 3
cult of normalcy, 168

D'Arcy, Martin C., 89n3
datum (gift concept), 36, 41–42
De civitate dei (Augustine), 44, 46–47, 46n38
Death and Immortality (Pieper), 133
deBlois, Jean, 16n4
deformity of nature, 20
Dementia: Living in the Memories of God (Swinton), 7–8n10, 43n30
Dependent Rational Animals (MacIntyre), 5–6n6
Desire of Nations (O'Donovan), 47n40
deviation and difference, 171
Didache, 23n13
dignity, 19, 127
"Disability, Bioethics and Human Rights" (Agius), 16n4
disability, term usage, 2
Disability and Christian Theology (Cremer), 7n10
Disabled Church—Disabled Society (Gillibrand), 7–8n10
The Disabled God (Eiesland), 7n9, 199
discipleship, 81
discontinuity, anthropology of, 122–24
diversity of human life, 37
donum (givenness concept), 36, 42
Donum vitae, 22–25
Down Syndrome, 162
durability of friendship, 84–85

Eiesland, Nancy, 7, 7n9, 200, 203, 207
emergentism, 163n15, 165, 167, 167n27
Engelhardt, Tristram, 5n4
Ephesians, Letter to, 194n10, 197
epistemological anthropology, 124
equality, friendship and, 69, 71
eros love, 53
essentialism, 131–32
eugenics debates, 7, 7n8
European Society for the Study of Theology and Disability, 8n11
existential anthropology, 20–22

faculties of reason and will, 29–31, 121, 126, 128
Fergusson, David, 138
Foundations of Bioethics (Engelhardt), 5n4
fragility of friendship, 85
Francis, pope, 15
freedom, 38, 38–39n20, 125–27, 169–70
French language publications, 8n11, 16n4
friendship
  agape love as, 54, 58, 71
  being included in, 103–5
  characteristics of, 84–87
  charity as, 63
  as context dependent, 76
  definitions of, 60, 65, 68
  downward movement into, 105–8
  equality and, 69, 71
  human beings as befrienders, 108–10
  human dimensions of, 63–66
  importance of, 32–33
  instrumental friendship, 72, 72n30
  Jesus of Nazareth and, 75–80
  meaning of, 222–23
  "no greater love," 80–84, 86
  of God, 56–57
  profoundly impaired and, 95–100
  radical friendship, 66–70
  rational friendship, 100–103
  Reinders' notion of, 58–62
  sources of, 90–95
  temporality of, 79
  theological accounts of, 88–90
  theological understanding of, 61–62
  types of, 85
  with God, 39, 56, 89, 131

Gaudium et Spes (Vatican II), 20–22, 114
Gaventa, William, 8n11
Geiger, Louis-Bertrand, 153–54, 182

Genesis
  creation of humans, 109, 137, 149, 173
  imago Dei, 13, 116, 117, 159, 179
  separation of God from creation, 138
"Genetic Anomaly or Genetic Diversity" (Iozzio), 16n4
gift of life vs. givenness of life, 36
Gillibrand, John, 7–8n10
glorified bodies, 143–44
glory and grace, 180–81
God
  existing in, 132–40
  friendship of, 56–57
  friendship with, 39, 56, 89, 131
  God/creation relationship, 138–39
  grace of, 149
  redemption, 141–42
  separation from creation, 138
good, human beings and, 33–44, 137–38
goodness, Augustine on, 44–52
grace and glory, 180–81
grace of God, 149
Grisez, Germain, 89–90n3

Haldane, John, 5–6n6, 167n27
Hall, Amy Laura, 7n8
Haslam, Molly C, 7–8n10, 113n6, 173n39
Hauerwas, Stanley
  friendship as virtue, 90n6
  Suffering Presence, 7n9
  theological reimagining of the disabled, 7
healing, in Gospel of John, 57
Health Care Ethics (Ashley, deBlois, and O'Rourk), 16n4
Hebrews, Letter to
  hope, 153
  human suffering, 199
  humanity, 204
  measure of man in measure of Jesus, 193–98
  nearness to Christ, 185–86

Hiding from Humanity (Nussbaum), 5–6n6
Hill, Edmund, 173, 191
Hill, William, 152n36
Holy Spirit, 161, 165
hope, 148–155
human beings
    as befrienders, 108–10
    being human vs., 3
    diversity of, 37
    friendship as dimension of, 63–66
    good and, 33–44, 137–38
    non-persons as, 4–6
    in Psalms, 188–193
    puzzlement and expertise on, 18–20
    treatment of, 24–25
human condition, measuring
    human beings in Psalms, 188–193
    human nearness to Christ, 184–88
    humanity of profoundly impaired, 203–6
    humanity under condition being impaired, 207–10
    impairment condition and suffering of Christ, 198–203
    lives lived, 210–11
    measure of man in measure of Jesus, 193–98
human dignity, 127
human nature, 29, 36, 48–49, 125–26
human person, 29, 127–28
human pilgrim, 144–48
human soul, 50–51, 167
human subject vs. human condition, 73
humanity
    achieving under condition being impaired, 207–10
    Catholic Church as expert in, 17–20, 17n6
    creaturely existence and, 118–22
    lived under condition being impaired, 220–23
    of profoundly impaired, measuring, 203–6
    transcending concept of, 33–40, 74

imago Christi, 154
imago Dei
    angels and, 176
    Aquinas' modes of, 179
    Aquinas' stages of, 175–76
    Catholic perspective, 13–14, 114–15, 123
    doctrine of, 111–18, 113n6
    in *Gaudium et Spes*, 20–22
    intellectually disabled and, 160–67
    Reinders on Aquinas and, 171–83
    Reinders on personhood and, 11–12
    right question of, 159–71
    St. Paul on, 154
    status viatoris and, 156–59
impairment, term usage, 2
impairment condition and suffering of Christ, 198–203
inclusion
    ambivalence of, 216–18
    descending the ladder, 219–20
    friendship and, 83–84
    as goal, 104–5
    moving beyond paradigm of, 213–16
    need for, 203
    paradigm of, 9–10
    Reinders on, 35, 71, 107, 107n31
infanticide, 23, 23n14
institutional inclusion, 217
instrumental friendship, 72, 72n30
intellectually disabled, *image Dei* and, 160–67
International Theological Commission (ITC), 113, 115, 117
Iozzio, Mary Jo, 16n4
Irenaeus, saint, 52n49
"Irresponsible Love" (Volpe), 7n10

Jeanrond, Werner, 89n2
Jerome, saint, 50–51, 50–51n44
Jesus Christ
    Chalcedon Council on, 6
    childlikeness theme, 26–27
    healing of man born blind,
        55–58
    human nearness to, 184–88
    image of God in, 21
    as incarnation of God's love, 59,
        144, 195–96, 200
    Judas' friendship, 96–97, 103n28
    love, types of, 86, 86n47
    McCabe on, 64–66
    measure of man in, 193–98
    model of friendship, 69
    "no greater love," 80–84, 86
    offer of friendship, 75
    person of, in His human nature,
        204–6
    personal encounters with, 75–80
    personhood of the other, 72,
        72n30
    profoundly impaired healings,
        26, 26n16
    Reinders on, 58–61
    suffering of, and condition of
        impairment, 198–203
    Swinton on, 66–68, 72, 75–80,
        94
John, Gospel of
    on charity, 63
    discipleship, 81
    durability of friendship, 85
    on friendship, 61, 65, 69, 82, 95
    friendship language, 78–79
    good shepherd metaphor, 79
    on healing, 57
    Jesus washed disciples' feet, 95,
        96
    measure of man, 197
    "no greater love," 80–84, 86
    Samaritan woman, 76, 77
    story of man born blind, 55–58
    total commitment to others, 76
    unconditional acceptance, 76
    vine and branches metaphor, 82
John Paul II, pope
    disabled as fully human beings,
        12–13, 16
    Donum vitae, 22–23n13
    Message, 28–29
    Reinders on, 28n20
    suffering and the disabled,
        200–201, 210
    "theology of the body," 114–16
    Vanier on, 28n20
    Veritatis Splendor, 124–29
*Journal of Religion, Disability and
    Health*, 8n11, 9n13
judgment, 197

Kasper, Walter, 20n11
Kavanaugh, John, 15–16n3
Keener, C. S., 86n47
Kerr, Fergus, 75
Kotva, Joseph, 90n5

ladder metaphor, 106–8, 219–20
L'Arche International communities,
    29, 105–6, 106n29, 213–14
learning, Augustine on, 51n47
Leo the Great, 144
Lewis, C. S., 91–95, 91n9, 96n21,
    97–100, 186–88
likeness, image and, 179–180,
    179n46
love
    concept of, 53–54
    definition of, 78–79
    friendship and, 84–87
    Jesus' "no greater love," 80–84,
        86
    sacrificial, 78–82
Luke, Gospel of
    childlikeness, 26
    mothering image metaphor, 79
    possessed, healing of, 26n16
    possessed Gerasene man, 76, 77
    profoundly impaired and, 26
    raise up the lowly, 181
    Zaccheus' calling, 76, 77

MacIntyre, Alasdair, 5–6n6
Mahowald, Mary B., 7n8

Mark, Gospel of
    childlikeness, 26
    possessed, healing of, 26n16
marriage friendship, 85
Matthew, Gospel of
    childlikeness, 26, 26n17
    friendship language, 77–78
    Jesus dining with tax collectors and sinners, 76, 77
    judgment, 197
    Last Supper with disciples, 76, 77
    mothering image metaphor, 79
    nearness to Christ, 186
    possessed, healing of, 26n16
    profoundly impaired and, 26
    solidarity with poor and marginalized, 76
Matthews, Pia, 16n4
McCabe, Herbert, 64–66, 80, 86, 103, 209
McEvoy, James, 88–89n1
Meilaender, Gilbert, 88–89n1, 91n9
mental health problems, medical mode of care for, 67
mental retardation, 28–29
Mitchell, Alan, 195–96
moral status of persons, 4–5
Moreland, J. P., 131, 136, 160n4, 167n27
mutuality of friendship, 97

nature
    deformity of, 20
    intelligent nature, 176–77
    of man, 134, 134n8
    term usage, 177
non-persons, 4–6
Norfolk, Duke of, 3
Nouwen, Henri, 39, 39n22
Nussbaum, Martha, 5–6n6
Nygren, Anders, 53–55, 53n51, 55n57, 58–59, 88–89

O'Daly, Gerard, 47
O'Donovan, Oliver, 47n40, 49n43, 50–51n44
On Hope (Pieper), 133

On Love (Pieper), 133
Ormerod, Neil, 141
O'Rourke, Kevin, 16n4
Ouellet, Marc, 114

Pailin, David, 37–38
Parfit, Derek, 4–5n3
Paul VI, pope, 17n6
Pentecost and Holy Spirit, 161
person
    being treated as, 22–25
    concept of, 6, 15–16n3, 15n1
personhood
    capacity of, 34n8, 35, 35n9, 35n11
    dignity of, 19
    Donum vitae on, 22–23
    imago Dei and, 11–12
    as lived reality, 221
    personal relationships and, 67–68
    person-with-disorder mode, 71–72
    of profoundly impaired, 2, 123
    recognition of significance, 2–6
    Reinders on, 45n34, 72–75, 215–16
    subject of, 70–75
Phenomenology of the Human Person (Sokolowski), 15–16n3
phileo love, 86n47
Pieper, Josef
    on friendship, 91, 91n9, 95, 98, 100, 109, 133
    on hope, 150, 151, 153
    humans as *viator*, 133–34, 143, 144–45
    provisional character of existence, 145–46
pilgrims, 133–34, 144–48
Pinches, Charles, 90n6
Pinckaers, Servais, 15–16n3, 30, 89n3
pneumatological imagination, 161, 165
Pope John Paul II and the Apparently "Non-acting" Person (Matthews), 16n4

Practical Ethics (Singer), 4–5n3
Practical Philosophy (Haldane), 5–6n6
profoundly impaired
   description of, 1
   John Paul II on, 28–29
   personhood of, 2, 4
   Sacred Scripture on, 26–27
   term usage, 1n1
Protestant tradition on hope, 151n33
Psalms, Book of
   on childlikeness, 26
   on human beings, 188–93
   on humanity, 18, 194, 195
   on nearness to Christ, 186

radical friendship, 66–75
Rahner, Karl, 114n72, 135
rational friendship, 100–103
Ratzinger, Josef, 15–16n3, 184–85, 184n1, 201
   See also Benedict XVI, pope
reason and will, faculties of, 29–31, 121, 126, 128, 172
Reasons and Persons (Parfit), 4–5n3
Receiving the Gift of Friendship (Reinders), 7–8n10, 10, 32, 39n21, 52n49, 55, 60
receptivity, 38–39n20
redemption, 140–44
Reinders, Hans
   agency-based humanity, 50, 101
   anthropological projects of, 10–12, 17, 111
   anthropological re-imagining, 30–31
   on Aquinas, 63–64, 171–183
   on Aristotle, 101–2
   assumptions of, 32–33
   capacity and personhood, identity of, 34n8, 35, 35n9, 35n11
   Catholic anthropology, misinterpretation of, 124–30
   creaturely form, a return to, 130–32
   creaturely principle for human existence, 118–22
   disabled as a specific theological theme, 7, 8n11
   on friendship, 58–62, 80, 92n14, 94
   good, human beings and, 33–40
   on goodness, 48–52
   on human faculties, 147, 215
   on *imago Dei*, 111–18, 120–21, 123, 171–83
   on inclusion, 107n31
   on Jesus Christ, 58–61
   on John Paul II, 28n20
   Nygren and, 52–54
   on personhood, 45n34, 72–75, 215–16
   transcending concept of humanity, 33–40, 54–58, 55n57, 74
Reinders' publications
   The Future of the Disabled in Liberal Society, 7–8n10
   Receiving the Gift of Friendship, 7–8n10, 10, 32, 39n21, 52n49, 55, 60, 111–12, 126n39, 215
relational aptitude, 131
relationships, types of, 81, 83, 83n45
religious images, 113–14n9
reliquiae, doctrine of, 52
Resurrecting the Person (Swinton), 7–8n10
resurrection, bodily, 143
"Retrieving the Tradition" (Ratzinger), 15–16n3
Revelation, Book of
   redemption, 141
   side-by-side friendship, 99
Reynolds, Thomas
   disability theology and, 7
   humanity of profoundly impaired, 203
   on *imago Dei*, 160, 167–71
   intellectually disabled, term usage, 160n5
   Vulnerable Communion, 7–8n10

Roman Catholic Church
    Christian anthropological
        perspective, 12–14
    as expert in humanity, 17–20,
        17n6
    on *imago Dei*, 13–14, 114–15,
        123
    perspective of Christian
        anthropological tradition,
        12–14
    Reinders' misinterpretation of,
        124–30
    voice of amid the human
        peripheries, 15–17
Romans, Letter to, 117, 152

Sacramentum Mundi (Rahner), 135
Sacred Scripture, on profoundly
    impaired, 26–27, 26n16
sacrificial love, 78–82
Schaefer, Konrad, 190
Schindler, David L., 21n12
Schumacher, Bernard, 146, 156–57
Schwöbel, Christoph, 135n10
Second Vatican Council, 18n17,
    20–22, 114
seeing, ways of, 56
self, Cartesian philosophy, 73, 73n34
selfhood, 43n30
servanthood, 82
Singer, Peter, 4–5n3
Sokolowski, Robert, 15–16n3
soul, human, 50–51, 167
The Sources of Christian Ethics
    (Pinckaers), 15–16n3
Spaemann, Robert, 119n28, 204
status viatoris (state of being on the
    way), 134, 134n8, 146, 149,
    150–51, 156–59
suffering, condition of impairment
    and, 198–203
Suffering Presence (Hauerwas), 7n9
Summa Theologiæ (Aquinas), 172
Summers, Steve, 89n2
supreme good, 47–49, 49n43
Swinton, John
    biblical evidence of Jesus'
        friendships, 75–80

creaturely existence of humanity,
    119n28
*Critical Reflections on Stanley
    Hauerwas' Theology of
    Disability*, 7n10
*Dementia: Living in the
    Memories of God*, 7–8n10,
    43n30
disability theology and, 7
disabled as a specific theological
    theme, 8n11
friendship concept, 80
on Jesus Christ, 66–68, 72,
    75–80, 94
radical friendship, 66–70
response to radical friendship,
    70–75
Resurrecting the Person, 7–8n10
on welcoming, 172n36

Terrien, Samuel, 192
theological accounts of friendship,
    88–90
Theological Anthropology (Rahner),
    114n72
Theology and Down Syndrome
    (Yong), 7–8n10
therapeutic relationships, 83, 83n45
"To Form a More Perfect Union"
    (Hall), 7n8
transcending
    concept of humanity, 33–40,
        54–58, 55n57
    immanence and, 74–75
triggers for friendship, 96–98, 96n21
*Twenty Opinions Common among
    Anglo-American Philosophers*
    (Anscombe), 5n5

ultimate good of being human, 42,
    46n37

Vacek, Edward, 89–90n3
Vanier, Jean
    on John Paul II, 28n20, 201n15
    ladder metaphor, 106–8, 219–20

L'Arche communities, 29, 105–6, 106n29, 213
Varro, Marcus Terentius, 47
Vatican II. *See* Second Vatican Council
Veritatis Splendor (John Paul II), 124–29
viator, term usage, 133–34n6, 144–45
Vincelette, Alan, 53n52
Volpe, Medi Ann, 7n10
vulnerability, 168
Vulnerable Communion (Reynolds), 7–8n10

Wadell, Paul, 38–39
Wannenwetsch, Bernd, 9–10, 107–8, 218
Who Counts as Persons? Human Identity and the Ethics of Killing (Kavanaugh), 15–16n3

will and reason, faculties of, 29–31, 121, 126, 128, 172
Williams, Rowan, 211
Wisdom, Book of, 137–38
"The Writing on the Wall . . . Alzheimer's Disease" (Mathews), 16n4

Yong, Amon
 disability theology and, 7
 image Dei and intellectually disabled, 160–67, 160n5, 170
 Theology and Down Syndrome, 7–8n10

Zimmerman, Nigel
 Facing the Other, 115n17
Zizioulas, John, 38, 38–39n20, 45n34, 59n63

www.ingramcontent.com/pod-product-compliance
Lightning Source LLC
Chambersburg PA
CBHW031732230426
43669CB00007B/331